Reimagining Christianity

Reimagining Christianity

*Reconnect Your Spirit
without Disconnecting Your Mind*

Alan Jones, Ph.D.

WILEY

John Wiley & Sons, Inc.

Published by John Wiley & Sons, Inc., Hoboken, New Jersey
Published simultaneously in Canada

The author gratefully acknowledges the following for permission to quote from:
"The Mower" from *Collected Poems* by Philip Larkin. Copyright © 1988, 1989 by the Estate of Philip Larkin. Reprinted by permission of Farrar, Straus, and Giroux, LLC.
"The Art of Disappearing" from *Words Under the Words: Selected Poems* by Naomi Shihab Nye, copyright © 1995. Reprinted with the permission of Far Corner Books, Portland, Oregon.

Design and production by Navta Associates, Inc.

For general information about our other products and services, please contact our Customer Care Department within the United States at (800) 762-2974, outside the United States at (317) 572-3993 or fax (317) 572-4002.

Wiley also publishes its books in a variety of electronic formats. Some content that appears in print may not be available in electronic books. For more information about Wiley products, visit our web site at www.wiley.com.

Library of Congress Cataloging-in-Publication Data:

Jones, Alan W., date.
  Reimagining Christianity : reconnect your spirit without disconnecting your mind / Alan Jones.
    p.   cm.
  Includes bibliographical references and index.
  ISBN 0-471-45707-8
  1. Spiritual life—Christianity.   I. Title.
  BV4501.3.J64   2004
  248.4—dc22   2004005662

Printed in the United States of America

10 9 8 7 6 5 4 3 2 1

In memoriam
Monica Furlong
Hugh Bishop
and Fielder Cook

For
The Community of Grace Cathedral, San Francisco

Contents

Acknowledgments

I owe a great deal to many great human beings who shared with me their vision of the fully human life. Three of them were great Christians: Hugh Bishop, Anglican priest and monk; Monica Furlong, novelist and journalist; and Fielder Cook, movie director. All three were generous artists of the soul and taught me a generous form of Christianity. I've also had the privilege of working in and with an extraordinary community—that of Grace Cathedral, San Francisco. That community gave me the freedom to preach and to teach. I was supported and encouraged from first to last by my wife, Cricket. Her energy and love know no bounds. My friend Diana Landau helped give the book shape and my editor, Tom Miller, brought the whole project together. I owe them a great deal and thank them for their patience. I also want to thank my agent, Tom Grady, for believing in the project and our friends David and Deborah Holloway, Jill and Buzz Kramer, Richard Pascale, Ann-Carol Brown, and Kat and Fielder Belk-Cook for providing quiet spaces in which to write. Finally, many thanks to my colleagues Ellen McDermott (for taking care of the final stages of the manuscript) and Rick Johnson (for providing the subtitle for the book).

Preface

The domain of morals is as chartless as the sea once was, and as treacherous as the sea still is. It is not too much to say that whoever wishes to become a truly moral human being (and let us not ask whether or not this is possible: I think that we must *believe* that it is possible) must first divorce himself from all the prohibitions, crimes, hypocrisies of the Christian Church. If the concept of God has any validity at all, it can only be to make us larger, freer, and more loving. If God cannot do this, then it is time we got rid of Him.

James Baldwin, *The Fire Next Time*

Religion is a funny business and isn't simply *one* thing. People have some funny ideas about it, too. This book is an invitation to give religion a second look—mainly through the lens of Christianity, since that's the religion I know most about. It's the result of a long journey through many *Christianities* as I have experienced them over the past sixty years. The fact that there isn't simply one Christianity may come as a surprise to some readers. But even in my limited experience, Christianity has ranged from extreme fundamentalist Protestantism to an extravagant papal Catholicism; from Pentecostal fervor to mystical contemplation; from political action to withdrawal from the world; from the Shakers to the Eastern Orthodox. I have encountered unparalleled meanness and unearned and unasked-for love. Some Christians make me want to throw up. Others touch and inspire me with their sheer presence and generosity of spirit. Many of them wouldn't consider me one and, if they're right, I'm not and grateful not to be one.

But I am a Christian and stand in a particular tradition—English and Anglican (Episcopalian)—a tradition that is confusing to anyone who wants to pin us down. Many of us say we are Protestants and others insist we are Catholics. At our best, we don't resolve the issue or relieve the tension. Without any sense of putting down any other tradition, Anglicanism is the one tradition that enables me to call myself a Christian. My tradition, as I have received it, assumes that human beings have far more in common with each other—before you get to the issue of beliefs—than anything that could divide us. We want to know how others respond to life's awful and wonderful questions. But I must admit that Anglicans are also deeply divided over issues of authority and sexuality.

"Anyone who claims to be totally uninterested in any sort of spiritual response to the ache of life is little more than a narrow-headed thug." So said the late playwright Dennis Potter. Potter puts it well. Religion, for me, is our response to the ache of life.

This book is my particular response and is written in the hope that it might resonate with yours. Religion becomes an issue when the ache and joy of life get too much for us—when we fall in love or someone dies or we lose our job or sense something we can't understand or when we're caught in a breathtaking moment looking at the sunset. A "religious" moment also can come when we see some awful cruelty or feel we have looked evil in the face or betrayed the best that is in us.

Some look to religion as that which answers all our questions about life's mystery, glory, and pain; others (like me) see it as that which deepens the questions. Right there, you have the two basic strands of religion. There are those for whom it answers questions once and for all and resolves the ache. There are others for whom it deepens the questions and there is no "once and for all." The people who loved and influenced me tended to love the questions. This book is for those whose questions are more numerous than their answers.

·   ·   ·

Here's something of my story. I need to tell a little of it because I have discovered that when we reveal something of our unique selves others can find it liberating. We give each other permission to acknowledge what appears to be most peculiar to us. When that happens we find that, as unique as each of us is, we have more in common than we realized. There is a resonance. I hope my story will tell you something about my peculiar take on Christianity and invite you to take a second look. How my pattern of believing and belonging came to me may help you see how you came by yours and how it still wields power over you. Mine came to me by way of reaction to my parents, who thought religion was for the middle and upper classes. Life was basically unfair, and the rich always win. They were rather like the porter in Bhutan who, when my friend Sam Keen asked him what he thought of karma, said, "Oh, that's for rich people." Religion was a kind of luxury for the leisured classes and was often used to keep people in their place.

I was born into a working-class family in suburban London in 1940 —the baby of the family with a brother nine years older and a sister seventeen years my senior. My dad was a bricklayer and stonemason. My mother was a cook and housemaid. She was from the country; he was from the suburbs. His parents were "in service" at a large house. His mother was housekeeper; his father was the coachman. When he was in his teens my dad ran away to sea and was captain's steward on a ship evacuating refugees from Russia after the Revolution in 1917. He came back an idealistic socialist. My mother and father tried being cook and butler, respectively, for a rising young couple, but my father got into arguments about "class" with their employers.

On my mother's side, my grandparents were country people: gamekeepers and poachers. My grandfather was killed in the Great War, leaving my grandmother with eight children. My mother, the oldest daughter, took on the role of being the little mother to her siblings. When she was eight she had infantile paralysis (polio) and was sent by a generous village matron to the Children's Hospital on Great Ormond Street in London. She said that her year there was the best year of her life.

My mother was a fatalist. Life was hard and there was no point in getting above yourself. She was proud of her three children, who all did well. She could imagine a different life for us but not for herself. My father was an optimist of great integrity and earthy humor who worked hard to send my older brother to public school (private school in England) and was very proud when he secured a commission as an officer in the army.

My father died suddenly when he was fifty-one and I was eleven. The years until I went to college were spent in a cold-water flat with my mother and grandmother. The cramped space, singing in a church choir, and my studies in grammar school all made for a rich interior life. I got lost in books and spent all my pocket money from a paper route and delivering groceries on taking the train into central London to go to the theater, mainly the Old Vic, where I saw most of Shakespeare's plays over a five-year period from age fourteen to nineteen.

My parents had the respect for and suspicion of religion characteristic of their class—neither went to church. Sunday school was handy, though, so off I went to a very evangelical affair with a mean minister and a kindly Sunday school teacher. When I was about eight I was admitted to the choir of the low-church parish (moderate evangelical) near my home, and this changed my life. I had given my heart to Jesus in Sunday school and now I sang my heart out for Him in the choir. In those days one could move through the whole ecumenical movement without leaving the Church of England. The church was a means of upward mobility—represented for me by being in the choir and singing in such exotic places as Westminster Abbey and St. Paul's Cathedral. Singing in the coronation choir in 1953 was a special honor.

The Christianity of my early years was that of a morally serious English gentleman: kind and honest, very repressed, and on occasion ruthless. In spite of its class-ridden context, I learned that I was loved. I have retained an affection for the hearty evangelicalism of my youth and the sense of the sacred from my conversion to a more catholic view of Christianity—all within the Church of England. I know this is confusing, but it's important to understand that for me being a Christian is a romance, a pilgrimage into the unknown, a process of continual conversion. It is not difficult for me to embrace contradiction. I can be Protestant, Catholic, agnostic, and devout believer all at the same time. In this respect I am very English. As far as I am concerned, the walls between people and traditions are very thin.

My "belief" began with an experience of being loved, and that experience was then tested in communion with others who were touched by the same images. Those who taught me helped me question and refine my experience. Above all, I was touched by the example of those who loved others, really loved them and believed that they had more in common with others (of whatever belief or disbelief) than could possibly divide them. Later, I would call this strong sense of solidarity *communion*.

The local Anglicans (Episcopalians) in suburban London took me under their wing and I flourished in a good church choir, found my way to grammar school and on to college. These members of the Church of England were good people, kind and compassionate and full of self-confidence about the role of Christianity and England in the world. And they loved Jesus. They read the Bible every day and they said their prayers. Our church had a relationship with one of the halfway houses in East London. There was a doctor who would give two months a year to do volunteer work in Iran. But he was a tyrant at home and a sanctimonious and harsh father. All his children rebelled. There also was a hearty major general who loved Billy Graham and was not sure that our vicar was truly one of the "saved." The religion was very tribal—very English—but wasn't all bad. I look back on it with great affection.

When I was about fourteen years old, I announced to my mother that I wanted to be a priest. The idea had been planted in my head on some teenager weekend. I must have been a smart-ass because all I remember of the weekend was my giving the young priest a hard time by making fun of the church to such an extent that, in exasperation, he turned to me and said, "If you're so smart, why don't you try it?"

Christianity as Love Affair

I was zapped—zapped by the romance of it all, the call to some great adventure. The idea wouldn't go away. My bemused mother told my grandmother, who spontaneously came out with the comment "I hope to Christ he doesn't." She didn't mean it piously! She was always a lively skeptic and thought all religious people were suspect. My other grandmother had a deep and attractive faith. Skepticism and faith: they go together. That's part of my story. They are part of the love affair.

Religion became a love affair with all the ups and downs you would expect from a passionate relationship. I loved the pictures and the stories. Above all, I was struck by the wonder of creation, the wonder that there was anything at all and not just nothing. Without knowing it at the time, I was drawn instinctively to the mystical.

Since whoever God was came to us in a personal, not private, way—through creation, through flesh and blood—I naturally gravitated in my teens to a more Catholic version of Christianity, with its emphasis on images, sacraments, and rituals. I left behind the kind of Protestantism that had no stomach for art and images and that found anything mystical suspect. I was brought up a fundamentalist, but it never took hold. God's generosity kept breaking in. I couldn't stomach the exclusive interpretation of Scripture, and when I was younger this caused me a lot of distress.

When I left for college, I went on an intellectual adventure in biblical interpretation. The Bible was taken apart in front of me. It is still being taken apart by scholars. Some of these scholars are my friends. Right now, the question of who Jesus is, is in the news. The New Testament is on the cover of *Newsweek* and *Time,* and the novel *The Da Vinci Code* (presenting a very different Christianity from that of the Vatican or the Southern Baptist Convention) is a bestseller. There is radical skepticism about the authenticity of the words attributed to Jesus. What is significant is not that all these "new" ideas are right but that they are in the air. To tell the truth, none of this makes much impression on me. It's not that I don't care, but from the very beginning when I heard those Bible stories, I believed them but I believed them in a mystical way—as a way of communicating deep truths by way of images. I instinctively read the Bible as allegory and metaphor, not as literal truth (even though the historical context was important).

Later I came under the influence of some Anglican monks who

introduced me to the mystical and intellectual life. The monks taught me to believe in God as a means of saving me from believing in anything else. They encouraged a kind of "atheism" with regard to my giving ultimate allegiance to anything else—to science, political ideology, instinct. It was the first time I encountered this kind of atheism—the kind of believing that's committed to questions and to not knowing all the answers. The kind of faith that encouraged a questioning skepticism and, at the same time, a deep compassion, was new to me. I have a feeling that some of the monks would have been considered nonbelievers by many of my friends because they were too open, too ready to entertain ideas and listen to stories from other traditions. The big problem with "God" (the monks said) is idolatry. "God" gets stuck to ideas like patriotism or personal virtue—things that give us the illusion of control. Most of what we *think* of as God isn't God. They taught me to be skeptical because *believing* was a moving target and its test was always love. A sense of belonging was necessary but it was the kind that didn't worry about self-preservation and was always breaking its own boundaries. Other religions and all honest questioning, they told me, are part of God's plan. Don't be afraid of them.

Even as a young kid, God was to me an impenetrable mystery, yet I experienced this deep reality as personal. God wasn't a person, but God was personal. By that, I don't mean private; I mean that the sense of the divine came to me through other persons and wasn't and isn't, in the first instance, a matter of belief. Eventually I came to appreciate the insight of the mystics that we are nothing else but questions and longings, and that these deepening questions lead us beyond tribe and class into a vision of humanity that leaves no one out. Beliefs are a kind of ladder. When we get to our destination, the ladder can be kicked away.

I began to see that an energy had been at work in my life all along that is more than "me," more than the longings that bubble around just under the surface of my life. I remember reading somewhere in the work of a contemporary French mystic, *"Il y a en moi quelque chose plus moi que moi-même."* There is in me something more me than myself. I'm grateful for this energy. I am also confused and frustrated by it. And most important of all, I find that I am in love with it (or is it a him? a her?—it has the characteristics of the personal). Being connected to this energy became the most important thing in my life. Life turned into a romance of being lost and found.

Through a series of events that now in retrospect seem providential, I was ordained an Episcopal priest and always nursed the vision in my heart of Christianity as simply a love story. I was shocked to discover that many Christians didn't see it that way. I was very naive. I never worried much about the fate of unbelievers. For one thing, they seemed very much like me, and as for the card-carrying believers, they didn't seem that much different from the unbelievers, and just enough of them seemed *worse* for me to feel uneasy. As a teenager and young man I thought, naively, that we—all of us on the planet—were part of one great adventure. We were one family, whether we believed or not.

Waking Up

There were several great awakenings that jolted me out of my naïveté. The first was a moral earthquake. I always believed that forgiveness was at the heart of the Christian enterprise, but I was brought up with a great sense of shame and guilt. The version of Christianity that formed me gave off conflicting signals. On the one hand, it was very moralistic and burdensome; on the other, it was supposed to have forgiveness at its center. The trouble was that when push came to shove, the former always won over the latter. I tried to lead a virtuous life—I still think it's worth a try!—but I couldn't. I kept messing up. The Christianity that had been passed on to me saddled me with a crippling idealism. There was no way I could live up to it. So I led something of a double life and in the end collapsed. I don't mean that I had a breakdown. I simply discovered the kind of liberating belief that was known only by those who feel themselves to be morally and spiritually shipwrecked and who experience the miracle of resurrection in knowing that they are loved. In the end it wasn't beliefs that saved me. It was other people. It was simply other people loving me.

The second awakening was intellectual and involved my daring to follow my inner instincts about the Bible and the dogmas of Christianity. From a very young age, instinctively I never believed them literally, even though literal acceptance was required. Yet I hung on to both the Bible and the teachings because I sensed there was something in them of infinite importance that had nothing to do with their being taken literally. This obviously separates me from the literalists but it also cuts me off from some of my liberal friends who want to throw too much—even everything—overboard. They seem just as fundamentalist as the people they ridicule. You don't have to surrender your intellect to be a believer.

In the first awakening I discovered true forgiveness, and in the second, intellectual freedom in seeing the religious quest in poetic, mythical, and metaphorical terms. My head was beginning to clear. My heart didn't feel so heavy.

As a romantic, what did I want? Perhaps the weakness of romanticism is the fact that one can easily get lost in it. It can lead to shipwreck. And so I noticed in myself an opposite pull toward clarity and stability. I wanted the bits and pieces of me to be in touch with one another. *Character, integrity,* and *integration* became important words for me. I didn't want either to be a victim of my emotions or enslaved to dogma. Early on I realized that the name of the game is freedom, and if religion doesn't liberate the soul it's not worth a damn. These early battles have still to be fully resolved and have affected my deepest relationships.

When did the world begin to slip? Was it when I got married? When we had children? When we moved back from England in the early 1970s? At any rate, the world began to slip away from me about twenty years ago, and I have never fully recovered. I believe that the slipping away of the world was the true beginning of my spiritual journey. There was breakdown and there was breakthrough. The road has been spiritually perilous, and I have been miraculously preserved. Looking back, the experience of therapy was central in helping me face that inner, unintegrated world. I joined a growing crowd of pilgrims who were realizing that their inner work was not a private trip but a way of helping to heal the collective psyche. Much of the violence perpetrated in the name of religion is largely due to people not recognizing their own demons. At last I came to see that the personal, social, and political were all of a piece. I was beginning to grow up. My body became a source of wisdom.

I have gone through two awakenings of the body; I think of them as wordless conversions. One was in the 1980s, the other fairly recent. I had to be pushed to discover the body's wisdom. I had always believed intellectually in its importance for the spiritual life; after all, "incarnation" is a key concept in Christianity. It tells us that flesh and blood matter, but in practice it has more often sent messages denying the sacredness of the body and its longings.

We need to acknowledge the damage done by the Christian tradition for making a mess of things by setting the body against the spirit, for our shame and embarrassment over the physical. It has left a terrible scar. But it took the better part of my lifetime to internalize and integrate this wisdom. The Protestantism of my childhood was hard on the body, and I hear similar stories from my Catholic friends. The two awakenings described were breakthroughs in this long, hesitant progress.

The first time my body spoke to me was at Esalen Institute on California's Big Sur coast, a retreat center devoted to exploring the mind/body connection. I had been staying at a Benedictine monastery not far away and had booked myself for one of these massages for which Esalen is famous. (Many clergy aren't at home in their bodies and look askance when I tell them that I have a massage whenever I can.) At the time, however, I was skeptical about what Esalen stood for. In my mind it was uncritically New Age and touchy-feely, and my skepticism only deepened when I learned that my massage therapist was called Lionesse (that's all).

She began the treatment on an open deck overlooking the Pacific. Speaking gently in what sounded like metaphysical gobbledygook, she claimed that she was "lining up my chakras" as she played a Tibetan flute over me. My critical mind was having a high old time with all this until another voice spoke to me—the voice of the body. It asked, "How do you feel?" "I feel great," I replied. "Do you trust this woman?" "Yes, I do," I answered. The body said, "Then shut up!" This was a wake-up call, and I have tried to listen to my body's messages ever since.

The second wake-up call came in the mid-1990s when I was diagnosed with prostate cancer. At first, since the cancer was termed "incidental," I suppressed the knowledge that I had the disease. In fact, my urologist never mentioned the c-word at all. It took me about three years to admit that I had cancer. Eventually I took part in a study led by Dr. Dean Ornish (whose pioneer work in heart disease is well known) investigating whether a change in diet and lifestyle could halt and even reverse prostate cancer (and by implication other cancers). The program requires not only a strict vegan diet (no animal or dairy products) but also daily yoga and relaxation practice, a routine of aerobic exercise, and regular sessions of group support.

As of this, I don't yet know whether this program will cure me of my cancer, but it certainly has put me on a wonderful road to health. I discovered that healing doesn't come in bits and pieces. I believe I am engaged in a healing process that's more than the localized curing of a particular cancer. When I opened myself up to changes in my eating habits and lifestyle, I found that personal issues of mind, heart, and soul bubbled to the surface, also demanding healing and attention. Physically, emotionally, and spiritually I've experienced a drive toward integration that has become the engine of my life. This means paying attention to the body's wisdom and making sure to use creativity and joy as well as woundedness and sickness.

I find that the daily routine of yoga and relaxation has deepened my prayer life and broadened my sympathies. I couldn't pray that I would be healed of my cancer without encountering questions of intellectual honesty and moral truth-telling. I had to face afresh my failures and relearn what an awesome and wonderful thing it is to be a human being.

So my experience of living with the disease has been an occasion of healing, creativity, and celebration. *It helps me to understand that belonging comes before believing.* The body has its own wisdom and is grounded in experience, not dogma. I'm grateful to both of these awakenings for bringing me face to face with the possibility and gift of integrity—of the relation of all things in a web of connection we call love.

At the beginning of this new century, my life is still going through upheavals caused, in part, by the attractions and repellent aspects of religion that I encountered when I was young. Religion does great harm because it fosters closed-minded beliefs and restrictive ways of belonging. But religion also is like a love affair. It opens up the world and extends the boundaries of belonging and believing. For a lot of people love is destructive, too, but that doesn't stop us from falling in love over and over again and getting hurt by it.

I believe myself to be on a journey with countless other people into the full religious experience of sin, doubt, and longing. There are many paths and many roads. We question. We have doubts. We get angry. We have bodies that need attending to. They have much to teach us.

So what is my religious tribe at this point? I am a Catholic Christian—something of an anomaly, because the Roman Catholic Church doesn't think I am, at least not officially. When I say this, people tend to respond, "Ah! Catholic with a small c—that means universal." I protest and try to explain that I believe in the unity of flesh and spirit, in the mystical path, in sacraments. I try to explain that I belong to a tribe in the making. My "Catholic" tribe has yet to come into being.

I feel blessed at the privilege of being able to stumble along the Christian way with some amazing companions. My faith has sustained me through many upheavals, experiences of betrayal, shame, and disappointment, and my failures have taught me something of what grace is about. I treasure especially the friends who seem to see right through me and still take delight in the fact that I am. I'm grateful to other friends and colleagues who, when I have messed up royally, never diminished me with condemnation or judgment. I have saddened these good companions at times but never lost them. They showed and still show me that being a human being is a glorious thing and that at the heart of being human is love—active, hurting, healing, and transforming.

Life is a continual process of reassessment and readjustment, which brings me back to that roving pain inside. It's a pain we need, one that calls us back to a life that cannot be controlled or manipulated, into the life of faith.

What about practice? I read and write every day. I say my prayers, which means morning prayer from the Book of Common Prayer. I find that the discipline it offers is liberating. I attend the Eucharist at least twice a week, and every morning, prefacing an hour of yoga, relaxation, and meditation, my wife and I recite the following prayers:

> In your hands we rest,
> in the cup of whose hands
> an ark sailed rudderless
> and without mast.
> In your hands we rest,
> and own a providence
> as large as sea and sky
> that could make
> of the aimless wandering of the ark
> a new beginning for the world.
> In your hands we rest,
> ready and content this day.

And

> We are the boat.
> We are the sea.
> I sail in you.
> You sail in me.

This captures my experience and that of many. Alongside the pain of the world there is abiding joy and peace.

Peregrinatio—pilgrimage—is a kind of journey for those who feel far from home and are in a state of exile. And all *pro amore Christi* (for the love of Christ). The cost? Becoming a stranger to all that is familiar and safe. The enemy of *peregrinatio* is thoughts that encourage us to be competitive and comparative, or anything that makes us lose touch with gratitude and wonder. Those who belong to any tradition or to none who, for the sake of love, are on pilgrimage are my brothers and sisters, my community.

To try following this path, I have had to go on a journey of the imagination. I believe that the way out of our decadence (the state of believing that futility and absurdity are normal) is to recover the life of the imagination and to see the religious impulse as natural to us.

I often think that mine must be the slowest conversion in history. I'm not, like St. Paul, the chief of sinners, but I do lay claim to being the slowest of learners. My mentors have been my children, my spiritual path, my broken marriage, and my miraculous friends who refuse to abandon me to despair and stupidity. The courage of a new spouse, the spontaneity of children, the faithfulness of friends—all have contributed to my salvation.

Life so far has been a struggle to evade the truth, and yet the truth—as relationship, as love—pursues me. Layer upon layer of self-deception has been peeled away, and it's not over. There have been moments of sheer grace and wild splendor when I have felt myself flying or floating. The illusions disappear and there is only grace.

This is how it is with me. How is it with you?

Prologue

Does Faith Have a Future?

We live in . . . a time of bad language. What new sorts of religious outlook might replace what we have lost?

—Don Cupitt, *After God: The Future of Religion*

Two Tales about Religion in Our Time

A friend confided to me that there were difficulties with an upcoming wedding because the groom's grandmother was "very religious." I asked, "Is she lovingly 'very religious' or pain-in-the-ass 'very religious'?" My friend confessed that Grandma was religious in the latter sense. People had to tiptoe around her, and she confused a spirit of condemnation with faithfulness.

After the September 11 bombings, the journalist and antitheist Christopher Hitchens wrote, "Here is the enemy, in as plain and clear view as it could possibly be: theocratic fascism, disclosed in its most horrific form. If that's the battle, if they want a clash of civilizations, they can have one, and I will never get bored with prosecuting it."

Only a few decades before this writing, our world—at least, the developed world—seemed headed for a safe, secular, scientifically enlightened future. God was dead, if he had ever existed. So what happened to bring us to our current pass, where issues of belief still intrude into everyday affairs like a family wedding and terrify us with nightmare images of bloody Middle Eastern street scenes or the World Trade Center collapsing in flames?

There's no quick answer to that question, but a few clear signs can be discerned. It's clear, for one thing, that many people born around the middle of the twentieth century, who once abandoned their religious heritage in relief or disgust, have started to grope their way back to some kind of spiritual practice, or at least felt the stirrings of spiritual need. It's also clear that in nearly every major faith, strains of radical fundamentalism have been rising up, renewing or reintensifying faith conflicts that go back, in some cases, for millennia. The causes of both phenomena are linked to global events that on the surface seem to have little to do with "religion." But as we'll see over and over, any attempt to isolate the spiritual life in a cloister today is doomed to fail.

As a Christian priest, thinking about the future of religion and humankind fills me with equal parts of hope, dread, and excitement.

This book is about Christianity, its expression in symbols and stories, and how its practice can be redefined as art. Writing it has not been an exercise in objective scholarship. Nor has it been a foray into religious journalism. It is a snapshot of the world in which I live. I wrote it because the Christian world for me is no longer as life-bearing as it once was. In fact, much of it is downright toxic. Yet I still see great hope in it and don't want to give it up. It has spoken to and sustained me through the ups and downs, the glories and follies of my life.

Much of my hope and sustenance rests with people I love and respect, from good friends to scholars and pilgrims I have never met. Their insights and wisdom are as vital to this book as anything I bring to it. I don't always agree with these fellow Christians or other faith practitioners, but they have one thing in common: others are safe in their presence. In the world they're seeking to build, no one is persecuted or ridiculed. They have helped me learn to inhabit a religious world where it's commonplace to argue without consigning anyone to hell.

I know many other people, however, who have an extremely uneasy relationship with religion, if they have one at all. I have often seen the light go out in someone's eyes when they learn that I am a priest, simply because their experience of religion has been of the hating or mindless sort. I believe that if we would give each other some attention, we would find that we have a lot in common. These are the people to whom this book is addressed, and I want to introduce a few of them.

Fellow Pilgrims

My friend Carol is not totally averse to coming to church, but as the mother of two small children she has doubts about having them baptized. That might be because it has something to do with Jesus. Talking about God is okay, but to her, Jesus-talk seems too narrow, and she's haunted by the memory of her grandmother, who insisted that only the "saved" were going to get into heaven. The rest would burn in hell. It's no wonder Carol is squirrelly about religion. She's convinced, however, that there's something spiritually worthwhile that's "beyond belief"— outside the boundaries of authoritarian belief systems—and she would like her children to be in touch with that.

The turning point for her was at an Evangelical summer camp she attended when she was fourteen (mostly because they had horses and she could ride every day). One evening in a talk about Christian faith, Carol was firmly told that her closest high school friend, who was Jewish, was one of the damned. She immediately called her mom to take her home, and a heavy door slammed in her soul. The Christian God was an unfeeling bastard. For Carol and countless others, Christianity seems irreparably tainted as a religion of a wrathful and capricious God.

Therapist Christina Grof gave up being a Christian for much the same reason. As a child and adolescent she was made to feel worthless, scarred, and unrighteous, and, like Carol, was told that her non-Christian friends weren't going to make it. Even Christians lived pretty miserable lives, exiled in a "vale of tears"—cut off from life. Making matters worse, the God of the Church was remote and relentlessly male, distant, and external. In *The Thirst for Wholeness*, she writes:

Chances are, there will be a priest preaching salvation by some vague external entity, or a rabbi talking about some God who is removed and unavailable and grand compared with us miserable human beings. . . . Even if God is represented as a loving God, he is almost exclusively male, and he exists apart from us.

Carol and Christina listened to what those in authority told them and, like many of us, believed that those in charge had a handle on what Christianity was really about. What they heard was so repellent that they wanted nothing to do with it.

Scholar Elaine Pagels, who hasn't given up identifying herself as a Christian, asks an important and refreshing question: Who gets to say what is "Christian" and what isn't? She refuses to accept the voices in authority as the *only* voices, and she writes extensively about these *other* voices from the tradition, thereby encouraging us to take a second look. In her book *Beyond Belief,* she writes:

> When I found that I no longer believed everything I thought Christians were supposed to believe, I asked myself, Why not just leave Christianity—and religion—behind, as so many others have done? Yet I sometimes encountered in churches and elsewhere—in the presence of a venerable Buddhist monk, in the cantor's singing at a bar mitzvah, and on mountain hikes—something compelling, powerful, even terrifying that I could not ignore, and have come to see that, besides belief, Christianity involves practice—and paths toward transformation.

Another friend, Jim, a former Roman Catholic priest who left the priesthood several years ago, also comes to mind. In a recent e-mail he wrote:

> I am feeling somewhat at sea in my life. I feel isolated, helpless, soiled, angry, horrified, fearful. Secondly, my Christian practice is wobbly. I am getting ideas and images of Christianity which, while illuminating and exciting, are a far cry from my traditional beliefs and education. I don't know of any others who are in my

position. Are there people who want to explore a different way of being a Christian? I am not going to Easter ceremonies this year; I do not want to hear "Jews" saying "Crucify him!" or participate in hymns with images of war and conflict. See, I have more questions and doubts than even firm sand to stand on!

Jim, I think, represents a growing number of the disillusioned and questioning, even among those highly trained in Christian theology. He hasn't quite abandoned the Church but he is concerned about the inauthenticity of much of contemporary Christianity. While aching for a spiritual life, he cannot find it in any of the Church's public manifestations.

I find myself at home with these four friends. I admire their questions and am encouraged by their honesty. For the past few years I, too, have felt something wrong about the way religion is presented by those "in authority." Until recently I've lacked the confidence to question my received view of Christianity, simply because it's hard to imagine something you've accepted all your life as something *other* than you've known it. I don't mean that I've been uncritical—I haven't been reticent about saying just what I think about the meanness and cruelty of much of so-called Christian behavior—but I rarely questioned the core exclusionary beliefs. The time has come, however, for a more comprehensive effort at reimagining the faith I live in and the role of religion in all our lives.

More and more often I meet people I respect who seem to be getting along fine without believing in God. In fact, they feel liberated from living in a God-infested world. Belief in God has proved exhausting and destructive. Some of the more spiritually inclined have turned to Buddhism with relief because it is a God-free religion with compassion and attentiveness at its heart.

It might come as a surprise to some that this aversion to God has a long history and is found deep within the mystical traditions—not least in Christianity. There are, classically, two movements: the liberation *of* God from our projections and projects, and our liberation *from* the God of those projections and projects. We need both. "God" needs to be set free from human prejudices and limitations, and we need to be liberated from allegiance to that God. Anyone, even the most ardent believer, who isn't occasionally repulsed by religion must be asleep. At the same time, the longing for a God who is beyond our projections and projects is surely as deeply felt.

If we take the time to explore and learn from Christianity's terrible and wonderful history, we might discover that it is different from how we'd imagined it. Recent scholarship reveals that there was, for example, much more variety of belief and expression in the early Church than previously thought. It emphasized the transformed life rather than acceptance of a belief system—an emphasis that many today are discovering. Many spiritual seekers today are able to live with diversity of practice and a wide variety of doctrine. They are looking for community and not dogma.

What I sense I and my friends long for is a community of free persons united in love and justice. As critic Frank Kermode notes, we "cannot be reconciled to churches that claim sole access to the truth of doctrine and discipline," and the reward of honest exploration "may be a truer knowledge not only of Christianity . . . but also of the other great religions." I share that hope and conviction. And I am beginning to experience it with a growing number of companions across the religious spectrum, including many who wouldn't call themselves religious at all.

Religion's Bad Record

Someone wrote to me not long ago about having attended a baptism at Grace Cathedral in San Francisco, where I work: "I have to say that as a total skeptic when it comes to religion—particularly when one considers the tribal brutality conducted in the name of the various religions in the Middle East—I entered the service thinking 'What relevance does any of this ancient ceremony, language, and procedures have in the context of today's world?'" It turned out that this man had a positive experience at the baptism, but his question is still a good one.

We're living in a world that seems dangerously chaotic. The human family, if it can be called one, is caught in a cycle of violence, often religiously sanctioned. Despite the fact that much of this violence finds its true source in conflicts over resources or tribal vengeance, belief is too often the justification or the trigger. The violence against children and women perpetrated or covered up by organized religion is another cause of much bitterness and disaffection with it.

A different kind of chaos is engendered by the fast-moving, voraciously materialistic culture that is poised to spread across the globe—sometimes provoking the religiously sanctioned violence. There are too many cracks in the fabric of things—fissures in the world—for us to discern any ground rules. This chaos is manifested in the cosmic (with the threat not only of war but also of apocalyptic disaster) and the trivial (our depressed consumerist culture). We aren't all reading from the same page anymore.

What makes the task of revisioning religion so urgent today are the velocity of change, the shrinking world of globalization, and the longing to keep the human community together before we blow ourselves to pieces. All three tend to make people fearful and attracted to religions that provide rest and answers to their anxious and exhausting questioning. One such answer is the promise of apocalypse—the assurance that we will be among the saved while the world burns up. There's a kind of relief in believing that the whole sorry mess will be swept away and there will be a new beginning. Apocalypse is in the air: many Americans believe that the end of the world is coming soon, probably at a movie theater near you. This juxtaposition of the serious and the flippant is deliberate. Religion has become a department of the entertainment industry, a dispenser of routine terror and packaged hope.

To some people, the destructive, ignorant, or escapist manifestations of religion today are simply of a piece with religion's bad record throughout history—which is all they know or choose to know of religion. "What about the Spanish Inquisition?" people demand, sounding like a Monty Python sketch. Or, "What about the burning of witches, the Crusades, mad Irish nuns, crazed televangelists?" But these are arguments in the shallow end of the discussion about religion. It becomes a pastime, a lazy and simplistic form of entertainment, to blame religion for all the world's ills.

Nor can all violence be laid at the feet of believers. It's reckoned that 85 million to 100 million were slaughtered in the twentieth century in the name of communism. Yes, much religion is mindless and cruel or just plain silly. Why not admit it? Human beings do daft and terrible things. No one would deny that religious traditions lose their way, get corrupted, become tyrannical; Christianity is no exception. It is also true that religion has attracted intellectually gifted people and done a great deal of good. Why not admit that, too?

Opium of the People?

My friend Carl has already made up his mind, so when I mentioned the idea of his taking another look at Christianity, he said, "Fat chance!" To him the evidence of history is overwhelming: religion is a failure. "Sure," he conceded, "there have been some great human beings caught up in it, but the verdict over time is clear. Religion sucks." To him and to many, atheism is the thinking person's only option.

Besides devaluing human life and breeding violence, Carl argues, religious belief is for the stupid. It is of the order of believing the earth is flat and in the existence of unicorns. It is infantile regression. Religions in general, he insists, teach people not to think for themselves, but to be satisfied with handed-down, authoritarian, traditional wisdom, never based on evidence. I tend to agree with Carl and point out that any ideologically driven people (including atheists) tend not to think for themselves.

A priest and theologian I admire, Kenneth Leech, points to "the sheer mediocrity and dullness of the religious life of the mainstream. Frankly, it is boring. It opens no windows in the soul." The culture in general isn't any better off. "The fate of the soul is the fate of the social order," Theodore Roszak once said, bemoaning the rise of the narcissistic, me-first culture of the 1970s. But we should expect that a consumer society would produce a consumer spirituality. Consumer spirituality assumes that each individual soul must seek to take care of itself. Each of us is on a solitary quest, and if we're lucky it will help us cope with our own sadness and mess. As for the unjust conditions that produce so much pain and destruction, there's nothing we can do about them. These are the lies this book seeks to confront.

But it's not hard to see why so many people are turned off. Religion is broken, and something needs to be done to fix it. It needs to be reinvented. The word *invent* suggests two things: a discovery of something genuinely new, and the uncovering of something that was already there. When it comes to religion, we need to do both— embrace the new and recover what has been lost.

Religion, after all, isn't about to die out. It's here to stay. The need now is to admit that we've got it wrong. As one wise friend puts it, "Christianity is a wonderful religion but it fell into the wrong hands!" More positively viewed, it may be that Christianity has yet to come into its own.

Reimagining Religion as a Shared Quest

When he listens to evangelists on the radio, Evangelical pastor Brian McLaren isn't sure he wants to be a Christian anymore.

> the very formulations that sound so good and familiar to the "saved" sound downright weird or even wicked to the "seekers" and the skeptics. These people come to me to ask questions, and I give my best answers, my best defenses, and by the time they leave my office, I have convinced myself that their questions are better than my answers.

Many of us feel that the old story of religion—the way it makes sense of our place in creation—is in need of serious revision. McLaren writes, "Either Christianity itself is flawed, failing, untrue, or our modern Western, commercialized, industrial-strength version of it is in need of a fresh look." Human beings have always told themselves stories about their longings. In fact, this need for stories binds us together. We need a new way of telling the Great Story.

And our search for how to revise it must start with questions. The poet Wallace Stegner wrote, "The guts of any significant fiction—or autobiography—is an anguished question." An anguished question brings things out into the open so the story can be told and retold. The same is true of our lives: the kind of questions we ask determine the kind of person we are. Educator Robert Fuller comments that "At any age, our questions define our growing edge. . . . In those places where we're most alive, we are questions, not answers." My friends Carol and Jim are asking urgent questions because the old story they were told doesn't work anymore.

A monk who greatly influenced me used to say, "The opposite of faith isn't doubt. It's certainty." Keeping the big questions alive is as important as answering them. In fact, deepening the questions is the task of mature religion. A religion of all answers keeps people in an infantile state. Once you have all the answers you have nothing to learn. But for the growing number to whom such an approach is irresponsible and unacceptable, there is another way. There always has been. It's both right in front of us and hard to find—hard because we naturally resist questions that lead us into the unknown and compel us to change.

Some take the path of least resistance and find their answers in a reassuring tribalism, which has both religious and political expressions. So strong is the need to belong that in times of crisis and insecurity, people band together for mutual support, but they do it in ways that can be destructive. Religion easily degenerates into a mechanism for excluding the stranger or nonconformist from the tribe. It's then that religion deserves to be criticized.

Sadly, we see much of the worst of religion in the world today. Religion-as-all-the-answers seems to have the upper hand. That's where we find the imperative to reinvent and reimagine the life of faith. But when we see the best of religion as a quest for meaning and community—which includes everyone—we find life and energy that heal rather than wound, love rather than hate, embrace difference rather than violently seek to eradicate it.

In light of the unstable times in which we live, questions like "Do I have to accept *everything* Christians are meant to believe?" and "Do I have to believe everything I read in the Bible?" become more frequent and urgent. Is there a chance that we might—together—reimagine the whole enterprise?

Is This Book for You?

The fastest-growing "religious" group is composed of the unaffiliated. This book is for them and for those who are ready to give religion another chance. It is also an attempt to apologize to those who have been wounded by some of religion's more bizarre and cruel expressions and manifestations. Perhaps we can walk together into a new way of understanding our longings, fears, and hopes.

If you're the sort of person for whom, as soon as you find the answer to a question, a deeper one wells up, this book is for you. It assumes that asking these basic questions (at deeper and deeper levels) is what the life of faith is all about. It also assumes that spiritually committed people, grounded in their own tradition, need not be afraid of other faiths and other stories. And it trusts that human beings have far more in common with each other than we have barriers that divide us.

- Questioning and faith go together.
- We needn't be afraid of each other.
- What unites us is stronger than what divides us.

These three assumptions have helped me appreciate traditions other than my own without my having to "give up" being a Christian. For example, I've learned a lot from friends who once abandoned Christianity yet come back to it by way of Buddhism. I have much sympathy with those who turn to that tradition for a breath of sanity. The traditional reward of Christianity is "otherworldly," while Buddhism pays off here and now in a practice that makes a difference. It is pragmatic and, at its best, leads to personal and intellectual independence. You don't have to *believe* in anything to be a Buddhist—not even in God. You are, however, called to be in the world in a certain way—a way of compassion and loving kindness. For some, this is like being led out of prison.

One of the attractions of Buddhism for Americans is that it's a set of instructions rather than a list of impossible things to believe before breakfast. That's where Christianity could do with some work—as a way of imagination rather than a set of dogmas. Timothy Radcliffe, the former head of the Roman Catholic Dominican Order, writes of seeing everyone of goodwill as a partner in building God's home with us. I like that image of everyone building a home, each of us building a shelter for the other.

> This can happen in wonderful and unexpected ways. Our Japanese brother Oshida founded a Christian community in the hill near Mount Fuji. In the garden he set up a statue of the Buddha, with the child Jesus on his lap. The villagers began to come discreetly during the night to leave offerings. A place was coming to be where people of different faiths could gather and prepare for the Kingdom.

The image of the child Jesus sitting on the Buddha's lap appeals to me and captures the spirit of this book. It is an image of the Kingdom. "The Kingdom" is a sort of shorthand signifying an inclusive community of faith, love, and justice. This book is an invitation to people of different faiths and of no formal faith to gather and make space for the coming of the Kingdom.

What Does Reimagining Religion Involve?

- Moving from the narrowly tribal and exclusive to the transformational and inclusive—seeing God, good, and dignity in those *unlike* ourselves.
- Exchanging the dogmatic stance of certainty for the way of imagination, which is not frightened by the thought that God is greater than religion.

- And, since this is written from a Christian perspective, exploring the three basic images of Christianity (Mary, Jesus, the Trinity). These images illuminate three basic longings: our struggle with the new (pregnancy); our enduring the past, present, and future (suffering); and our desire for love (communion). These longings bind us together as human beings whether we are "believers" or not.

I hope that readers, if believers, might deepen their faith, and that nonbelievers might give religion a second look and find in it the love, healing, and transformation they need. For those on spiritual journeys other than mine, I welcome and need your companionship.

1

Belonging and Believing
Getting Past Tribalism

Oh, how we hate one another for the love of God.

—Cardinal Newman

Human beings are tribal and scribal. We can't live without a sense of belonging: we are tribal. And we can't do without appealing to texts, stories, customs, and creeds that support our tribal identity: we are scribal. But there are many tribes and thousands of texts, so we go to war over territory and over whose tribal story is true. For example, I heard someone say, "How could the Christian West abandon Christian Serbia to the Muslims? What a betrayal!" The point of religion for her (in this case Serbian Orthodoxy) was to cement and protect ethnic solidarity *against* others.

Belonging and believing are indispensable to us, but they get us into trouble. It requires great skill, discipline, and dedication to honor belonging to a particular community without becoming defensive and exclusive. It is equally difficult to affirm deeply held convictions without being threatened by or contemptuous of those held by others. Reimagining religion calls us to a new level of spiritual maturity that is open to questions and unafraid of difference, and sees the call to unity stronger than the call to divisiveness.

The physicist Freeman Dyson wrote in 2002, "I have no use for a theology that claims to know the answers to deep questions but bases its arguments on the beliefs of a single tribe. I am a practicing Christian but not a believing Christian. To me, to worship God means to recognize that mind and intelligence are woven into the fabric of our universe in a way that altogether surpasses our comprehension." The phrase "I am a practicing Christian but not a believing Christian" is extraordinarily wise. Dyson realizes that a single tribe doesn't have all the answers.

A few simple affirmations or principles are a good place to begin because they unite all people of goodwill—nonbelievers and believers alike. Compassion, respect, and working for justice transcend religious and ideological differences; if we look deep enough, they can be found in all the great stories of various tribes. Our first task in reimagining religion, then, is to move from the narrowly tribal, where our story is the only story, to a wider definition of "tribe" that can embrace stories other than our own, told by people who are different from us.

Demonizing the Other

The world is alive with religious conflict about believing and belonging. Although they occupy they same geographical space, competing tribal stories set the Serbian Orthodox against the Bosnian Muslim; the Belfast Protestant against the Belfast Catholic; the Hindu Indian against the Muslim Indian; the Palestinian against the Israeli. We don't like being in the hot seat and being questioned about who we think we are. We love simplistic solutions to explain complex political and religious realities. It would make life easier if people on either side could simply say, "Muslims are mad," or "The United States is evil." Is there a way of imagining religion that does justice to the differences in the various traditions and, at the same time, is able to bring them together into a higher unity? Can we believe and belong without consigning to hell those who don't?

Believing and belonging don't just affect us personally. The world community is in agony about them. For millions, fundamentalism and tribalism are the two clear and secure solutions to a world falling apart. This isn't a dig at conservatives. I am a conservative, in that I want to keep intact and pass on to the next generation all that's good in the life I have received. Liberals, in their own way, are just as prey to tribalism and fundamentalism as conservatives.

Most of us feel the need to take refuge in one enclave or another—in political ideologies, in gated communities, in gangs or exclusive hideaways—anywhere to feel safe and among our own kind. But boundaries are breaking down, people are on the move, and safe havens are hard to find. It's no wonder that many seek communities based on narrow identities that build fortresses of security against enemies with no face and no return address.

Think about what you believe. Do you really believe it, or is it just a way of you're saying that you belong to a particular tribe? And does it matter? Perhaps simply belonging is more important to you than believing. We shy away from beliefs because they can send us off into a fantasy world in which we think our constructions of reality are reality itself. But we also know that the longing to belong can degenerate into our throwing ourselves into a prejudiced "in" crowd made up of people who spend their energy building walls thick enough to keep others out.

What's the remedy? Shouldn't we all be working for communities that not only tolerate but also celebrate differences and yet maintain an overall unity? This vision of *E pluribus unum* is a political principle familiar to Americans. It's time it became a religious one. In this country we talk about the checks and balances of our government. Democracy demands a never-ending conversation (sometimes bitter and contentious) about those checks and balances, and nowhere are they more fiercely debated and contested than around the issue of the separation of "church" and "state." We are committed not to enact laws that impose a particular religious viewpoint over others. There is no sign that the argument that Americans belong to a tribe that transcends all other tribes is coming to an end.

Tribal Christianity

Believing always has a context; we don't suddenly come up with a set of beliefs that we swallow whole. Even those who claim to have had a sudden conversion were "prepared" for it psychologically and spiritually by their prior experiences. Where we are born, who our parents were, make a difference.

For example, I was born in England in 1940. The world I grew up in was an Anglican/English world, which generally looked down on other forms of Christianity, let alone other religions. We also viewed people from other parts of the world—those who had the misfortune to have been born outside England—as not quite right. We found foreigners interesting but puzzling and odd. Even other Christians were suspect: Protestantism of the Baptist variety was no religion for civilized people, and Roman Catholicism was considered exotic and corrupt. No one had ever heard of Mormons. As for other religions, they weren't even on the horizon except when visitors arrived from "the mission field" where our agents were busily converting pagans.

Christians have a lot of housecleaning to do with regard to claiming to know who's in and who's outside the Celestial City. We tend to demonize people unlike us or people who were once our enemies. My tribe, when I was growing up, never liked the Germans and often despised the Irish. They came to symbolize rigidity and unreliability, just as black people came to symbolize indolence. Housecleaning in the house of belief cannot be avoided because prejudice and racism are never far from the surface.

My friend Jim reminds me that we still go on using some texts of which we should be ashamed (like those readings that kept him away from the Church at Easter). Much written in the New Testament gave Christians the justification to be anti-Semitic. Scholar Elaine Pagels told me of a commentary on St. John's Gospel written by the eminent German theologian Rudolf Bultmann in the 1930s that baldly stated that references to the Jews were only symbolic—as if that excused them. When asked what the references symbolized, Bultmann said that they represented total evil! These interpretations need to be acknowledged and apologized for and rejected permanently. Imagine today describing Muslims or gay people as evil but then naively claiming that you only meant it "symbolically."

Jim also asked me how I reconciled my preaching with some of the sentiments in the hymns and prayers we sing and recite in church. To me they are part of the archaeology of belief, and from time to time we go on a dig to explore the layers from which our longings spring. Some of the language is archaic, but insofar as it points to wonder and mystery, I'm all for keeping it. I tried to explain to Jim that I no longer cared so much about beliefs. I was more interested in how these beliefs played themselves out in human behavior. Does their believing turn people obnoxious and possibly dangerous? Or does it turn them into lovers? I, for example, get very excited about the doctrine of the Holy and Undivided Trinity. The test of Trinitarian faith is Trinitarian love. It's a doctrine about how love works. And if it isn't that, it's not worth a nickel.

Making Space for Difference

Rabbi Jonathan Sacks asks, "Why, if God is the God of all humanity, is there not one faith, one truth?" He suggests that God calls us to be unique, different, and for all of us to rejoice in the dignity of difference. The test of faith is whether I can make space for difference. A friend of mine comments, "If, every day, I could welcome just one small point of difference that separates me from someone I'm close to, or cannot avoid, the inner freedom this brought might, like the grain of mustard seed in the Gospel story, grow to visible proportions." Rabbi Sacks makes this point:

> As the great rabbis observed some 1,800 years ago, when a human being makes many coins in the same mint, they all come out the same. God makes every human being in the same mint, in the same image, his own, and yet we all come out differently. The religious challenge is to find God's image in someone who is not in our image, in someone whose color is different, whose culture is different, who speaks a different language, tells a different story, and worships God in a different way. This is a paradigm shift in understanding monotheism.

In a remark after September 11, 2001, the writer Gore Vidal suggested that the real menace in the world today is monotheism—

and he's certainly not alone in his anger at it. Each of the mono-
theistic religions has its own peculiar neurosis: Judaism is obsessive/
compulsive; Christianity is sadomasochistic; Islam suffers from
megalomania. Each religion has its own particular mess to clean up,
and in any case, monotheism as a rigid "we're right and everyone else
is wrong" affair has to go. It won't go by fighting or dismissing it, but
each religion's adherents can transform it by going deeper and
deeper into the questions it raises.

We need a paradigm shift to see the real miracle of monotheism.
According to Rabbi Sacks, the miracle is "not that there is one God
and therefore one truth, one faith, one way, but that unity above creates diversity here on earth." As we deepen and love the questions,
there are shifts in consciousness and behavior that draw us together
and make violence less likely. Our believing and belonging take on
a different shape. It might not sound like much, but you have to
begin somewhere.

The New Tribe

James Joyce frequently used the phrase "Here comes everybody" in
Finnegans Wake, and I have always loved it as a way to describe the
great tribe from which no one is excluded. For Joyce, the phrase had
many meanings: on one level, it's a description of the Catholic
Church as it is supposed to be.

"Here comes everybody" appeals to me because belonging is
everybody's birthright. I am convinced that many long for an inclusive community that is liberating and not confining and in which
they are allowed to think for themselves. I believe that a critical
mass of people (though by no means the majority) long for a communion that is not authoritarian. And I do see a different kind of
tribe emerging, one that doesn't eradicate tribal differences but celebrates them.

This new tribe will have to look at believing and belonging
through two lenses: the global and the personal. Something "big" is
happening in the world. Something enormous is dying. Something

enormous is being born. Barriers are breaking down or becoming more and more porous. It's no secret that the growing accessibility of knowledge and information is bringing about a worldwide movement of democratization. The World Wide Web has brought us closer together. Yet it also has brought us closer to outbreaks of violence. The largely Western global consciousness is changing, and we're changing along with it.

The way we talk about God is being democratized, too. For some the challenge is to choose sides. Which side are you on? The side of love or the side of hate? This is a question that crosses all lines— political and religious. Fear increases our passion to belong to a community or tribe that will take care of us. We want to be on the winning side. It's hard, in stressful times, to work for a world that includes everybody.

We are having to make room for others in ways that we haven't had to before. The early dominant Protestant culture in the United States had to make room for Roman Catholics, and they both in turn had to make room for Jews and later Muslims. Ours is now a nation of many religions and spiritualities—a pluralistic culture that, in spite of its diversity (sometimes degenerating into fragmentation), is developing certain common values of tolerance and inclusion. Just how stable and firm these values are remains to be seen.

Distinctions within Community

Working for an inclusive community of love and justice doesn't mean throwing all of us with our various beliefs into a big blender so that our believing and belonging become homogenized. It means being able to celebrate difference and argue for our point of view without wanting to imprison or kill those who differ from us. The United States, for all its problems and faults, is a remarkable achievement in this respect. As Americans, we have no particular ethnic identity to celebrate. Our ethnic community is the whole human race. At our best, we have an identity based on individual character, not on skin color or class or status. This is worth sharing with the rest of the world. The fact that we still have a long way to go should keep us humble. As a country, we still need to learn that forging respectful relationships comes before struggling to be united all under a common belief.

I love living in the United States and in San Francisco. My fellow citizens are people who used to live far away in other countries and believe "strange" things. They now live on the same block, still believing whatever they believe. The United States is a Muslim country. The United States is a Buddhist country. I discovered that the nice woman next to me on a plane recently is a witch who values the spirits in trees, rivers, and mountains. She struck me as strong and gentle and full of love. I thought, "How great to be a member of such an interesting and caring family."

The great religious traditions are having to live side by side in an intimacy never before experienced. As the world gets smaller, we are bumping up against each other more and more—sometimes with deadly consequences. When you add to this closeness the acceleration of change, there are bound to be both tensions and opportunities. Conflict and violence seem inevitable, but at least individually we can make choices. Will we choose coming together or will we be agents of polarization?

Opportunities to deepen levels of understanding and mutual respect are always available, but we have to *choose* them. Religion can no longer exist by the mere force of authority and custom. The world is very crowded, and we have to find ways to live together. Hosni Mubarak of Egypt said not long ago, "Our global village has caught fire." And since we are one village, a fire in one place soon becomes a blaze in another. Let's choose the way of dignity and respect.

Columnist Ross Werland of the *Chicago Tribune* puts it well: "The real power in churches and synagogues and mosques and temples is the honest-to-God believer whose religion in simple: love, not hate. Potentially that makes many atheists and agnostics the spiritual brothers and sisters of the 'believers,' whether nonbelievers like it or not." This simple test for religion—is it love or hate?—is an instrument of discernment that comes as naturally to little children as to adults.

Global Souls

We are seeing more and more fledgling "global souls" who travel the world and are at home nowhere. Such "in-betweeners" can provide models in the flesh of how the new tribe might come into existence and hints as to how it will experience the world. Such global souls often seem to have a gift for living responsibly and generously, or at least the sense that such living is their goal.

I know of several notable in-betweeners. One is journalist Pico Iyer: born in England of parents from Bombay—the largest British city outside London when they were growing up. When he was young they moved to California but shipped Pico off to an English boarding school. His parents were Hindu-born Theosophists, and he was educated entirely in Christian schools. He now works mostly in Buddhist countries and spends a lot of his time in Japan and in a Catholic monastery. Iyer writes, "The country where people look like me is the one where I can't speak the language."

Another, Richard Rodriguez, is an American of Mexican heritage who lives in San Francisco. To me he looks like an Aztec prince. He's gay, Catholic, a Ph.D. in English, and definitely Richard (not Ricardo). Richard writes cogent essays on culture and appears frequently on the PBS *News Hour*. Unafraid to speak his mind, he left a university post because he found out that he was hired not because he was good but because he was Latino. He has, therefore, strong views on affirmative action as a debilitating and destructive work of social engineering. We should help people, he believes, but based on poverty, not on race or ethnicity.

Kazuo Ishiguro is the author of the novel (made into a great movie) *Remains of the Day*. He is Japanese, writes in English. His wife is Scottish. They have a daughter, and they live in an England with a growing number of Muslims. Who is he culturally? He's an in-betweener. And their numbers are growing.

I presume to claim kinship with these three; at least I feel in junior partnership with them. I am Celtic, Anglo-Saxon, and (family legend has it), through my maternal grandmother, Romany. My grandchildren carry the bloodlines of most of Europe (if you're interested in bloodlines). Where am I religiously and psychologically?

Born of working-class parents during World War II, I was brought up an Evangelical Christian and became a Catholic (not Roman) within my own Anglican tradition. I have experienced Jungian and neo-Freudian analysis and was blessed with being schooled in a generous vision of Christianity. Given all that crisscrossing of references, how could I not seek membership in a new, expanded, global tribe?

Somos Todos Mestizos

A retired cop friend of mine is half Portuguese and half Norwegian/ Danish. His wife is Japanese. His children are quintessentially American mestizos (mixed bloods). Most Americans are in-betweeners, living with at least two identities. It's just that some of us carry it more visibly than others, such as Secretary of State Colin Powell, who is more visibly of African than Scottish descent. Of course race matters, and racism is still a great evil, but one of the ways to combat it may be for us to appreciate what it is to be a mestizo. Understanding that we're all, in some sense, in-betweeners is the beginning of a cure for our spiritual migraine.

This sense of being mestizo affects our understanding of religion and tends to make us a little less sure of our identity as only *one* thing. When we begin to accept our inner plurality, we get less frightened of others who manifest a different tribal mix. Some of us feel that there is an emerging tribe—the global soul—that is able to see religion as a great work of the human imagination. Seeing it as a work of the imagination doesn't make it any less true. Religion becomes a collective enterprise of cooperation between us and the unknown. Some of us identify the unknown with Spirit. Others leave it as the unknown. But we all participate in the same work of imagination.

The emerging tribe need not be put off by the three great themes of Christianity because they touch us first on the level of the imagination before they engage the intellect and invite belief. The woman and her baby, the broken and ruined man, and the community of persons (which Christians acknowledge as *Incarnation*—God in the Flesh; *Redemption*—God in the healing of the world; and *Trinity*—God revealed as a community of persons) connect us with each other on the level of common human experience. Anyone with an open mind and heart can respond to a woman and her baby, to a man in his suffering, to the longing for a loving community.

In the same way, Christianity's central sacrament of communion (the Eucharist) is a sign of what the human project is all about—all of us gathered around a table where there is plenty of food and room for everyone. It is a vision of love and justice. These themes are worthy of contemplation by all people of goodwill, whatever they believe, and resonate in the emerging tribe. And the same themes come back at me in a different form and in different stories from the other traditions.

Somos todos mestizos. There is only one tribe, and that's all of us—without exception.

2

Literalism and Other Headaches

God is the hidden God.

> —Isaiah 45:15

Anyone who thinks that God can be named is hopelessly insane.

> —Justin Martyr (paraphrased)

In David Lodge's novel *Thinks,* two characters have a conversation typical of many of contemporary conversations concerning religion. Ralph Messenger, a linguistic scientist and an easygoing unbeliever, likes Helen Reed, a lapsed Catholic who teaches literature. Ralph had been watching her walk across the university campus when he lost track of her. Later he asks, "Where were you?"

"I went into the chapel."

"What for?"

"Why do people usually go into a chapel on a Sunday morning?"

"Are you religious, then?" There's a note of disapproval, or perhaps disappointment, in his voice.

"I was brought up a Catholic. I don't believe anymore, but—"

"Oh, good."

"Why do you say that?"

"Well, it's impossible to have a rational conversation about anything important with religious people. I suppose that's I why I didn't think of looking for you in the chapel. I had you down as an intelligent, rational person. So what were you doing there, if you're not a believer?"

"Well, I don't believe literally in the whole caboodle," she says. "You know, the Virgin Birth and Transubstantiation and the infallibility of the pope and all that. But sometimes I think there must be a kind of truth behind it. Or I hope there is."

"Why?"

"Because otherwise life is so pointless."

"I don't find it so. I find it full of interest and deeply satisfying."

Helen and Ralph represent, I believe, a growing number of people on two sides of a great divide. Ralph has dismissed religion altogether, while Helen can't. There's no meeting of minds. If you're looking for common ground, it's enough to give you a headache.

Similar conversations go on between different kinds of believers within religious traditions. Take, for example, the Lutheran parish in the seaside village of Tarbaek in Denmark. Its pastor, Thorkild Grosboll, is well liked, but he's thrown the Danish Church into a tizzy because he's publicly confessed that he doesn't believe the doctrines of his church literally. "I do not believe in a physical God, in the afterlife, in the Resurrection, in the Virgin Mary. And I believe that Jesus was a nice guy who figured out what man wanted. He embodies what he believed to upgrade the human being."

Grosboll was suspended, and Denmark—not known for its religious fervor—is in a bit of a turmoil. People in his village are asking, "Must a minister believe in Christ and in the Resurrection to be a good pastor? Isn't it enough to spread Christian values and help people in need?" The controversy opens up a churchy world in which people have forgotten or never learned how to talk about God. One of the parishioners says, "The pastor's beliefs mirror mine. I don't think the earth was created by God in six days. I don't believe it's a problem."

Arguing about the Wrong Things

Such tragicomedies are being played out in churches all over the world. The argument is between two sides that have both forgotten the ground rules for talking about God—have forgotten that God talk is poetic and metaphorical. We move ahead by means of analogy. Both sides fall into the trap of literalism. The pastor rightly rejects it, but fails to see that the very things he rejects can come alive again as analogies and metaphors, not just as good life models. The authorities are in a bind because they are in the business of sustaining tradition, and the general public want easy yes-or-no answers.

What do you do with a popular pastor who is half right? "I don't believe in a physical God," he says. I should hope not. If God were a physical reality, we might be having arguments about the weight and size of the divine. If we could recover Christianity as a work of art and of the imagination, the things this pastor rejects—Jesus as divine; Mary as the Mother of God; the promise of Resurrection— might come back as signs of realities that cannot be put into words. It might illuminate the colossal assumption that human beings matter, and that Pastor Grosball's or my life is significant. For me, that's a much harder thing to believe.

In his book *Am I Still a Christian?* Gordon Jeff answers questions such as "Do I have to accept *everything* Christians are meant to believe?" "Do I have to believe everything I read in the Bible?" "Why do Christians have so many hangups about sex?" and "Why doesn't being a Christian make me more happy?" He notes, "Belief, as I understand it, needs constant testing against the hard reality of experience. . . . It is becoming clear, in the light of recent scholarship, that early Christianity was far more varied than has often been imagined." We shouldn't be upset by that variety. We should rejoice in these varied and even contradictory voices from the past that contribute to the ongoing conversation about our faith. Tradition is a living thing. Our task is to keep questions open rather than suppress asking them. To ask no questions is to fall into a deadening trance of spiritual boredom. The past is always being reinterpreted through new stories. In the light of these new interpretations, we can retell our own story.

Someone supposedly wrote to Lewis Carroll on reading his nonsense poem "Jabberwocky": "It seems to fill my head with ideas, but I don't know what they are." Is that where some of us are? We can't shake off religion and don't want to entirely, and we wonder why. Something is missing in our lives. We want to honor the longing in our hearts but can't believe the words anymore—at least not in the old way.

The Headache of Literalism

Over a hundred years ago, in *The Varieties of Religious Experience*, William James said, "We must, I think, bid a definitive good-bye to dogmatic theology." It has been a long good-bye. And even some of those who still hang on to dogma can't digest it very well, or it makes them dyspeptic.

There are still millions, however, for whom the words associated with religious belief pose no problem. They take the words literally and feel whole and complete—in either their belief or disbelief. Words, for them, have simply one flat literal meaning. It's either true or it isn't, and that's that. I respect that no-nonsense attitude, at least from a psychological point of view. I have friends who believe pre-posterous things, yet I can see that their beliefs have helped them cope with horrible and crippling situations brought on by divorce, disease, death, or some other kind of collapse.

So I don't want to be in an attack mode, claiming that I'm right and others are wrong. I simply want to acknowledge that for a grow-ing minority, literalism is unacceptable and, at the same time, a rationalist/secularist view of the world won't do, either. One always seems to end in violence; the other in despair or just a flatness of soul. Like Helen in the novel, we think that there must be some kind of truth behind the words.

It's not just a private and personal thing, either; something is missing in our social and political life, as well. We're in this together but we don't know how to talk about it. We look for things that bind us together without enslaving us.

Writing about religion is difficult because of the either/or men-tality prevalent in our culture. How do you communicate with some-one who thinks that literal belief is the only option? Clergy who don't believe literally are often accused of hypocrisy. On August 1, 2002, the *Times* of London published two articles about how Christians are to believe in the Virgin Birth and the Resurrection: one from the liberal point of view, the other the conservative. One headline ran, "Are the pulpits of Anglican Churches occupied by closet atheists?"

I believe the Bible and the creeds but not literally, and I am no atheist. I love the tradition and am nurtured by it. I have a great devotion to Mary the Mother of God but am agnostic about her literal virginity—or, to put it bluntly, I couldn't care less about it. It's all right by me if people believe it literally as long as they get the point that it turns your idea of God upside down. To me it is an amazing image, and the point of the doctrine is not to teach us about Mary's sexual status but to show us the awesome humility and availability of God. That's what the doctrine is *for.* Every day I invoke the protection of holy angels but I hear no flapping of wings. Belief in angels is a way for me to affirm the presence of God in a personal way, permeating the whole of life. Angels are a metaphor pointing to something real, and the only way to get at that reality is through poetry, myth, and metaphor.

So Christianity *as a set of beliefs* doesn't work for me. At the same time, I acknowledge the need for ritual and celebration in my life and find fulfillment and joy in many traditional practices. I light candles and ask for the prayers of the saints. These disciplines and habits are the way I get in touch with depths inside me that aren't accessible in any other way. They do not require me to believe literally in angels and the Virgin Birth.

Literalism cripples the imagination because it cannot fathom that something could be true on one level and not on another: true as metaphor and teaching but not true literally. Even most adamant literalists know that God isn't a real father with arms and legs and body parts. They know that calling God "Father" is an analogy. Yet they insist on literal acceptance of the Bible and of church doctrines not found in the Bible. A friendly Mormon acquaintance of mine believes such doctrines literally and knows exactly where the Garden of Eden is located and when its restoration will occur.

Longing for the Past

Since religion is inherently conservative and resists reformation, it often appeals to an idealized past. There is a tendency in any belief system to insist that its view of reality is eternal and changeless. This is the deep flaw of fundamentalism. All has been revealed, and the genuinely new isn't possible. Views about sexuality, the roles of men and women, are seen as unchangeable. Christians tend to think that if they get "back to the Bible" or to "the faith once delivered to the saints," they will recover some pure, better form of Christianity. The Bible tells us that God gave the Chosen People the Promised Land in perpetuity. No one should mess with the Word of God. This isn't simply an eccentric view held by a few individuals; it's the conviction of millions. And they influence the fate of the world, including U.S. foreign policy. Beliefs can be dangerous when they are based on absurd and unquestioning interpretations of ancient texts.

In Islam, for example, one senses a great disappointment because many Muslims dare not believe that the poverty in their world may result from the pious practice of their religion. That is unthinkable. This is not to say, of course, that Islam is the cause of poverty. Rather, like the rest of us, Muslims look for causes of their distress outside themselves. The fault must lie *outside* Islam. Behind this conviction is belief in the imminent appearance of the Umma, the world Muslim nation dreamed of in the Koran, which will accommodate no other ideology. But that happy day hasn't arrived, and it must be the fault of the rich, indolent, corrupt Christian West. Surely something satanic is at work. At least, one can see why some Muslims might think so.

Religion finds it hard to take in new information and new insights and to adapt to new situations, such as human rights and democracy. Instead of asking simply, "What is the truth?" or "Who teaches the truth?" religious people tend to ask, "Who preserves the tradition best?" The irony, in the Christian world, is that we have access to doctrines that invite and expect change ("The Spirit blows where it will"), but we are not open to our own teaching! We believe that God is not confined or constrained by human ideas and institutions, yet we try to capture God in our formulations. We don't like things to be open and unresolved. We are made uncomfortable by ambiguity, yet the acceptance of ambiguity is a sign of spiritual maturity.

Think of the early settlers from Europe in the new colonies of America. As historian Robert Wilken has written, the early "Pilgrims never dreamed of establishing religious freedom in their colonies. Indeed, they had no idea of toleration. 'Tis Satan's policy to plead for an indefinite and boundless toleration.'" And a pope has reminded us that "Error has no rights." Religious people, throughout history, haven't been notably tolerant and inclusive.

For many Christians, the idealized past of the so-called Apostolic Age is the test of all subsequent ages. It comes as a shock to learn that, as Wilken writes,

> the apostolic age is a creation of the Christian imagination. There never was a Golden Age when the church was whole, perfect, pure—virginal. The faith was not purer, the Christians were not braver, and the church was not one and undivided. . . . It is not the wholeness, perfection, or completeness that impresses the historian of early Christianity. Rather, it is the incompleteness, openness, and newness that strike us.

I think of the many versions of Christianity, Islam, and Buddhism now playing in the world and I wonder: Why label? Why ask is it Christian, Muslim, Buddhist? Why not ask simply: Is it true? Diversity of belief and practice have existed from the beginning, at least in Christianity. Wilken continues, "There is no original Christian faith, no native language, no definitive statement of the meaning of Christ for all times."

The past is not necessarily the judge of the future. Our problem is not so much that we are unfaithful to the past as we are unfaithful to the future, jeopardizing it for the coming generations by a cavalier indifference to the environment (Why bother, if the world is going to end?) and by a callous disregard for the so-called unbelievers caught up in the coming apocalypse. Religion easily becomes an individual affair—a private deal with God that leaves out others, the world, and the future.

Believing beyond Words

On the other side from the believing literalists are the nonbelieving literalists, whose minds can be just as closed. I find myself at a loss with some of my intellectual friends whose view of religion is still stuck in the old catechism they long ago rejected. They want religion to be "stupid" so they can go on rejecting it. One friend insists that any religion worth a damn is, by definition, fundamentally intolerant; he would deem ecumenical—let alone interfaith—overtures anathema. He finds me dependably wrong. He is a "literal atheist" because he thinks there's only one way to be a believer, and to him it's a crazy way. We are often talking at cross purposes.

Staying safely behind walls of literalism or nonliteralism may be comforting, but it's intellectually and spiritually cowardly. Simone Weil once said, "Anyone who isn't confused in the latter part of this [twentieth] century simply isn't thinking straight." And thinking is hard. Very few of us can do it well. We resist it because hard thinking tends to puncture our view of the world and let all the gas out. This process of deflation is both disastrous and necessary. We labor to amass facts but don't know what to make of them when we've got them. That is why we need the intuitive artist to pump the air back into tired and deflated imaginations. From the point of view of the consumerist, utilitarian world, artists are useless. But artists know that facts aren't enough to make sense of things or to express the struggle, darkness, and passion that haunt our spirits.

Helen, in David Lodge's novel, sensed that words were important but instinctively felt that they weren't enough. Two people can speak the same set of words yet be forever at cross purposes: one is full of love, and the other is gripped by a repellent obsessiveness. Sometimes they kneel side by side in the same pew. So the *way* we hold our beliefs is as important as the beliefs themselves. I've met people who are adamant about literal belief in the Resurrection but whose lack of love and compassion empties the belief of all content. Of course, the fact that some people are fanatical doesn't invalidate the truth of a doctrine. Wicked and stupid people can say true things. But when it comes to matters of faith, there has to be some practical value. Beliefs should make a difference in the way we behave and think.

The controversy between evolution and creationism is the quintessential battleground of literalists and their "enlightened" opponents, and there's plenty of foolishness on both sides. Those who make fun of creationists often fail to see the arrogance of science when it steps beyond its competence. Creationists seem to profoundly miss the point. I once asked the president of a fundamentalist college, a sad gentleman, why he insisted on believing in a literal Adam and Eve and repudiating any theory of evolution. "To deny the special creation of humanity would be to deny the meaning and purpose of life under God," he replied. I asked him why, but he seemed puzzled by the question and we dropped the subject. The more interesting and revealing part of our conversation came later, when I asked him what the most difficult part of his job was. "Everyone here, faculty and students, is a born-again Christian," he said, "and we have had food stolen from the kitchens, books stolen from the library, and there's even been a suicide." His sadness was explained, at least in part, but he was naive to hope that "right" doctrine was enough to ensure right behavior.

The Plural Consciousness

We are experiencing a vastly increased consciousness of plurality and diversity that is unsettling. It causes people to leap for one refuge or another: literalism, or total rejection of the mythical and metaphorical. Every generation goes on a journey of reappropriation and rediscovery. In spite of its impossibility, we are always trying to rewrite history (our own personal story as well as national and international history), in the hope that we will be able to get to the bottom of what "really happened." It's our way of trying to understand our pain. We reject the views of our parents who, in their turn, reacted against the views of theirs. We are always in the business of rewriting history.

What seems different this time around is that we're more aware of the differences. Living in a big city, I am aware that human consciousness is uneven. Primitive levels of thinking exist next to sophisticated ones—sometimes in the same person. In conversing with someone, I often feel as if I have been transported back to another time and place. Some of my fellow Christians seem stuck in the sixteenth century, still fighting the issues of the Reformation. For others it's 1860, and Charles Darwin lives next door and is to be resisted.

Still others seem centuries ahead of me, exploring terrain I have yet to discover. My friend Robert lives a cosmos full of intelligence and love. He sees in the history of the evolution of consciousness a divine direction and purpose. I cannot quite see what he sees, but I glimpse it through his eyes. He has a sympathy for other religious paths and psychological insights of which I have only the slightest hint. He has taught me that in the universe of belief you have to be a bit of a time traveler and good at "languages." When I am with Robert, my head doesn't hurt.

Reconnecting Our Spirits

We are in a time of unsettled meanings. When it comes to Christianity, many are no longer sure what it's about, and this causes great anxiety. Others are convinced that they know what it's about, but other Christians don't. If Christianity is about what most TV evangelists say it is, I want no part of it. No doubt they would say the same of my version, seeing it as "liberal," watered down, corrupt. The words conservative and liberal are bandied about carelessly. I am a "liberal" in the sense that I find myself living in deep mystery. This doesn't mean that I wander through the world in a fog of mystification. It means that for most things concerning belief I am a reverent agnostic. I think that religious people, in general, claim to know too much.

I am concerned about rethinking and reimagining Christianity because I believe that history has a purpose (in sum: communion with God and with each other), and that Christianity in an important sense hasn't happened yet. This is a relief! There is still a chance it may be true to itself.

The whole Christian world is changing. What this means for us is unclear, but the immediate prospect is daunting. It may mean a dominant form of Christianity, which I would want to repudiate and which would disown me. I don't even feel at home in what passes for the "religious" world of the West—all those people who are likely to go to church and are likely to vote Republican. Neither do I feel at home in the so-called secular world (or the world of the religious left), which is likely to vote Democratic. There is a cognitive dissonance between what is often mistakenly called "traditional beliefs" and mine. And the dissonance is also there with the so-called progressives as well. My head hurts! I find life in the tradition and part company with some liberals. I am open to the new and as a result am thought to be suspect by many conservatives.

Where I work we have a slogan: *Reconnect your spirit without disconnecting your mind.* In my search for meaning, I don't want to leave my brain behind. And, more important, I don't want to leave you or anyone else behind. I don't have a label for that. I am feeling my way and discovering allies in the culture who have no direct religious affiliation. There's Molly, brought up Jewish, who runs an arts organization. When we meet there's a look of recognition between us about what the world is truly about. There's Peter, who runs a local think tank. He is intellectually rigorous and deeply compassionate but has no time for institutional religion. Yet we are soul mates.

Such friends and allies help me get a feeling for the emerging culture of respect and inclusion, even as it becomes increasingly hard to find someone who is a credible spokesperson for a religious tradition. But a new community is emerging, one capable of living with questions. We're living in a period when the old maps have been found damaged or inaccurate and when new maps leave out many of those parts of the old that still can be trusted. I live in hope because I find that there are far more things that unite human beings than divide us. We are bound together by common questions, whatever our position on religion.

- How should we respond to human frailty?
- What are we to do about suffering?
- How are we to face death?
- What should our social and communal arrangements be?
- What are the paths to self-knowledge?
- What kind of language do we need to express and probe these questions?

Keeping these questions vibrant and alive is already to be committed to a community, which could help heal the world.

3

The God-Shaped Space in Our Hearts

A human being is a *capax Dei*—a capacity for God; *Deo congruens*—God-shaped.

—The Medieval Mystical Tradition

When I was eleven, a speaker at our elementary school told us that every one of us had a God-shaped blank in his heart. I was very taken with that comment at the time, although I wasn't sure what he meant exactly. Later I came to interpret my longings, the open and incomplete side of my life, as that God-shaped emptiness. When I got to college, my mentor there told me that we all have such empty spaces inside us, which only God can fill.

That space was described another way by Helène Aylon, an artist of Orthodox Jewish background in her seventies living in New York. She is in conflict and conversation with the tradition of her parents; grandparents; and deceased husband, a rabbi. Her conflict is often expressed through her art; in 1996, for example, she staged an exhibit titled "The Liberation of G——d." Writing the name of God in this manner is her way of acknowledging its ambiguity and strangeness.

More recently Helène was responsible for a controversial installation at a Jewish center in New York on the subject of the *niddah*— the time of "impurity" for a woman during menstruation. The background to this exhibit was the memory of her husband's death from cancer when she was only twenty-nine. When she menstruated while he was dying, she tells us, "We never held hands, we never touched. Religious observance was more important than love."

It's no wonder that she is ambivalent about her faith. Her Orthodox mother—well into her nineties—is still observant. "She does everything in the most beautiful way," Helène says. "She does the holidays with candles. She cooks fantastically. But I . . . have a hole in my soul." She means two things by this, I think: one, that there is still that "God-shaped space" in her waiting to be filled. But also, that she can't allow it to be occupied by the God of her ancestors. The hole has become a wound.

She might have added that institutional Judaism—indeed, all forms of institutional religion—have a hole in their soul, too. When religious observance becomes more important than love, religion begins to die from within. It deserves to. That "God" needs to be rejected.

Wounded and Lost Souls

For some people, the word *God* is so contaminated that it's no longer usable. I have a friend who cannot enter a church without feeling sick. He came to hear me preach once and, out of friendship and the promise of lunch, stood uncomfortably at the back of the church. He had no stomach for God as he saw him in his followers.

The word *God* seems to wound people and is deeply wounded itself. That's why many have given up using it. Besides, people who believe in God tend to be losers, don't they? There seems to be a connection between the word *God* and our being lost. Whether you use the word *God* or not, there's a hole in the soul.

I see the remains of this dying or dead religion in many of my Roman Catholic friends. They are not so much lapsed Catholics as disappointed lovers, alternating between rage and sorrow at the loss of or betrayal by a loved one. Patrick, a successful businessman—Irish, articulate, bright—is still so pissed off at the Church that he can't see straight. He supposedly let it all go thirty years ago, but his early Catholicism so structured his thinking and feeling that he can never get rid of it. He is nostalgic about the old structures and habits that gave him his identity. When he was growing up in Chicago, people didn't ask him what part of town he was from. They asked him his parish. The saying of the rosary, fish on Fridays, tipping your hat as you passed the church, the structure of the liturgical year, Holy Days of Obligation—all served as reminders that there was something above the daily grind, holding out the promise that your life might mean something after all.

Patrick and many others, however, couldn't take the repressive nonsense about sex and judgment that went with it. I wanted to go out and buy a rosary for Patrick, just to give him something to hold on to. There's something sad, even tragic, about how we deprive ourselves of the reminders and structures we need because we allow the worst of the traditions to set the agenda. I wanted to introduce Patrick to some of the Roman Catholic priests and nuns I know, who celebrate the best of the tradition and refuse to give the worst the upper hand.

On one hand, religion keeps us rooted and grounded (which we need). On the other, its powerful roots can engulf and strangle us. Religion includes and excludes, inspires and dumbs down, enlivens and kills. Religion appears to be dying, but it is here to stay. Human beings are wired for it—and need to be unplugged from it. We never seem to get it quite right. But God or G——d isn't going away. The divine presence/absence is felt all over the world, and it drives people mad.

In the movie *American Beauty*, the hero, Lester, is hurt and lost. His wife and daughter see him as "this gigantic loser." He reflects, "They're right. I've lost something. I don't know what it is, but I know I haven't always felt this sedated. But it's never too late to get it back." He, too, has a hole in the soul. Lester doesn't want to feel drugged all the time. He's hopeful that he can get his life back. Can God fill the hole in the soul? Maybe—but we shouldn't use the word *God* too easily or too soon. It needs its poison drained.

Not long ago there was the case of an Eagle Boy Scout who confessed that he didn't believe in God. What should the Boy Scouts of America do about it? Asked to comment for NBC News, I said that

I was delighted that a nineteen-year-old was having some questions and doubts about God, that this gave America the opportunity to deepen its conversation about belief. I also said that there are many people who believe in "God" and I wish they didn't. Their God makes them callous and hard. And there are others who don't profess any belief and yet practice what I would call a godly life. In many ways *God* is a useless word, yet something important is lost when we abandon it altogether.

The Transforming Experience

Before we can get back to talking about God, we may need to spend some time talking about what happens to our lives when the "God-shaped space" is filled by something that makes us feel truly alive. It doesn't matter what we call it, but there's no mistaking it when it happens.

I'm trying to get at something Viktor Frankl described in his account of his concentration camp experiences. He speaks of the "intensification of inner life" that came over the prisoners in the camp, so that sunsets, remembered lines of verse, and even the most ordinary actions of the past (riding on a bus, answering the telephone, turning on lights) become filled with beauty and longing. He quotes a young woman who knew that she was going to die: "I am grateful that fate has hit me so hard. In my former life I was spoiled and did not take spiritual accomplishments seriously."

Pointing through the window of the barracks, she said, "This tree here is the only friend I have in my loneliness." Through that window she could see just one branch of a chestnut tree, and on the branch were two blossoms. Frankl writes, "'I often talk to this tree,' she said to me. I was startled and didn't quite know how to take her words. Was she delirious? Did she have occasional hallucinations? Anxiously I asked her if the tree replied. 'Yes.' What did it say to her? She answered, 'It said to me, "I am here—I am here—I am life, eternal life."'"

That's why the words that interest me more than the word *God* are *authenticity, honesty, integrity, transformation,* and *love.* These come first and *God* comes later, much later. And concerning Christianity, I am not interested in its survival, in its adapting to the so-called modern world. Christianity doesn't need anyone to save it. If it has any truth, it will continue. If it hasn't, it deserves to die. As for me, I'm waiting for a more generous and inclusive version of the Old Story to emerge. I don't want so much to reinvent it as for it to reinvent me. How I understand myself is at stake.

I find myself as part of an odd community with people caught between credulity and cynicism who want less talk and more love in action. They want to attend to their hole in the soul. Practices such as lighting a candle and receiving some bread and wine regularly help me attend to the hole in my soul. I experience a presence that draws me out of my feeling lost—a presence that tells me I am not (and no one is) a loser. The presence is a sign that I'll never get to the bottom of understanding anything. There will be always more, and if I persevere I will find the unfinished quality of experience both deeply satisfying and wildly hilarious.

Getting a Fix on Religion

I get frustrated when I'm with my more academic friends because they have an expertise in a particular field. I know nothing about engineering and next to nothing about Chinese history, but they know enough about religion to have an opinion. When it comes to nuclear physics or geology, there are plenty of holes in my knowledge, but everyone feels free to shoot his or her mouth off about religion. Everyone is an expert. Some believe it to be the source of great good; others blame religion for all the evils of the world. What about all the evils done in the name of religion? Well, all I can say is that human beings have a genius for messing up and missing the point. We act in contradiction to our cherished beliefs. There are also interminable arguments about what the essence of religion is. What is its basic message? There is no *one* answer for Christianity, Islam, Judaism, Hinduism, and Buddhism (to name five of the biggies).

It might be argued that the oddness of religion (its crudeness and idealism) is nothing new. Why be particularly concerned about it now? Because we're in a new situation. There's a special urgency now because the world is shrinking and the velocity of change is increasing. Christians in what were once "Christian" countries are now waking up to the fact that Christianity isn't the only game in town. The word *religion* is used to designate anything from Devil worship to deep, contemplative practice, from the best and the worst of the various traditions. A Mozart Mass and a Mormon baptizing the dead are both religion. A blessed sense of the unity of all things is religion, as is the belief that most human beings are damned.

What Is God and Who Are You?

But it's not all hopeless. When we sit down and try to talk about God and religion, the tables are often turned. Instead of our sitting in a class and expecting the teacher to give us answers, the teacher turns the tables and interrogates us. We ask, "*What* is there to know?" The teacher responds, "*Who* is it who wants to know?" Questions about God and religion end up as mirrors that reflect back to us questions about ourselves. It all comes down to identity. Who do you think you are? What kind of creature are you? Are you lost? Are you a loser?

So it's not enough to ask questions *about* religion. Religion has a way of turning the tables on us by asking questions about *us*. It's as if we've summoned God and put the divine in the witness box, which is a bit like trying to tame the wind or defy gravity. We seem to have turned into gods ourselves.

Kevin Kelly in *Out of Control* writes, "We have become as gods, and we might as well get good at it." In his introduction to *The Iliad*, Bernard Knox writes, "To be a god is to be totally absorbed in the exercise of one's own power, the fulfillment of one's own nature, unchecked by any thought of others except as obstacles to be overcome; it is to be incapable of self-questioning or self-criticism." Gods tend to be childish and monomaniacal. Technology has improved the human lot and given us godlike powers. But it also has debased these powers. The Internet brings us all together. The Internet allows the terrorist to move in next door. We are gods and not very good ones. There is a radical distinction between the narcissistic gods of Greek mythology and the God who might fill the spirit-wired space in our hearts.

A Hole in the World

There's not only a hole in the soul but one in the world, as well. Does the world have a future, or is everything running down? A couple of cartoons I saw recently help me understand the kind of world I'm living in. The first is of a man reporting to the directors of a company. They are all looking at a chart, and the caption reads, "And our *ultra*-long-term strategy will be to burn up when the sun becomes a red giant." The second cartoon is of a secretary reporting to her boss as he removes his coat: "Sir, the following paradigm shifts occurred while you were out."

Religious questions are inescapable. In light of our ultra-long-term strategy, what really matters in the end? Mere secularism won't do. But how do we tell the difference between "good" and "bad" religion? How do we find a place to stand when things are unstable in the realm of the spiritual? And what is the relationship between religion and spirituality? The latter is in; the former is out. People repeat the mantra "I am not religious but I am very spiritual" without realizing that their spirituality depends on deep strands of religious tradition.

A friend of mine says that if you don't laugh every time "spirituality" is mentioned, there must be something wrong with you! He doesn't say this cynically but with passionate generosity toward his fellow pilgrims. He knows that we tend to take ourselves too seriously when it comes to the inner life. Our self-absorption can be very funny. The voice changes and the face assumes a special "spiritual" expression. It is no wonder that playwrights and novelists have been able to take this tendency and create characters such as the religious hypocrites Uriah Heep and Tartuffe.

Moreover, we tend to make religion only of the nice bits and pieces of our experience and repress the rest. That's why so much about the spiritual life can sound hollow and silly. We have no room for nasty bits such as anger, resentment, and lust. An honest spiritual life must have room for all our feelings and be wise enough to help us look them in the face. That's why there is often something slightly ridiculous about how-to books on prayer and spirituality. Many leave vast areas of human experience untouched. Such books are part of the self-help industry—part of the spiritual welfare system for the narcissistic—as if there could be four easy steps to enlightenment.

And what about those paradigm shifts that occurred while you weren't looking? What happens when the sun becomes a red giant? These are both serious jokes and, for anyone who is awake and aware, there is a sense of urgency and anxiety in the midst of rapid change. In reality, paradigm shifts are heart-wrenching and leave gaping holes inside us. We must change, but we don't know how. It is the best of times, it is the worst of times. Technology has improved the human lot and yet has made it more barbaric. On average the human condition is surely better now than it was a hundred years ago. But technobarbarism also has degraded it and deepened the spiritual void inside us.

How Do We Recognize God?

A key question is "How do you know when you've found something to fill the God-shaped space? Something, that is, that isn't toxic or simply a result of some restrictive fantasy. Issues of authority (who gets to say what it is) and discernment are central. How do we know what is true? And by what or whose authority? How are truth claims to be pressed? Since Christianity isn't the only show in town, how should it relate to other religions?

How shall we move forward? How shall we heal the hole in the soul? Should we begin with an examination of beliefs? I think not. Today experience is more highly valued than beliefs, so we should begin with experience. But this has its dangers, partly because experience doesn't exist on its own. It needs some filter to help us understand what we've experienced. Few realize that they rely on unexamined beliefs to interpret what happens to them. They just know that they have a hole in the soul. They feel lost. Some of them feel like losers.

Shopping for Religion

Think for a moment how having a hole in the soul affects religion and religious practice. For millions of people religion is mainly a function of tribal or ethnic identity. It is a given. If you're Italian you're a Roman Catholic—even if you're an atheist. An Italian Jew or an Italian Protestant is an oddity. Everyone is Italy is an honorary Catholic or used to be.

But for a growing critical mass, religious identity is becoming more and more a matter of free choice. You can see this in the Muslim world as it struggles for and against democracy. You could argue that religion at its heart was always a matter of free choice, and you'd be right, but this idea is only just coming into its own.

The downside is that people are free but rootless, and even the ones who are not antireligious tend to go shopping for a religion in the same way that they go looking for a new car. Religion becomes a matter of lifestyle, not life—a hobby. You could almost make up slogans: Baptists like Buicks. Catholics like Cadillacs. Religion is merely a matter of individual taste. You like stamp collecting and I like football. You're a Buddhist and I'm a Catholic. Religion becomes a harmless hobby. Some like it that way. It does less harm as an accessory to a lifestyle. But others cannot stand the supermarket approach to religion.

We know from ecology that stability requires variety, yet many people find variety and diversity in religion intolerable. They want people to shape up and believe just the way they do. But religion, either as a hobby or as a rigid system applicable to everyone, doesn't quite do it. The hole in the soul is still there, and we can trace a link between the hole, our loss of a sense of who we are, and the open wound, which we call G——d. Religion as lifestyle accoutrement doesn't come anywhere near filling the need inside us for significance. And a rigid approach may give the illusion of security, but it kills the spirit.

Commitment and Tolerance

Knowing you have a hole in the soul—like Helène Aylon—makes you vulnerable and sympathetic to others. Being willing to wait in the emptiness makes it possible to be generously hospitable to other views of the world and at the same time stick to one's guns with regard to deeply held convictions. Holding these two things together is surely what spiritual maturity is all about. We need to develop a tolerance for ambiguity without making ambiguity an excuse for never making a commitment. Sometimes we have to choose one form over another if the times demand it. Some people, during bad times, have chosen the ghetto of "purity" over the messiness of the world. The monastic movements come to mind. Withdrawal from the world *for the sake of the world* is always a viable option. Perhaps we need, as philosopher Alasdair MacIntyre suggested several years ago, a new St. Benedict to lead us into a new community of love and service. The point is that whatever we do, we must choose it *freely*.

Reinventing Ourselves Whole

Having a hole in the soul isn't all bad. Helène Aylon has the soul of an artist, and her struggles with Judaism seem to have formed a passionate and sensitive soul. There are many like her, and perhaps a new kind of soul is emerging. It's too early to say exactly what this soul looks like, but some of us are finding our identity in many places. And even though it's hard (impossible?) to create a self from scratch, a freely chosen faith liberates us from tyrannies of family, tribe, and tradition, yet without losing valuable connections to those primordial roots.

There's something heroic if naive about moving to Phoenix to start again, or taking one's life savings and going around the world. It is a heady thing to act as if one had no binding history. In the end it is impossible to live that way, but it is not stupid or naive to imagine that we can rewrite our personal history. In fact, that's what religious conversion is all about—the retelling of a life from a totally new perspective. Conversion gives us a new history and makes us accountable to it. It provides the roots we need and rescues us from the howling void of the lonely self.

As journalist Pico Iyer has written, we "have never lived with quite this kind of mobility and uprootedness before (indeed the questions themselves may be the closest thing we have to home, we live in the uncertainties we carry around with us)." This puts us under enormous strain, and sometimes I feel like a plane that is forever circling looking for a place to land. Religion, for me, has more to do with living in the uncertainties, with loving questions, than with answering them. In the end, the hole in the soul is not filled by answers. It is healed only by deeper questions.

A Safe House to Talk about God

I live in San Francisco, one of the last places for people moving west before they fall into the ocean. It is a city of religious and cultural pluralism—gay, Asian, and secular. Sometimes I feel as if I'm living in the middle of a refugee camp—a safe haven for people fleeing or recovering from repressive forms of upbringing or religion. And people drift into the cathedral where I work, looking for something. They are not looking for beliefs. They are looking for roots. They are looking for a place to connect their soul. Many of them have no religious story to help them interpret what is happening to them. Sometimes something tragic hits them and there's no context to look at and interpret it. Tragedy happens, and they try the methods available to get over the suffering. They turn to art, music, sex, drugs, sports, and religion.

We keep coming back to the theme of our being lost. The fact that so many of us are depressed points to the fact that we are, in some sense, losers. It's often hard work to cheer ourselves up so that we can truly believe life is good. Look around. What do you see? We need places to meet—such as a cathedral.

At its best, a cathedral is a place of meeting and safety for people on the move spiritually. Sometimes a great crowd gathers for a celebration or memorial—such as the one for Mimi Fariña (the singer and founder of Bread & Roses). Her sister Joan Baez was there, and Boz Scaggs sang a haunting version of "My Funny Valentine." The building was filled with laughter and tears. And, of course, there was a party. My guess is that most of those who showed up had left organized religion behind long ago, but they were glad there was a cathedral in which to gather. "It was great to be in church again," said one. "I don't go anymore, but I miss it. It was good to be here. There's something missing in my life and there's something here I need." Those who came to the memorial service loved the space and the music, but many had a hole in the soul. They also sensed a hole in the soul of the Church. They were looking for God—not the institution but the presence that told them they weren't losers.

Just as there are massive movements of population—millions always on the move, looking for a new home—so there are religious and spiritual migrations. Some people, I suspect, are rather relieved at being spiritually homeless for a while, since the "home" they have left was all torment and guilt at worst, and dislocation and a sense of not belonging at best. But religion won't go away. The hole in the soul is never fully filled. Even my friends who are skeptics and would call themselves atheists (often out of self-defense) are rather like the Dublin taxi driver who, when asked if he believed in leprechauns, replied, "Of course not, but they're there just the same!"

There is something "there" at the heart of things, and it looks as if religious language is the only way to get at it. We have to find a way to interpret our experience. That's why you can't get away from texts (the Bible, the Koran) when it comes to religion. In our probing of religion and politics, the skeptic and the believer need each other, and there's no reason why they shouldn't respect each other. Both have holes in their souls.

Sometimes I feel like one of the old rabbis in the Hasidic tradition who told the story about the people gathering in the forest around the fire to tell the story of redemption. As time went by, they forgot the story and could not longer find the place in the forest. But they did remember that there was a story. All they could do was light a fire and tell the story that there was once a story. This isn't as gloomy as it sounds, because it is a story about the power of stories. And the rabbis knew that God loved stories.

Love Heals the Hole in the Soul

Meanwhile, we might be able to appreciate the God story afresh by seeing it in a more generous light: as global and inclusive, as primarily a work of the imagination before it is a work of the intellect. The intellect is important, but it follows as well as guides the heart. Love is the highest form of knowledge. Thus, if we are to truly understand, we need to learn to love. We need to be drawn in by a picture or a story. We are attracted first to the truth of the pictures, stories, and images and only then do we work through to their meanings. I don't want to be told; I want to be shown. I want to be able to taste, touch, hear, smell, and see the love for which I long and of which the Good News in the Bible speaks. Experience first. Explanations later. As Eliza Dolittle sings in *My Fair Lady,* "Don't talk of love . . . show me!"

Our ignorance is at its most brilliant when it comes to religion. Everyone thinks he knows about God. We don't know a whole lot, and we don't know that we don't know. So what do we know? St. John of the Cross put it simply: "In the end, we shall be examined in love." That's all we need to know—but the trouble is that we have to go through a long process of initiation into the school of love before we find out.

Hannah Arendt, in one of her letters to Heinrich Blücher, wrote: "You see, dearest, I always knew, even as a kid, that I could only exist in love. And that is why I was so frightened that I might simply get lost. And so I made myself independent. And when I met you, suddenly I was no longer afraid. . . . It still seems incredible to me that I managed to get both—the 'love of my life' and the identity with my own person. And yet I achieved the one only since I also have the other."

This (that love and, therefore, religion are about union and identity) is what I learned was the heart of things when I was in the monastic seminary where I trained to be a priest. It is what I have learned from Dante's vision of Paradise. It is what I am learning from experience in trying to love my neighbor as myself. It is, at last, what I am learning as I glimpse unconditional love in the love of lover and children. This is true religion. Love heals the hole in the soul.

4

Poles Apart

Skeptics and Believers Choose Sides

Here's a story about the world I live in. Not long ago I was a guest at a fancy dinner party, styled as a sort of salon. Other guests included a philosophy professor known to be an atheist; the intelligent and witty director (Jewish and secular) of an art museum, and an elderly Roman Catholic priest, who was the guest of honor. After an excellent dinner, our hostess introduced Father X, who was invited to stimulate the conversation. He started off with some innocuous truisms about human history and how we came to be the way we are, droning on for a long time in a rather flat voice, so that the rest of us began to lose interest.

We woke up, however, when he said, "The answer, of course, is UFOs." People around the dinner table tried to cover their embarrassment, faces freezing in a bewildered look of polite attention. Father X serenely continued, "The ancient sites of the Middle East are full of traces of the visits of early spaceships from Andromeda, and all our DNA came on those ships." He went on for another twenty minutes, as if reciting a well-rehearsed script from which there could be no deviation. He was so completely on automatic pilot that actual conversation was impossible.

The cynics at the table had a field day. The philosophy professor muttered under his breath, "There's a technical term for all this.
Bullshit." The museum director thought that "as a metaphor" our
coming from Andromeda was interesting. When Father X insisted he
meant it literally, the director was flabbergasted. "I'd rather believe
the whole meshuga of Christianity, including the Virgin Birth, than
this nonsense." The room was polarized. When, as the sole other
clergyman, I was asked what I thought, I mumbled something
about our being made of the same stuff as the stars, about taking it
all as metaphor rather than literal truth. But I also said that even
if it were literally true, what difference would it make? How would
the improbable, even if proved true, help me decide how to live in
the world?

My dinner companion wouldn't let me off the hook, whispering
in my ear, "What do you really think about all this nonsense? You
don't *really* believe that the Bible is the Word of God?" She expected
me to say "Of course not!" I tried to explain, however, that such
questions don't lend themselves to easy yes-or-no answers. Demands
to take sides on matters of belief are often a lazy shorthand for a
whole raft of other questions about longing, meaning, and communication. It's rare that someone wants to do the serious thinking
required to get to a "yes" or a "no" of any depth.

What frustrated me was the lost opportunity for real conversation about God, reality, and the hole in the soul. We all left with our
prejudices intact; to be honest, I couldn't wait to leave. The butler
winked as we left and whispered, "Your spaceship awaits!"

The Trap of Cynicism

Thinking back, that evening was a cartoon version of the extremes
of credulity and skepticism that exist in our society. It was easy to
make fun of what Father X believed, but to many skeptics, the idea
of praying to an invisible, omnipotent God, not to mention some of
the other "supernatural" Christian doctrines, is just as lunatic. They
tend to be more polite about it because religion is socially sanctioned, but privately the skeptics are just as put off. To them religion

is nothing more than fairy tales. In a way, they are right. Much of religion is fairy tale, but it can't be totally reduced to that. Besides, there's a lot of truth in fairy tales. But these people come by their skepticism honestly. Many of them are refugees from a mindless and anti-intellectual upbringing. Some of them freely admit that when they shut out all but the purely rational, they feel emotionally impoverished.

My antireligious friends are spiritually schizophrenic in that they hunger for experience on one hand, but on the other, they have been so infected by what they *think* is the scientific method that they have swallowed its severe distortions of religion. Even the most intelligent are religiously confused. So they fall into the trap of dualisms such as "science deals with facts" while "religion is about meaning." Science is fact, religion is fiction. Science deals with the here and now; religion, with a fuzzy future. My friends have forgotten how to think metaphorically. The poetry has gone out of their life. They have a hole in the soul.

And while we have to be honest and admit that religion— because it is a receptacle for human aspirations and disappointed hopes— can turn nasty, this doesn't vitiate religion itself. Tolstoy once protested that while he himself was a bad example of Christianity, like a drunk wandering from the path, this didn't invalidate the path.

It is difficult for any of us to reimagine the truth of a tradition if we are, for example, fixated on a specific outrage done in its name. In the case of Christianity, its despisers have a view filtered through something like the burning of heretics or perhaps something more personal—a vindictive nun or a crazed fundamentalist pastor. I once cut a radio interview short when I realized that the interviewer had only one item on his agenda: the burning of witches, for which I was somehow responsible. Something had happened to make the interviewer tone deaf when it came to the music of religion. Argument was pointless. Religion was about the burning of witches, and that was all.

When I talk to some people it's not that we disagree on a particular issue, it's as if we are living on different planets. There are no grounds for disagreement. We have no common language. The conversation is on the order of "My wife was taken up into a space-craft, impregnated by an alien, and has just delivered its baby," to which theologian John Dominic Crossan tells us the only appropriate response is, "How nice! I hope they're both doing well." There's no point in arguing.

Science and Religion— Mutually Incomprehensible?

Skeptics have always raised their voices—sometimes to their own peril and sometimes to the great benefit of society. Galileo did so almost 400 years ago, and as Pope John Paul II observes, that affair "has been interpreted as a fundamental opposition between science and faith." But in the past century or so, science has gained ascendance, and skeptics have claimed it as their ally, deepening the gulf between themselves and believers. The creationist wants to talk about meaning and gets it confused with science. The evolutionist wants to talk about science and can't help sneering at religion. Many biologists seem to think that the theory of evolution (revised or otherwise) denies the possibility of design and order pointing to the possibility of God. The creationists respond negatively, and neither side understands the other.

I have to confess that until recently, I wasn't really aware of the reductionist assumptions of the evolutionist establishment. I'd always had a benign view of scientists, so I'm surprised to find myself thinking that creationists have a point—not a scientific one, but a theological one. Scientists as *scientists* have no business affirming or denying purpose in the universe. And people of faith err when they come to scientific conclusions based on creedal or biblical texts.

I have often taken part in entertaining but frustrating discussions on religion and science and have always assumed that the battle is false because they are basically two different languages that shouldn't be confused. For many people, however, a modern understanding of evolution implies that there is no ultimate meaning in life. In *Why Religion Matters,* Huston Smith quotes Steven Weinberg as saying, "The more the universe seems comprehensible, the more it seems pointless." This makes me marvel at the arrogant claims of some scientists—thinking *they* have a point.

Ironically, we are being diminished by the very "progress" we think is so great. Isn't it time to abandon crude Darwinism? In fact, it has already been discredited by scientists themselves. The National Association of Biology Teachers used to officially define *evolution* as "an unsupervised, impersonal natural process of temporal descent with genetic modification that is affected by natural selection, chance, historical contingencies, and changing environments." As a result of Huston Smith's challenge to those assumptions, the definition was changed in 1999: the processes of science are characterized by asking questions, proposing hypotheses, and designing empirical models and conceptual frameworks for research about natural events. It's also worth repeating Fred Hoyle's assertion that the chance of natural selection's producing an enzyme is on the order of a tornado's roaring through a junkyard and coming up with a Boeing 747. Other critics insist that "our modern understanding of evolution implies that ultimate meaning in life is nonexistent."

My experience with scientists is that they are not so much arrogant as ignorant of how to play the game of theology. Some think it's a game so silly that it's not worth playing. Yet they cannot help but dabble in the "meaning" to which science points.

There are actually three conflicts going on at once: one is between, among, or within religions, another between science and religion. The third is within science itself, centering on whether science reveals the world "as it really is" or whether it, too, is a construct. Scientists themselves are beginning to question some deeply entrenched assumptions. Is the random variation and selection of Darwinian evolution enough to explain something as complex and self-sustaining as life? Or could there be a deeper source of order? Isn't science part of a larger story? George Johnson in *Fire in the Mind* says, "Our brains are wired to see order, but we are prisoners of our nervous systems, cursed with never knowing when we are seeing truths out there in the universe and when we are merely inventing elaborate architectures."

It is no wonder that many turn from the worship of the warring gods of religion to worship at the altar of science. Our liturgy becomes "technology" and technique. We imagine that they provide endless possibilities for us. In reality, they are means of control, narrowing of horizons to make human life all the more manageable. But we aren't managing all that well. We are a depressed people. A friend of mine found the following note next to the body of a young man who had killed himself: "I just couldn't make the connections."

True Believers

There is a mind-set that infects believers and unbelievers alike. Both are tempted to make assumptions that they take for granted about reality and about their opponents. Encounters between them are frustrating because each thinks he or she knows what the other believes and is convinced at the outset that the other is wrong.

Believers and unbelievers alike, we all live—albeit unwittingly—according to principles that cannot be proved. That isn't an excuse for being stupid or lazy, however. At some point our beliefs should be capable of public scrutiny and discussion. I tend to get frustrated and a little depressed when I am with people for whom the questions have dried up. With some Mormon friends, for example, I get stirred up because I can't get them to *talk* about their beliefs. All they can do is to affirm them and smile. I admire and envy their sense of belonging, but when I ask simple questions about the authenticity of the Book of Mormon, they reply that it is self-authenticating. If you read it with an open mind and heart, they say, you'll know it's true.

That's actually the argument about all sacred texts. You either believe or you don't. It seems to me that the Book of Mormon, as interesting as it is as a myth binding a community together, has nothing outside itself by which to judge it. I don't know of any Mormon sites or excavations validating the provenance let alone the details of the book. At least when it comes to the Bible, there's a wealth of public controversy, scholarship, and archaeology. There's something there to argue about. And when it comes to doctrines, there's a philosophical tradition behind them as well as a long history of human experience. We can say where they come from and what they mean. When it comes to structures and institutions, there have been enough revolutions and reformations for endless debate about their value. In other words, we have a lot to talk and argue about—even though, in the end, faith is not about argument.

The weakness of all tribal texts such as the Book of Mormon (and, for that matter, the Koran and the Bible) is that for millions, they tend to exist behind a wall of uncritical faith and refuse to come into the arena of public debate. They are beyond question. And when believing gets to that point, we may gain a sense of tribal security in the short term, but in the long run we're heading for disaster. At the very least, the gulf separating us deepens. For a few skeptics and believers, there is a place of meeting where each is able to listen to the other without the filter of prejudice. Any believer with an open mind and heart should be skeptical about a glib lapse into "meaning." And any skeptic who is open and compassionate can see a "point" to life, even if it is limited.

Perhaps the chief flaw of believers is a complacent resting in a faith that has ceased to make them think and struggle. This attitude is summed up in the statement of the Evangelical bishop in Michael Arditti's novel *Easter*: "A liberal Christian is a contradiction in terms, because liberals believe in asking questions, to which Christians already have the answers. If you don't believe me, you haven't read your Bible." True conversation is closed to people who have all answers and no questions—whether they are believers or unbelievers.

Religion does not and cannot exist in isolation as a merely private deal we have with divinity. There are social and political consequences. Religion will make demands. It will piss you off if it's worth anything. It will make you uncomfortable.

We need a way of speaking that opens and suggests and does not conclude or define. I have to admit that the people who appeal most to the Bible as absolute truth don't see it that way. It is hardly, for them, a vehicle of imprecision. The late distinguished Methodist preacher Donald Soper, when challenged by two fundamentalists to choose between an infallible Bible and an infallible pope, told them he would choose the latter because "at least he says less."

The Trap of Fatalism

When we cease to ask questions and surrender totally to external authorities (or to the most insidious authority of all, our own uncritical judgment), everything is fixed, decided ahead of time. This leads to fatalism. It is one of the most damaging doctrines, and it comes in many forms to believers and nonbelievers. For the nonbeliever it sometimes hits as a debilitating nihilism—the view that nothing matters and nothing makes a difference. For the believer it strikes as a form of predestination. God had everything figured out from the beginning: some of us are predestined for heaven and some for hell. Our place in the scheme of things is fixed. We know where we belong, and there's nothing we can do about it.

Listen to the seventeenth-century Puritan John Bunyan: "I was more loathsome in mine own eyes that was a toad, and I thought I was so in God's eyes too: sin and corruption would as naturally bubble out of my heart, as water would bubble out of a fountain." Bunyan lived in torment and self-hatred until he heard a sermon on the text "Behold thou art fair, my love, thou are fair." The words "my love" stuck in his mind. And he went home repeating "thou art my love," "thou art my love," "thou art my love"—believing that God meant these words for him.

The irony is that it was religion that damaged Bunyan—believing he was predestined for damnation—but it also was the remedy that saved him. Religion is so often part of the wound and part of the healing. Many of us have been deeply wounded by religion. Some, however, are able to move from religion as debilitating moralism to religion as a moral adventure.

I think of two men I admire—both Jewish, both atheists; one a musician, the other a psychiatrist. They are both, to my mind, far closer to the mystery of God than literal-minded "believers." Why? Because of their rigorous honesty, their generous spirits, their open minds and hearts. One (the psychiatrist) thinks that God is *always* a projection—something made up by the hungry and needy psyche. The other sees the harm that received beliefs have done over the course of human history. They might be atheists, but they are also

Jewish and have in their blood strong antidotes to idolatry. They know their Bible.

God du Jour

There are life-bearing places where skeptics and believers may meet, but there are also some dead-end paths that some blunder into while seeking a way across the gulf. Among them are a consumerist approach to an ill-defined "spirituality" and misguided attempts to merge all religious traditions into one homogenized faith. My daughter, Lena, laughingly talks about the "God du jour" of contemporary culture. I don't want to put all the religions into a blender, and I think that deep intellectual questioning is important. We need a public and passionate discourse about God—not the God of a comfortable traditionalism but not God du jour, either.

Many people I meet are looking for communion and community but are adrift. They are tired of the old way of believing and belonging. They tend to dabble in religion but find it hard to commit to a particular spiritual path. Huston Smith, an expert on world religions, recalls a conversation with someone who was a taster of spiritualities. "My problem is that I am 'convictionally impaired.' I can believe something for a year or two, and then it dissolves and I start searching again," she told him. I couldn't help think of the remark of a character in one of William Golding's novels: "My beliefs are me; many and trivial." Being "convictionally impaired" and caught up in the trivial are part of the cost of living in a consumer culture that treats religion as if it were something you can pick up at the supermarket.

The human mind needs to cut things down to size. We manage our world by limiting our horizons. Think about the movie *Jurassic Park* and its poor sequels. The original book is about the limits of technology and the possibility of chaos and the awesome unpredictability of life—rendered at once horrific and cute in the movie version and with great special effects. Life is reduced to a theme park. The horrendous is made not only manageable but also amusing. Our religion becomes domesticated and our spirituality becomes trivial as we reduce our longings to needs and our promises to one another to contracts.

In our society cultural options are presented as consumer goods, and religion becomes so much window dressing. Just read magazine ads such as "What is enlightenment?" to get a feel for the spiritual supermarket. The consumerist mentality has infected everything, including our dying and death. We negotiate our way around death by buying things that make us look younger or move faster, when what we need is the patience and courage to look death in the face.

I recently read some promotional material from Maharishi Veda Land, a proposed "enlightenment" theme park that was to open in 1996 in Canada. The park was to occupy some 1,400 acres and cost $1.5 billion. The brainchild of magician and entertainer Doug Henning, its purpose was to "combine enlightenment, knowledge, and entertainment" in one facility. "Each of the park's attractions will expand visitors' appreciation of their own infinite potential. They will experience reality and illusion, immortality and change, unity in diversity, infinity within a point, and the universe within the self." There were to be thirty-three rides, including "Seven steps to enlightenment—Feel enlightened as you visit seven wondrous pavilions radiating out like the spokes of a wheel. Your path has been carefully designed to lead you, in an entertaining way, step by step to enlightenment." This may be a far cry from the offerings of mainstream religion, but even there, the tendency to provide entertainment and promise cut-rate, quick-fix enlightenment or salvation is apparent.

Followers of the God du jour school treat religion as a do-it-yourself kit bought off the shelf. The assembly process can be bewildering because instructions are nonexistent or confused: a friend compares it to the often garbled instructions in half a dozen languages that come with some appliances or toys. Moreover, do-it-yourself spirituality takes a certain amount of leisure and affluence, because having to earn a living can be exhausting and distracting. Not everyone can afford to belong to a spiritual gymnasium. Being ordinary tends to disqualify one. And those who feel "qualified" easily become self-absorbed and uncaring in the name of being "spiritual."

I experienced this in an uncomfortable way while staying with friends one summer. We all decided on a strict discipline of diet, exercise, and yoga. One morning, as we were stretching our muscles, the maid was cleaning up in the kitchen. I felt humbled and blessed at the same time. My spiritual practice is supported by countless others, and I pray that I'm somehow supporting theirs. Spirituality can be isolating and narcissistic and always needs to be examined. We need to be rooted and grounded in particular practices that help us make connections with others and the world. We can't help living in a particular place at a particular time and walking a particular path, but we don't have to despise others for their particularities.

Theologian John Dominic Crossan helps me understand the particularity of my commitment to Christ without my having to dump on other traditions. He writes about his marriage to a particular person:

> Imagine this. I wake up tomorrow morning next to my wife and say, "If I had not met you, fallen in love with you, and married you, I would probably have met someone else, fallen in love with her, and married her, and be waking up next to her this morning." That would be a very imprudent way to start my day, yet it is probably true. It is also unspeakably crude in its denial of human particularity. Or imagine this. A young couple have just lost their firstborn child and I tell them, "Don't worry. You can always have another one." That, too, is unspeakably cruel in its denial of human particularity. So also, then, with your religion; you must experience it as if no alternative were even possible. But at the back of your mind, you must also recognize that alternatives are always present. Particularity is not relativity, not the belief that anything goes or that everything is the same, but the acceptance that our humanity, at its deepest moments and profoundest depths, is individual and specific.

Crossan is asking a lot of us, but it is a demand that is crucial for the future of religion in the world if it is not to lose all meaning or spiral down into tribal violence. When I say that my non-Christian friends are, to me, more Christ-like than many Christians, I am not slipping the Christian God into every other religion by the back door. Indeed, as Crossan points out, I am trying to go in the opposite direction. I want to honor and protect the integrity of the particular experiences of others.

I see the world through the images of Christianity, which teaches me that I encounter God in everyone I meet regardless of what they believe. My way of understanding who they are is to see them as an image of the divine. That understanding allows me, to quote Crossan, "to accept my own religion with utter fidelity without having to negate the integrity of everyone else's. Particularity is not relativity. It is destiny."

A woman in North Carolina once took me to task for being disparaging about those who prefer "spirituality" to "religion." She asked, "What are people to do when the tradition that once nourished them has gone dead on them? I have to make do with the scraps and fragments that lie to hand to feed my soul, now that the life that nurtured me has dried up." She is one of the growing number who cannot fit Christianity into their heads if it is presented as a list of literal facts, but are drawn to it nevertheless because of the love and integrity at its heart.

Beyond Belief and Doubt

The philosopher Paul Ricoeur tells us that we need to come to the "second naïveté," a childlikeness on the other side of doubt and skepticism. His "wager" is that the naive in the best sense can be recovered in a critical form. You can be truly simple without being simplistic. You can be transparent and open without being a simpleton. Neither the naive nor the critical has a monopoly on truth. And this second naïveté comes to us when we have exhausted our minds with our thinking and come up against the sheer mystery of being. It doesn't mean being stupid.

In an accelerated world of unsorted information, we can't close ourselves off to questions, whether we are naturally inclined to skepticism or belief. We must all be learners and seekers—at least if we're awake. Just when we've figured something out, new information comes our way, and we have rethink things. We have to move ahead even when we don't have the wit or the energy to sift through the piles of information lying all around us. We have to muddle through. It's no wonder that millions turn to ideology (in both religion and politics) as a cure for self-doubt, a way to cut through the muddle, while millions more turn to cynical apathy. Others respond to ads such as "How to meditate deeper than a Zen monk . . . literally at the touch of a button."

Those who manage to resist ideology and/or the promise of instant enlightenment find themselves in a situation of lifelong learning. Modern life requires us to learn new ways and new habits, not least of which is to live with more uncertainty yet with more trust, with less control but with more openness to new possibilities. Those who resist being "managed" by ideology (theirs or somebody else's) must learn to think and act like a leader, but a different kind of leader from the ones we're used to. A leader is a person who isn't seduced by the "certainties" of ideologies or quick fixes and who doesn't surrender his or her will to someone else. In this sense we're all called to be leaders.

We need the point of view of both believers and skeptics to keep the urgent dialogue open. To use an old analogy, we need both foxes and hedgehogs. The fox knows many things, but the hedgehog knows one big thing. The fox enjoys the freedom of ambiguity but finds it hard to focus and settle on any one thing. The hedgehog has a single vision but is in danger of embracing a restricting Utopian fantasy. Foxes find it hard to make up their mind. Hedgehogs know what's what, but their single-mindedness can turn fanatical. The hedgehogs and the foxes—absolutists and relativizers—are at war and do not know that they need each other. We read about them in the newspaper every day. They yell at each other on television, write editorials, and preach sermons.

There's another option besides "God du jour" for those seeking to reconcile belief and skepticism. It's a harder road, but it leads somewhere other than a maze of dead ends. William Golding's last novel, *The Double Tongue,* is about a priest named Ionides, who presides over Apollo's shrine at Delphi. It's his job to train the new priestess, Pythia, who in her trances will give voice to the oracles. Literary critic Frank Kermode notes: "Ionides, whom in so many ways we resemble, did not believe in the holy, did not believe that Pythia was inspired, but honored her all the same."

It seems to me that there are a growing number of people like that, and we need more of them. They are not hypocrites but in-betweeners. They are more comfortable with poetry and metaphor than they are with dogma, yet comfort is not their main concern. They're looking for traditions of belief that honor their own experience and don't ask them to believe something on the mere say-so of authority.

Some of us are looking for allies and, given the parlous state of human affairs, we're not too particular about pedigree. We look for generosity of spirit, a certain vulnerability brought on by experience, and an eagerness to form transforming connections for healing and celebration. I don't care who you are—what tradition you embrace or reject. It's too late for that. Let's first acknowledge our connection (since there is more that unites us than divides us) and *then* argue: argue with passion about real issues—not about the tepidities of much modern spirituality.

In looking for a common language and common purpose, I'm not looking to found a theocracy—the Kingdom of God on earth. History is littered with the debris of the righteous who tried to speak for God. Theocracies are totalitarian and autocratic. They assume there can be an end to dialogue and discovery. That's why they're so attractive! Believers would have the right to outlaw unbelief. They would have nothing to learn. This is why there's some urgency to reimagine and rework the religious quest, if only for the sake of those who come after us. We need to revive the ancient versions of Christianity that see God as an ever-receding horizon calling us into endless possibility. Or explore traditions such as in the Eastern Church, which sees the Holy Spirit as celebrating the endless diversity of human life and the work of Christ as the setting free of human possibilities.

Living in a world where the loss of transcendence—the spiritual dimension of life—is felt everywhere, I find that I cannot do with the language of science alone. I need the language of faith. Beyond physics, I need metaphysics—a term that simply means that there is something more or "above" physics, something binding all things together. Transcendence also speaks to the search for more than the eye can see. We are always looking for more. Is this looking for more a foolish quest, or is it something built into us?

The human heart needs to give itself away, but to whom? To Lenin, to the apostles of science and progress? To technology? To Freud and Darwin? To a domesticated and tribal Christ? To an avenging Allah? To Allah, the All-Merciful? To the free market? Allegiance—falling in love—is inescapable. But who and what we love matter.

5

Living with Anxiety, Rushing to Belief

I wouldn't want to belong to a club that would accept me as a member.

—Groucho Marx

There was no ambiguity, no room for doubt and no room for faith at all. The whole world knew for certainty that Christ was the Son of God. It was only a dream, of course, only a dream but nonetheless Father Quixote has felt on waking the chill of despair felt by a man . . . who must continue to live in a kind of Saharan desert without doubt or faith, where everyone is certain that the same belief is true. He had found himself whispering, "God save me from such a belief."

—Graham Greene, *Monsignor Quixote*

O ur roving anxieties and desire for control often cause us to leap into and cling to belief. When we feel ourselves shipwrecked, it makes sense to grab hold of anything that floats. Indiscriminate and unconditional love may be at the heart of reality, but that's too vague a thing to bet your life on. You want to know where the next meal is coming from and if the building where you work might be blown up. Those of us who live on planet Earth know in our gut that reality (whatever it is) and religion are chiefly struggles for power. At least that's what they feel like. Therefore we want to be right and with the "in" crowd, which controls things.

When it comes to religion, exclusion is the preferred way of exercising control. Talking about it is like belonging to a club. When most people you know belong to the same club, the conversation goes along pretty easily. Sometimes, of course, there are controversies and upheavals, palace coups and revolutions—even in well-run clubs such as my own Episcopal Church. The disaffected form their own clubs. But at least the combatants have a shared history. There's a relationship (even if a soured one) between or among rival factions.

Occasionally you run into someone who is definitely not in any club you know about. When that happens, the most common response is to assert the superiority about your own club, and then the conversation can turn ugly. On the other hand, if you are disillusioned, you may be irresistibly tempted to romanticize the new revelation.

I once spent a weekend with some Mormons. I've got nothing against Mormons; I just don't know many. Staying with this couple was like visiting another planet, which seemed familiar, except now and then you'd turn a corner and be in a landscape so strange that you'd begin to doubt your senses. It was very confusing. They were loving, friendly, and open; we shared many interests. And then, wham: a different world. It looked to me to be a cartoon world of bright colors and clear beliefs, but I couldn't find my way in and through it. They looked at me with affectionate pity, as if to say "If you really had an open mind and heart, you'd come to see the world as we do." I looked at them as if to say "You're crazy if you believe that stuff."

Conversation with them was respectful and congenial, but there were things we simply couldn't talk about. I bumped up against what's called incommensurability—our differences were so great they couldn't be measured. When it came to being respectful and kind to each other, we inhabited the same universe. When it came to beliefs, we lived in different worlds.

When we meet members of a club of which we've had no experience, the conversation goes something like this: "I am so radically different from you that we have absolutely nothing in common. Even having a good fight is impossible." This experience in religion is mirrored by identity politics: voting for people because they're white, black, gay, straight, male, or female rather than because of their views or values. Sometimes it feels as if we're in a process of resegregation: "I'm white, you're black. I'm straight, you're gay. I'm male, you're female. I'm an Episcopalian, you're a Mormon. We have nothing to say to each other besides you just don't *get it*; in fact you *can't* get it."

If we feel threatened by someone else's club, attempts to exclude can go to extremes. In 2002, incoming freshmen at the University of North Carolina were assigned a book called *Approaching the Qur'án: The Early Revelations*. It's a fine book and an apt choice for incoming freshmen, given the pervasive ignorance, fear, and prejudice surrounding Islam, especially then. Three anonymous students, however, supported by out-of-state fundamentalists, objected to the assignment and took the university to court. The matter was even taken up by the state legislature, some of its members trying to undermine the modest funding for the freshman reading program. No distinction was made between learning about another religion and owing allegiance to it. On the TV news, one protester with a placard shouted truthfully but irrelevantly, "Muhammad didn't die on the cross to save you from your sins!" He'd gotten that right but betrayed his ignorance of a tradition other than his own. Even to know about another tradition was anathema. The protester's anxiety was expressed as a thoughtless dogmatism. When a friend of mine (having just come back from six months in China) suggested that millions of Chinese who weren't Christians were, nevertheless, in the hands of a loving God, his pastor told him that by merely raising the question he was revealing his deep-seated atheism! Anxiety breeds a crippling certitude that leads to violence. Supreme Court justice Sandra Day O'Connor was rightly puzzled and shocked when evangelist Pat Robertson urged all good Christians to pray for her death because she and others on the Court didn't conform to Robertson's vision of Christianity. Listening to each other and respecting each other aren't just nice ideas. They are matters of life and death.

Jumping to Conclusions

We tend to talk about "beliefs" prematurely and jump to conclusions about other people's intelligence and depth. Listening to each other on more than one level is a challenge, and an important one—for beneath and behind professed beliefs, something more is always being said. Questions are silently being asked: Would I be safe in your world? Does anything really matter? Even, Do you love me? Do you wish me harm?

Rodney Stark, who teaches sociology at the University of Washington, tells us that "success [in religious movements] is really about relationships and *not* about faith. What happens is that people form relationships and only then embrace religion. It doesn't happen the other way round." The trick in religion is, evidently, not to push dogma up front but to give people things to do. No one can be *argued* into a life of faith, but if you invite them into a community and give them something to do, believing will follow. The best and most mature religious communities encourage questions and foster conversation because conversation is an essential gift of being human. Through dialogue we come to deeper meanings.

The way in which religion is usually presented misleads people into believing that they cannot enter into a faith practice unless they wholeheartedly believe the doctrines of that faith. But to expect belief before doing the work is getting things backward. Patient practice, sometimes a lifetime's worth, is a prerequisite of true faith. As scholar Karen Armstrong points out, "In all the great traditions, prophets, sages, and mystics spent very little time telling their disciples what they ought to believe." They were invited to trust that "despite all the tragic and dispiriting evidence to the contrary, our lives did have some ultimate meaning and value. You could not possibly arrive at faith in this sense before you have lived a religious life. Faith was thus the fruit of spirituality, not something that you had to have at the start of your quest."

The Need for Ritual

S. Brent Plate, a professor of religion and the visual arts at Texas Christian University, stresses the importance of religious practices rather than beliefs—especially the importance of performing rituals. But when he asked his students to define *ritual*, they used terms such as "routine" and "boring." He comments, "They've been raised on marketing slogans that would have them believe that they think for themselves, and that participation in a prescribed set of actions indicates that they are lesser beings."

In response, he points to the shrines and memorials that sprang up around New York City in the aftermath of September 11: "all those 'boring,' 'unproductive' symbols, like candles, poems. Flowers, photos, mementos, people standing around for hours and doing nothing except being together or maybe singing and praying."

Lighting a candle, reading a poem, eating a little bit of bread . . . all these carry more weight than we realize. They draw us deeper into being fully human. They may even elicit from us forms of freedom and ways of being truly ourselves, which invite new initiatives, new forms of leadership. These small acts don't tell us what to believe. They don't impart new information or give us a way of controlling our lives. In fact, they do the opposite. They help us wait in the chaos and confusion until a new way of being human reveals itself.

Why Do We Need to Believe?

There's an old story about two frogs—let's call them Bill and Ted. Ted lived by the ocean, Bill lived in a well. When Ted tried to describe the vastness of the ocean, Bill was impressed. "You mean it's so enormous that it's half as big as this well?" Ted tried and tried to convey the ocean's hugeness, but Bill, so impressed by his own little world, just couldn't get it. In the end, Ted persuaded Bill to make the long journey to the ocean to see for himself, and after a series of adventures they came to a hill from which the mighty ocean could be seen. Ted told Bill to close his eyes and wait for his signal to open them. Leading Bill up to the crest, Ted finally said, "Open your eyes." When Bill did, he was so overwhelmed by the vast, shining presence of the ocean that his head exploded in a thousand pieces.

When it comes to our beliefs, we need to begin "farther back" and "lower down," to see how they function psychologically and spiritually. We believe certain things for good reasons, and those reasons aren't always readily perceived. If we take this inner exploration seriously, we discover much wisdom. Some of it is very personal; some points to the universal.

If we're open, we nearly always learn, for example, that religion at its heart is a work of the imagination. We find that the body has a wisdom of its own; it can tell us much about solidarity with others and with the earth. We realize that our need for affiliation and community runs very deep, making us vulnerable to belief systems that can be repressive and cruel. We endure them because our need to have something to hang on to outweighs the awfulness of the beliefs. At least they keep us in the dark well of certainty and protect us from the immensity and depth of the ocean. Our hearts may be small and ungenerous, but at least our minds haven't exploded in a thousand pieces.

I told the frog story to a group once and was taken by surprise when one man reacted to it in horror. He was angry and shocked that there might be some kind of knowledge that would destroy a person's well-constructed and defended universe. This man, I learned, clung to the belief in eternal punishment as if his life depended on it. This was the particular well he lived in. The belief was the linchpin of his universe; without it everything would fall apart. He was frightened and worried that people "were getting away with things and they shouldn't be allowed to."

I asked him, "How many people need to be in hell for you to feel safe?" He blinked and couldn't answer at first, but something lit up in his mind. He began to relax and climb out of his well. He didn't abandon his belief in eternal punishment—he still believes judgment is essential in a true view of the world—but he seems to hold it more gently. It lost a lot of its energy, as he shed some of his burden of fear and anger.

Beliefs are tricky and take time to understand. They come at us at many levels and can be true on one level and not on another. With my Mormon friends, though I couldn't accept the claims to the objective truth of their beliefs, I came to see their value psychologically. They gave comfort, provided rules of behavior, and shaped a community. Theirs was a morally sound and caring universe. This is what belief systems do, from the dark, destructive systems of the Nazi Party to the vows of Benedictine and Buddhist monks. And because all belief systems perform this function but clearly are not equal in value, the ability to discriminate is vital.

All I'm suggesting, for now, is to hesitate a little before jumping all over someone else's way of believing. Sit still and listen. Find out not only *what* they believe but also *why.* Sometimes, when you get to the "why," the "what" makes more sense. And occasionally a moment of insight arrives when the link between the "why" and the "what" is severed, the wacky belief withers and dies, and something deeper takes its place. This can be a shattering experience. One's inner world falls apart when the walls we have erected begin to crumble. Under pressure to grow and change, people beat up on themselves, and institutions become repressive. If you live in a closed belief system of certainty, resistance to new information is intense, and the breakthrough feels like death. You feel as if your head might explode.

This fear and resistance is in all of us. Before we get into a contest about whose beliefs are better, we might try to back off to recover what we have in common.

Living with Anxiety and Ambiguity

One of the things we have in common is our anxiety, and the greatest anxiety is that of annihilation. We naturally resist what we think contradicts our view of things, especially thoughts we fear can destroy our world. Jungian psychiatrist Tom Singer points out that we make our annihilation anxiety manageable by finding an enemy.

Religion is often used to relieve our anxiety and resolve ambiguities, and it's good at finding enemies. It is no accident that religious traditions are both nurturing and ruthless at the same time: nurturing to those within the club, and ruthless to those who are outside or who want to leave. In our own time, for example, it's a tragedy that Islam appears to present only this ruthless side to the world, and the world cannot see this great tradition's glory and depth. Religion under siege presents its most steely front to the outside.

Religion and violence seem to go together. In psychological terms, they constellate complexes that play havoc with our emotions and express themselves in compulsive and repeated acts. People so beset and inflamed resist anything that might disturb their world. They will do anything to shut out new interpretations from consciousness. In fact, they will see to it that their "experience" of the world confirms their beliefs about it. For example, if you believe that people are basically rotten and unreliable, then, sure enough, they are. It's easier to settle for certainty than to wrestle with emotional ambiguity.

Mature religion, far from doing away with ambiguity, gives us the grace to live with it. That's why it's important to get at *why* people believe what they do. If we can get to the "why," we might be able to change the "what" into something closer to the truth. If we jump to conclusions and try to resolve all the tensions inherent in being alive and aware, we get trapped in a world that might feel secure but is so costly to hold together that violence becomes our only defense.

There will always be tension between stability and change, tradition and innovation, but learning to live with this tension is vital. In a letter to his brothers, the poet John Keats described the concept of negative capability as "when a man is capable of being in uncertainties, mysteries, doubts, without any irritable reaching after fact and reason." Coming to that capability is the beginning of a mature faith.

Keeping Belief Nimble

Roger Lundin points out that Emily Dickinson's poetry "is in large measure about belief—about the objects of belief and its comforts, as well as belief's great uncertainties." Near the end of her life she wrote: "On subjects of which we know nothing, or should I say *Beings,* we both believe, and disbelieve a hundred times an Hour, which keeps Believing nimble."

Belief is kept nimble when we become aware of just how flimsy our constructions of reality are. In *Roger's Version,* novelist John Updike captures a moment when another kind of truth intrudes into consciousness. Updike's protagonist takes time to notice a tree:

I even stopped, on the pavement of this unsavory neighborhood, to ponder more deeply that tall gingko with its gong-like golden color; there are few things which, contemplated, do not, like flimsy trap-doors, open under the weight of our attention into the bottomless pit below.

The old name for this is contemplation, which means being willing to stand still and look—really look—at an object: in this case, a gingko tree. Under the weight of our attention, things open up to either the pit of terror or the abyss of wonder. As we struggle to break free from the cage of our received beliefs and self-images, we find we don't know ourselves as well as we thought. The truth of who we are has to be made and found all over again.

How Do We Know Anything?

Waiting in an openhearted stance becomes a challenge as well as an imperative when things appear to be up for grabs. It takes courage to ask the simple question "How do we know anything?" Knowledge remains an intractable problem for philosophy and a mystery for people of faith. It drives people mad. We want certainty so much that we will cling to almost anything and make it an absolute. That's why many believe that the pursuit of absolute truth is a dangerous illusion.

The word *absolute* is confusing because it can be used in two senses: as a way to close down debate, or as an affirmation that life has meaning. It can close down conversation with rigid dogmatism and arbitrary authority. We are pilgrims *to,* not possessors *of,* the absolute. Yet the *absolute* can start and nourish conversations about the purpose or worth of the human enterprise. This can be as simple as affirming that it is *absolutely* worth getting up in the morning. But is it? Why get up in the morning? How do you *know* it's worthwhile? Are you willing to question the very things you take for granted?

When you ask a question as basic as "How do we know any-thing?" it's rather like sawing off the branch you're sitting on. It begins to dawn on us that there are two truths that seem at war with each other: one, we invent our world, and two, the world is *real*. And there's another unnerving question waiting in the wings: "Who wants to know?" True seeking after knowledge always turns the tables and asks us questions. True spiritual discipline opens us up to images that will revolutionize the way we are in the world.

Any journey toward belief must begin with the task recognized by mystics throughout history. They realized that merely knowing about things (science) wasn't enough. In fact, it was a distraction. They recognized that there was a deeper and potentially frightening task of self-knowledge. Knowledge of God and knowledge of self were sides of the same coin. It was a knowledge that had no end. And the endlessness of it—its known unknowability—makes many of us turn away to embrace something we can pin down and control. This is one mystic's conviction about the soul's journey: "And yet although its search is unending, by some miraculous means it finds what it seeks for: and again it does not find it, for it cannot be found."

We know by "not knowing"—by wise and learned ignorance. Those on a spiritual path share this vision of the universal and unending character of our journey to and in God. The principle is that all things are lights guiding our way—even a stone or a piece of wood—but they are not what we seek. What stops our drive for facts from going haywire? The discovery of a higher form of knowing. This form of knowing requires giving up control. It is called love. It was the twelfth-century mystic St. Gregory the Great who coined the phrase "Love itself is a form of knowledge."

Right Belief or Right Action?

I know people whose beliefs are all over the map but whose moral compass seems right on—Catholics who believe in reincarnation; New Agers who go to Mass; sensible types who take astrology seriously; Buddhists who are more Jewish than Buddhist in that they embrace Buddhist practice but retain their quintessential Jewishness; atheists who sniff around religious institutions, drawn to the practice but wanting none of the dogma. I'm not talking about the intellectually lazy. The seekers I speak of may be confused but they're not lazy. These people might not have thought through belief systems, but I find that I can trust them. They behave in a loving and trustworthy way. They remind me that belief or disbelief in God isn't the first thing we should think about. Actual behavior and character come first.

Believers who claim to be truly orthodox often exhibit a gap—sometimes a wide one—between what they profess and what they practice. Many don't seem to have made the connection between belief and behavior. I'd rather go with those I can trust and who act lovingly than with those who are religiously "correct," feeling that there is plenty of time to do some intellectual tidying later. I am more interested in pursuing integrity—in trying to be who I say I am—than in being a doctrinal purist. So I take my friends where I find them. Some are believers, some not. Some have abandoned any form of institutional religion, some show up every week. Some find that the old rituals have gone dead and are making up their own. Each has his or her blind spots. Having been in the crossfire myself occasionally, I would rather be with the intuitively loving than with the doctrinally correct. One thing I've learned in trying to follow Christ is that there are more important things than being right.

I am no longer interested, in the first instance, in what a person believes. Most of the time it's so much clutter in the brain. I am more interested in what role belief plays in shaping the believer's personality. I wouldn't trust an inch many people who profess a belief in God. Others who do not or who doubt have won my trust. I want to know if joy, curiosity, struggle, and compassion bubble up in a person's life. I'm interested in being fully alive.

An Unreliable God

There's an aspect of Judaism and Christianity that runs counter to the God-is-on-our-side certainties of most institutional religion. In Anne Mary Doria Russell's novel *The Sparrow,* a character (also called Anne) muses on the mystery of faith:

God was at Sinai and within weeks, people were dancing in front of a golden calf. God walked in Jerusalem and days later, folks nailed Him up and then went back to work. Faced with the Divine, people took refuge in the banal, as though answering a cosmic multiple choice question: If you saw a burning bush, would you (a) call 911, (b) get the hot dogs, or (c) recognize God? A vanishing small number of people would recognize God, Anne had decided years before, and most of them had simply missed a dose of Thorazine.

Russell herself is a convert to Judaism after having been raised Roman Catholic. Both religions have their fanatics. She seems to be attracted to Judaism because it is at home with the ironic and the ambiguous. Jewish comics couldn't perform their routines without that basic Jewish anxiety to play with. Russell writes, "If you read the Torah, you realize that God has a lot to answer for. God is a complex personality. I wanted to explore that complexity and that moral ambiguity. God gives us rules but those are rules for us, not for God."

I believe that Christianity at its deepest shares this sense of irony and ambiguity for the sake of truth. Coping with the constant changing images in our consciousness of God, ourselves, and our world is a humbling experience; it can even be humiliating and painful. Yet our journey into these truths helps us get out of useless and damaging fights about whose beliefs are better. It enables us not only to love and respect each other but also to argue with passion and compassion, because the final test of anyone's belief is in how we treat each other. Believe it or not.

6

See How Those Christians Love One Another

I love your Christ, but I hate your Christians. They are so unlike him.

—Mahatma Gandhi

The ethicist and pacifist theologian Stanley Hauerwas has a poster on his office door: "A Modest Proposal for Peace: Let the Christians of the World Agree That They Will Not Kill One Another." If accused of Christian-centeredness, he replies, "I agree that it would certainly be a good thing for Christians to stop killing *anyone,* but you have to start somewhere."

We live in a world where people who claim to be Christians kill each other. Now, *that* is a contradiction. The venom of excommunicating self-righteousness runs through Christian history. Pope Urban II, launching the First Crusade, declared, "Let the army of the Lord, when it rushes upon his enemies, shout but that one cry 'Dieu le veult! Dieu le veult!'" God wills it.

You do have to begin somewhere, and promising not to kill each other isn't a bad place to start. Once we've agreed to that, we might be liberated to look at some of our strange beliefs—beliefs that lead some of us to the conclusion that it's legitimate if not to kill then to condemn and excommunicate others. So, having looked at the divides between believers and skeptics, and among people of various faiths, we'll focus here on the apparently unending failure of Christ's followers to get his message.

A woman recently wrote to me about what it was like to belong to her parish church, saying, "I feel as if I am a member of the Flat Earth Society for Christ." She loves the community and the liturgy but cannot enter into the web of words that are part of the deal when she goes to church. When asked by the exasperated rector why she stayed, she replied, "No human being brought me in here and no human being is going to run my ass out." This is how I feel sometimes about being part of the Christian community—the Flat Earth Society for Christ. We share a great vision for the human family. We forgive each other as we go along. We embrace those in need. And yet we tend to try to straitjacket the whole enterprise by framing it in a literalistic way.

We're lucky; at least we no longer arrest people for not believing the way the theological police insist. In the past there were ways to make people conform. In John Calvin's Geneva of 1551, Jerome Bolsec publicly criticized the doctrine of double predestination, protesting that "those who posit an eternal decree in God by which he has ordained some to life and the rest to death make of him a Tyrant, and in fact an idol, as the pagans made of Jupiter." He was arrested on the spot by Calvin's people. Truth suffocates in a system of thought that already has all the answers.

When I was eight years old and in primary school, an angry teacher smacked the kid next to me over the head while declaring, "God is love!" The words may be true, but the action denied them. St. Francis of Assisi was supposed to have said, "Preach the Gospel to every creature and, if you must, use words." There has to be a congruity between what is said and what is done for any creed to maintain credibility. But faith is practiced by humans, who are weak, quarrelsome, forgetful, and fearful. Enchanted by Christ's message, we act contrary to it again and again.

So the questions today are much the same as those of our forebears. Not only "What are the Christian claims?" but also "How should they be pressed?" "On what basis?" "By whose authority?" Christians can't agree, and the issue is raised time and time again in all sorts of situations. Even those who appeal to external authority (the Bible, the pope) can't escape from their interpretation of the authority they invoke. There is no objective authority—only authority as interpreted by individuals. When people say, "Back to the Bible!" they think there's some objective truth to be found in its pages. In reality, we read the Bible through the filter of our presuppositions and prejudices.

The Christian Debate

All the great religious traditions are in upheaval, and the divisions are within rather than between or among them. I have more in common with my friend Stephen, the rabbi at a large synagogue in San Francisco, than I do with many fellow Christians. I don't mean that we simply find each other congenial. I mean that I am more theologically compatible with Stephen than with, say, any Christian fundamentalist.

In my own Episcopal tradition, which is notoriously generous and open, there are bitter divisions. We have Catholics and Protestants, progressives and conservatives. Some of these acrimonious divisions are expressed in Michael Arditti's novel *Easter*. The bishop is a hearty Evangelical and the archdeacon a bigoted Anglo-Catholic: "the Bishop finds God in the pages of the Bible like a lazy schoolboy cribbing for an exam; . . . the Archdeacon finds God in a ritual meal the way the primitive warriors ate their dead chiefs." Although there are some Christians who are unafraid of other spiritual paths and have learned from them, and still others who are postdenominational, battle lines are being drawn between "orthodox" and "progressives." And some people, like me, are at home on neither side.

There's a celebrated couplet by the poet William Blake that sums up for me much that is disturbing about exclusionary versions of Christianity:

> That vision of Christ, which thou dost see
> Is my vision's greatest enemy.

Rowan Williams, archbishop of Canterbury, writes, "People who say to one another, 'If you think *that,* you shouldn't be here,' are . . . implicitly echoing Blake's horrifying couplet." It is a terrible thing to hate and fear someone else's vision of the thing we love most—whether it be Christ, our nation, or our way of life. We attack one another with amazing ferocity around the things we love.

I sometimes wonder if there's an ingrained Christian misunderstanding of Christianity itself. Does it inevitably degenerate into religious imperialism? Christians get imperialistic when they think that their religion is being watered down to accommodate others. Sometimes I have been accused of "selling Christianity down the river" because of my openness to other traditions. Yet I am a Christian for a reason. I really do believe that Christianity, as I have received it, has a fullness of truth, which I cannot find in other traditions. That conviction is humbled by the fact that many non-Christians are more Christ-like than many Christians.

Many like to claim, echoing Gandhi, "I love your Christ, but I hate your Christians." You can't make a clean division between Christ and Christianity, however, since there'd be no way of knowing the Spirit of Christ except through the witness of particular Christians nurtured in specific institutions. But the impulse is still valid. Somewhere in the back of your mind you think you know what Christianity is. Even the atheist knows something of what he's rejecting.

Where did the idea come from? How deep does it go? Where does it need correcting? If you're attracted to Christianity, whose version are you going to go for? The pope's? Billy Graham's? A New Age version? The Ku Klux Klan's? And what if you're attracted to Christ but not to the local Christians? Christ seems to have followers everywhere, in and outside the Church, and there are those who, while keeping their denominational allegiance, know themselves to be part of something bigger.

Endless Zones of Contradiction

There are endless contradictions in being fully committed to a particular religion and yet open to others. The Old Testament teacher and writer Walter Brueggemann has helped me understand this without despairing about it. We might be more gentle with one another, he notes, if we took to heart the impossibility of putting what we believe into words.

Brueggemann points out that the language on which both Judaism and Christianity depends is Hebrew, and Hebrew is endlessly imprecise and unclear. There's an openness to the language because it lacks connecting words: "it points and opens and suggests, but it does not conclude and define." You have to infer meaning. I love Judaism because it is an endless yet fruitful *argument* about God and meaning. No one has the last word. The language is

> a wondrous vehicle for what is suggested but hidden, what is filled with imprecision and inference and innuendo, a vehicle for contradiction, hyperbole, incongruity, disputation.
>
> Now the reason this may be important is that in a society of technological control and precision, we are seduced into thinking that if we know the codes, we can pin all the meaning down, get all mysteries right and have our own way without surprise, without deception, without amazement, without gift, with miracle, without address, without absence, without anything that signals mystery or risk.

What Christians (and, to be fair, people in general) can't stand is not being able to pin things down. We resist having to negotiate what Brueggemann calls "endless zones of contradiction . . . [and] endless layers of interpretation—no one of which can ever be more than provisional." The irony for literalists is that the Bible doesn't lend itself to literal, single-voice interpretation. There's always more to learn, another layer of meaning. To this many a Christian might respond, "No, thank you. This doesn't sound like true religion. It sounds like fuzziness, compromise, and lack of faith. I want to be absolutely clear." It's a short step from this to hating one another.

Christians live in a tradition based on two apparently contradictory principles: "Error has no rights" and "Faith cannot be coerced." We want to honor the pursuit of truth, and at the same time we know that people cannot be forced into faith. All arguments between Christians—political or theological—have to do with what is or isn't a legitimate part of the tradition.

How do you distinguish a true development in the Christian tradition from an aberration? Can Mormonism be a valid development? Are Jehovah's Witnesses beliefs aberrations? Where are Baptist beliefs in relationship to those of Roman Catholics and Eastern Orthodox Christians? And what does all this family squabbling look like to outsiders? From one perspective, it's all part of being human. Controversy is normal. And a sign of human maturity is the ability to negotiate these endless zones of contradiction. We never get to the bottom of things. There are always more things to learn, more idols to smash, new images to discover, new journeys to endure, and fresh adventures to take us off into the unknown.

In *The Theological Orations* of St. Gregory Nazianzus, which appeared just before the second ecumenical council, at Constantinople in 381, the question is posed, "Why did it take the Church so long to come up with the doctrine of the Trinity, especially the doctrine of the Holy Spirit?" Gregory's answer: "We weren't prepared. We had to be ready for the doctrine of the Holy Spirit."

What are we getting ready for now? I am grateful that no one has all the answers and that I am part of an ongoing, never-ending theological discussion. This could seem off the wall to someone looking at Christianity for the first time, but all I am saying is that to be a person of faith is to be part of a conversation in which no one has the last word. This open-ended conversation is a source of frustration to believers and unbelievers who want everything settled and decided, but it's what gives religion its resilience and freedom.

Evangelicals vs. Progressives

Meanwhile, Christians remain polarized. Among Protestants, this takes the form of the Evangelical option set against the progressive option—as if there were only two. On one side is the parachurch of "Young Life" or "Campus Crusade," with its stress on "wholesome fun, sports, and warm mentoring relationships tied to Bible study and a personal relationship with Jesus." That sounds pretty good to me, especially in the light of the violent culture young people have to navigate. Theologian Ellen Charry notes that "While the soft-rock, just-love-Jesus quality of some of these ministries may belie the strenuousness of the Christian life, in truth, the ability of sev-enth graders to refrain from oral sex takes a lot of strength." A little soft rock and a just-love-Jesus message might not be half bad.

At the other extreme is the progressive option, catering to the professional managerial class. This option cares "about people who find organized religion irrelevant, ineffectual, and repressive." In some versions it's a form of post-Christianity where you make it up as you go along; in others, it's an adventure of the spirit to experience the tradition's continuities and revolutions. As Charry characterizes this version:

> Jesus Christ is not longer the Son of God, the second Person of the Trinity, the redeemer, but one of the many gateways into the realm of God. The Lord's Supper is not a sharing in the body and blood of Christ, but a ritual meal that projects the vision of world peace. The Church is not to be defined by standards of belief, but should equally embrace believers and agnostics. It is a com-munity in which doctrines and beliefs are simply not very impor-tant and where questions are more important than answers. This may appeal to those with answers they found uncongenial.

I find some of this true but other parts of it shallow and hardly com-pelling. For example, why can't the Lord's Supper be many things? A sharing in the body and blood of Christ *and* a ritual meal that pro-jects the vision of world peace? I have already cast my lot with the progressives in affirming that I think questions are often more important than answers, but that doesn't mean that there aren't great affirmations and genuine content to our believing. There's no way we can get ourselves off the hook of *choosing* which way to live our lives. This is why I'm not entirely at home in the progressive camp. I do believe Jesus is the Son of God, the second Person of the Trin-ity. I believe the creeds—not literally, but I don't want to see them updated or revised, any more than I want someone to update Shakespeare's *Hamlet*. I want to recover them as amazing works of the human imagination.

When Christians are spitting at each other from across some faith divide, I am caught in the middle. If push comes to shove, I want to follow Jesus and discern in the old formulations a struggle to articulate the dynamics of love. Mistrusted by both extremes, I see the mystical and contemplative as the necessary grounding for social action and involvement in issues of justice. I see the spiritual life as a summons to astonishment, and this recovery of wonder as an antidote to intra-Christian warfare. It is primal because life comes to us as sheer gift, and to talk about this amazing gift, we have to use analogy, metaphor, and symbol. In this realm, however, both of the two popular options strike me as lacking.

Who's Included?

Imagine a great cathedral in Western Australia packed for the celebration of Commonwealth Day. There's been a lot of preparation for the service, and tough questions were asked about what "commonwealth" might mean in such a multicultural society. Who should be included and how should the Church celebrate the present reality that is Australia? What's the relationship of Christianity to the other faiths represented in the Commonwealth?

John Shepherd, the dean of St. George's Cathedral in Perth, Western Australia, invited the abbot of the Bodhinyana Buddhist Monastery to preach at the service, which was a Eucharist—the central Christian sacrament. The abbot accepted in full knowledge of this. Aboriginal dancers led the procession into the cathedral and later led the offertory procession to the altar. During communion, representatives of the Jewish, Hindu, Muslim, and Baha'i faiths read passages from their sacred writings, and after communion an Aboriginal reader offered a dream-time reflection. Was this Christian? The answer, as far as I'm concerned, is "Of course."

For others, however, the service was an act of betrayal. Outside the cathedral two people stood in protest, holding placards bearing biblical texts. One protester briefly interrupted the abbot's address with a cry that they were all heading for hell. The two lone objectors believed that the Christian witness was being compromised. And from their point of view, they were right. Either Christianity is true or it isn't. If it is, the other religions, however well meaning their adherents are, must be false. Right? And it's hypocritical to think and act otherwise.

But another ancient strand of Christianity teaches that we are all caught up in the Divine Mystery we call God, that the Spirit is in everyone, and that there are depths of interpretation yet to be plumbed. "In the beginning was the Word, and the Word was with God, and the Word was God. . . . What has come into being in him was life, and the life was the light of *all* people" [John 1:1–18; italics mine].

Christians often get stuck on the interpretation of texts such as the generous one above. Some claim it is contradicted later in the same gospel. The text they like to quote is John 14:6: "I am the Way, the Truth, and the Life. No one comes to the Father except by me." John Shepherd voices the inclusive tradition when he points out that "What is being said, as with all the other 'I am' statements, is that the Way, the Truth, the Life is a person, and that no one can come to the Father without experiencing Christ 'as a person.' It is a person, not a creed, who, according to the writer of John's gospel, is the bread, the light, the door, the vine, the carer (the good shepherd), the Way, the Truth, the Life, and the Resurrection."

More important, we don't worship texts and verses. We don't put our faith in paperwork. "The documents have no value apart from the Christ to whom they testify," Shepherd goes on. "They are not to be worshiped of themselves. That would be idolatry. They are accounts of believers' beliefs. . . . Above all, they should never be alleged to mean what they were never intended to mean, nor to be conscripted illegitimately to try to infer a divine policy of rejection and lack of love."

All in all, the Christian service at which a Buddhist abbot spoke caused quite a stir. John Shepherd wrote to me that "It was an eye-opener for me to realize how much biblical texts can be used to stir up hatred and violence." Some Christians carrying placards that read "God hates fags" once picketed the cathedral where I work. Whose Christianity is closer to the truth? There are forms of it that need to be repudiated. But how do we get to the essence of Christianity in the midst of such diversity of practice and opinion?

At the cathedral we "break the bread" for those who follow the path of the Buddha and walk the way of the Hindus. We pray for our brothers and sisters of Islam and for the Jewish people from whom we come. Recently an e-mail correspondent assured me that Buddhists in many parts of the world worship or are dominated by demons. It's true: there are crude forms of Buddhism just as there are dark forms of Christianity. And it's a dirty trick to compare the best of your tradition with the worst of theirs. The Buddhists I know are serious practitioners of a way of compassion and don't worship demons. And there are Christians who seem to be possessed. So, whose Buddhism? Which Christianity? While it seem obvious to *me* what the Christian character is like (even when I feel far from it), others see a very different picture.

The Treadmill of Perfection

Unlearning Christian hate starts with the self. I was brought up with a form of Christianity that emphasized the fact that I was not only a sinner but also a miserable one. The Morning Prayer confession in the 1662 Book of Common Prayer had a profound effect on an eight-year-old choirboy, especially the phrase "and there is no health in us." Are we by nature sinful and unclean? Sunday after Sunday we would acknowledge our wretchedness; later I would gain an intellectual understanding of the depravity of human nature when details about the concentration camps started to become available.

Many Christians or lapsed Christians of a certain age could tell similar tales. It's not that humans aren't sinful. We mess up, and history is bloody. But the version of Christianity I received was a very mixed bag. On one hand, I knew I was loved, and I felt drawn to the picture of Jesus painted by my teachers and mentors. On the other, a damaging division was set up inside me between my idealized self and my hidden self. I received one message that I was utterly unacceptable. At the same time, I was told I could come to Jesus "just as I am."

For one thing, there was a split between body and soul, with the body always placed second. Sexuality was so idealized and sanitized that, as a teenager, I always mistook my racing hormones for signs of being madly and even nobly in love. I also absorbed much judgmentalism and condemnation of all those who didn't see things our way—especially other Christians. Roman Catholics weren't considered Christians at all. This was part of our narrow, English Protestant way of looking at others.

The biggest "sin," and one that was actually encouraged by the Church, was an irrational belief about myself. I could be perfect. And when I failed, I either denied the imperfection or hated myself. The perfectionism was spiritually deadly and isolating. We certainly did not love one another, mainly because we were weren't encouraged to love ourselves first.

This perfectionist form of Christianity has left its followers in despair or driven them to a place outside the Church altogether, where the air seems less toxic. It has turned some of them downright nasty. It took me a long time to unlearn the fundamental errors about life that I picked up from my early Christian training. At that earlier time in my life, the intolerance I learned toward myself was easily projected onto others. It became part of my received theology. Condemning others became an integral part of my "Christian life." I had a lot to unlearn.

The Cycle of Sacrifice

Seeing yourself as a victim of those who would destroy your way of life and threaten your safety allows you to marshal your resentments, disappointments, and fears and forge them into a political platform—all in the name of religion. The world cannot do without the cycle of blood sacrifice, it seems, even if Christianity is supposed to be more advanced than the pagans who practiced literal sacrifice. So who gets sacrificed? As life gets more insecure, we look for someone to blame, and we identify whole classes of people to sacrifice. We are all priests of the cult whether we know it or not, all sacrificing to some god or other—the Market, the Self, Pleasure, Pain, Security, the Tribe.

Generous versions of the great spiritual traditions tend to enrage people. When God's generosity gets out of hand, sacrificial victims become difficult to control and victimizers can no longer be proud of what they do. We can't get away with our strategy of security, which always sees to it that we are on the top of the heap both economically and morally.

Shifting blame has always been used as a screen to conceal the anxiety and chaos stirring in the dark recesses of our hearts. Much of what passes for religion is simply attempts to turn spontaneous acts of scapegoating violence into something sacred. Bloodletting then is not just a sport but also a divine mission. The Church needs to repudiate some of its nonsense and cruelties: the fate of unbaptized babies and the unbaptized in general; the refusal to bury suicides in consecrated ground; the grotesque absurdities of its sexual fixations—to name a few of the suffocating lies that do violence to others.

Denying the suicide Christian burial was quietly dropped in a 1983 revision of canon law. But imagine what it was once like for people to have the Church place an unbridgeable chasm between God and the one they loved. Patrick Henry asks, "What does it mean about Christian certainties that they so often change? By what *right,* during all those generations, did the Church, which now acknowledges that there is hope for suicides and no longer segregates their corpses, presume to know otherwise?"

Michael Mayne, the former dean of Westminster Abbey in London, writes movingly of the suicide of his father, who was the vicar of a Northamptonshire parish. On a Saturday afternoon in May 1928, "my father wrote a note to my mother, who was out, climbed the tower of his church . . . and threw himself down. . . . My mother was left homeless, and with £40 in the world." In those days, of course, his father could have no Christian burial, no marked grave or memorial. Sixty years later, Michael stood in his father's pulpit and addressed him:

> We shall never know *why* you did what you did, for that is known
> only to you and to God, but your desperate cry for help came out
> of so much unrecognized anguish of spirit that it demands not
> our judgment but our deep compassion. . . . One thing your
> action has taught me is that none of us really understands the

heart of another human being, and none of us dares pass judgment on the life and death of another.

I wonder what our successors a hundred years from now will think of some of our current "certainties."

The chief hope of some Christians rests with the Day of Judgment, the Second Coming, the Apocalypse they are convinced is imminent—a kind of final mass sacrifice. They don't seem fazed by the promised slaughter of billions. Some Christian Zionists look for a battle in the Valley of Megiddo (Armageddon), which will settle things once and for all. They expect and hope for the end of the world so that the whole mess can be cleared away and God's elect can make a fresh start.

Historically, people who hope for a great cleansing Holocaust move from disappointment to disappointment. Those with power and influence do a great deal of harm. Christians with this point of view are in our government and affect foreign policy. In his novel *In the Beauty of the Lilies,* John Updike describes the frustration of Apocalypse postponed with regard to a peculiar American Christian sect of the mid-nineteenth century:

> Adventism should have died near its beginning, when the predictions of its founder, William Miller, met, in 1843, the First Disappointment, and then, revised to October 22, 1844, the Great Disappointment. For all the chances they gave Him, Christ declined to come. This sect of Millerites had grown over their fantastic elaborations a skin or scar of worldliness, of conventional dress, business success, and pleasant manners; yet underneath burned a pus of frustration, and inflammation of hope deferred.

Today's doomsday mentality is all too reminiscent of a "final solution"—words that freeze the heart, used not that long ago by the Nazis as a euphemism for the extermination of the Jews.

Those in need of a sanctifying text for violence have only to open the Bible. There is plenty of violence there. But the Bible is too full of contradictions to be possessed by would-be avengers. Samuel hacks Agag in pieces before the Lord, and Jesus dies on the cross. Jezebel is thrown to the dogs, and Mary gives birth. David gets rid of Uriah so that he can have Bathsheba, and Isaiah speaks movingly of the Suffering Servant.

These are wonderful if troubled texts, and what troubles them is the truth of human experience. The narrative is always correcting itself, always taking us by surprise, and never compromising the truth by editing out the nasty bits of human encounter. We'd like to turn the messy Judeo-Christian story into a comfortable myth—a story that explains everything, but (as theologian Gil Bailie points out) the Hebrews were clumsy mythmakers. They recorded stories in which they did not come off best or look good. He writes, "The true biblical spirit works like a lie detector."

Giving Up Scapegoating

There is a moral imperative to discover how murderous we can become in the name of our own culture or religion. We need to allow ourselves to experience a wide range of emotions and not edit out the nasty bits of our experience. If we do this, those bits are never wasted. We can use them to tell stories about ourselves and others. True storytelling is hard work, and we get depressed when we come to the parts of the narrative that shame us or make us feel guilty. We assume our own modest share of the sacrifice life demands when we do our inner work with painful memories and refuse to empty our garbage onto others in an orgy of blame.

It takes courage to choose for ourselves without external assurances, courage to live without scapegoating someone. Like Abraham, who was prepared to sacrifice his son Isaac, we can learn to hold back the knife of our resentments and disappointments and see that we do not have to hurt others to be healed and to feel safe. When we face and resist our own attraction to violence, we contribute to the peace of the world.

After two thousand years, the Gospel has yet to come into its own. I don't think Christianity has become Christian yet—or better,

Christ-like. An inclusive spirituality reveals the perversity of scape-goating mechanisms and the pernicious logic that finds violence morally acceptable. No wonder we resist it. It's hard to be convinced that we do not need victims to live our lives. Yet the transforming energy of a new vision initiates in us the process of inner disarmament. The arsenal of destruction we have amassed inside ourselves can be dismantled—and we don't have to be committed to a complicated belief system to begin that important inner work. Christians can make a start by loving one another.

7

A Faith to Live By

Religion and Cultural Politics

When I first came to the United States, in 1964, as a student to live in New York City, I was captivated by the energy of the city and was struck by what to me was the strange take on religion that many Americans took for granted. My education in the American attitude to religion began with ads and slogans on cars and on the subway. It was an election year, Barry Goldwater was running for president, and there was a bumper sticker that read, "Keep God in America!" I was a bit puzzled because I thought God, while willing to *visit* America, spent most of his time in the United Kingdom.

There was also an ad on the subway that read, "Give your child a faith to live by. Worship this Sunday." God was acknowledged, but in a generalized way. I had a fantasy of people practicing various forms of sacrifice in their backyards and teaching their children to hate as well as love—and all in the name of a general all-purpose religion. It took me some time to come to a grudging respect for the marketplace of religion. I soon came to the conclusion that a supermarket approach was better than having one religion established over a nation. I came to realize that there was a particular psychospiritual landscape to the United States. It was not named the New

World for nothing. The separation of Church and State is a part of the American genius, but it was often invoked in strange ways. On one hand, religion in some generic form was everywhere, yet in some places it couldn't get a look in. Religiosity was pervasive, and yet secularism relegated it to the private.

I was also struck by the physical landscape, the wide-open spaces. In the summer of 1965 I took my first trip driving across this country, with my seminary roommate. It was breathtaking, and this was the first time I realized that geography had something to do with the particularities of religious outlook, from a reverence for nature to the taking for granted the right to own guns.

What I discovered was that being "spiritual" or "religious" was not simply some generalized feeling of goodwill or awe and even terror before the unknown. It has something to do with time and place, with particular people and their group memories, their history. It is intensely political, too, because questions of spirit are partly questions about what kind of world we want to build. We are all possessed by one vision or another of the American Idea, and that idea is inextricably bound up both with the use of religious language and with philosophies of inclusion and exclusion. We are always being forced to reexamine the very *idea* of America (or the idea of Ireland or Palestine or Serbia).

Within this outer and inner landscape, it seems that Americans are always looking to revitalize ethics, affirm transcendent moral truths, and reestablish public virtue in a more perfect commonwealth. This makes us vulnerable to rigid religious simplifications that serve certain political ends. Congress becomes a debating chamber for complex ethical issues, yet its senators and representatives are no wiser than that rest of us.

"Keep God in America!" Whose God? The word *God* rolls off our tongues a little too easily. At the same time, I have secularized friends whose ignorance of religion is appalling. They give the word *barbarian* new meaning. They are religiously illiterate.

The word *God* also has a history. As the nation developed, so the idea of God got more and more vague to accommodate the growing number of immigrants who were neither Christians nor Jews.

Human beings are masters at domesticating the divine. To be a believer requires a sense of the past, and we specialize in the present and the future. Abraham Lincoln in 1861 spoke of "the mystic chords of memory" as being at the heart of a united people:

> Though passion may have strained, it must not break our bonds of affection. The mystic chords of memory, stretching from every battlefield, and patriot grave, to every living heart and hearthstone, all over this broad land, will yet swell the chorus of the Union, when again touched, as surely they will be, by the better angels of our nature.

We once talked of a manifest destiny, and we go on looking for ways to legitimize the present and reinforce social cohesion. God is often the glue, at least for those who want to influence political direction. Society needs the illusion of social consensus. Human beings need divine sanction so they can be free to act *as if* the world made sense. Even Huey Long, governor of Louisiana and U.S. senator, found God useful. Before Long began his electoral campaign in southern Louisiana, an aide pointed out that there were a large number of Catholics there. Long began his first speech: "When I was a boy I would get up at six o'clock in the morning on Sunday, and I would hitch our old horse up to the buggy and would take my Catholic grandparents to Mass. I would bring them home, and at ten o'clock I would hitch the old horse up again, and would take my Baptist grandparents to church." Later a colleague remonstrated with Huey: "You've been holding out on us all these years. I didn't know you had any Catholic grandparents." "Don't be a damned fool," replied Long. "We didn't even have a horse."

We live in times when it is politically expedient to be "religious" and for presidential candidates to profess belief in God—preferably a Protestant one—although the Catholic variety has proved acceptable as long as private beliefs don't slip over into the public sphere. Leaders of the former Soviet Union find it politically helpful to attend the Divine Liturgy—some, no doubt, expressing a genuine faith.

I appreciate the fact that America is forward-looking and basically optimistic. That's a good thing. It holds out hope for the future and promises progression for justice, inclusion, and the common good. But there are dangers. We tend to divide the world into two camps: one good, the other evil. We lack self-awareness. And while we don't want to be crippled by self-doubt, a little self-questioning would do us good. Historically things do not always "work out for the best." And we tend to put too much faith in turning the world into consumers just like us.

Yet there is something in the national spirit that is admirable. Tom Paine expressed it in 1776, in the pamphlet *Common Sense*. "We have it in our power to begin the world over again. A situation, similar to the present, hath not happened since the days of Noah until now. The birth-day of a new world is at hand." This mixture of hope and naïveté is an American characteristic, but it contains a great error. As admirable and heroic as the sentiment is in some ways, it is surely wrongheaded and even dangerous because it fails to take the tragic in human life seriously.

The Promise of America

Richard Rorty, a professor of philosophy at the University of Virginia, has his own version of the story and is a kind of "priest" of the liberal left. He, too, cannot live without texts. He wants our children

> to come to think of themselves as proud and loyal citizens of a country that, slowly and painfully, threw off a foreign yoke, freed its slaves, enfranchised its women, restrained its robber barons and licensed its trade unions, liberalized its religious practices and broadened its religious and moral tolerance, and built colleges in which 50 per cent of its population could enroll—a country that numbered Ralph Waldo Emerson, Eugene V. Debs, Susan B. Anthony and James Baldwin among its citizens.

I value his vision even though he doesn't have any time for God.

To him all God-talk is projection and wishful thinking. But there is genuine belief in a God who is beyond our imaginings and manipulations. This is where those open to intellectual and spiritual exploration could meet. Atheists and believers alike might be able to talks about belief in a God who makes us uneasy because we are continually being presented with an alternative view of the world. In fact, our deeper belief functions as a sign of contradiction about what we take for granted; for example: the view of the self as autonomous; the assumption that the bottom line is the budget rather than, say, issues of life, death, and love; the belief that some other countries are deeply wicked, whereas we make only well-intentioned mistakes. Religion is either chaplain of the status quo or something pushing us into the untried and unknown. Most of us like religion as a supporter of the status quo, something that is psychologically useful and spiritually comforting.

Religion points to a very different system—one that is all answers and no questions. An open, supple system is not wishy-washy but morally challenging. The God who stares at us from the pages of the Bible contradicts the Nike version of reality—"life is for winners"—for people "who live well, are self-indulgent, but who never get involved in anything outside of their own success." The predominant narrative in our culture pushes us to do the "right" thing, wear the "right" clothes, get the kids into the "right" schools. The story that has captured our imagination in our culture is that we are rivals of each other for finite and limited resources. The biblical story, however, is not of a God of achievement but of a God who makes everyone a neighbor.

Under the title "In the Culture Wars, There May Be No Winners," Martin Marty quotes a letter to *Christianity Today* by Paul Schlitz: "What is sobering is that evangelicals have gotten used to a culture that is terrible by any conceivable standard. Is anybody going to contend that Christian Contemporary music, the paranoid novels of Peretti and Jenkins-LaHaye, the Conservative Book Club, or the architecture of today's suburban sprawl megachurch is great art? If anything, it implies that evangelical culture is very unhealthy and pretentious." Would you want to live in such an "evangelical" culture? I certainly wouldn't.

God on Our Side

Michael Kammen, in *Mystic Chords of Memory,* draws attention to an 1853 painting by Asher B. Durand called *Progress* (also known as *The Advance of Civilization*). It sums up the American Myth. It is grand icon of a time when nostalgia and progress weren't at odds, and it helps us get inside the American imagination. There is a superficially serene landscape containing, on close inspection, a great deal of activity. Livestock are being driven to market. There's a busy canal plied by steamships. Across the cove there is a steam locomotive. We can see a bustling town with belching smokestacks, large mills, and small workshops. A few Native Americans complete the scene. It is a glimpse of a tamed Eden, a picture of the way we like to see our past.

We use the word *God* a bit like Americans in the middle of the nineteenth century viewed that painting. It made them feel good about themselves and their country. That is precisely what the word *God* is supposed to do. But our memory is very selective and the god we invoke is, more often than not, the projection of our wishful thinking. What aspects of our history are conveniently "forgotten" or turned into a myth? As a people, we're not very good at history. We tend to prefer looking to the future than learning from the past.

For us, the best is yet to come. That's why we're a country that is fascinated, not to say mesmerized, by the hope for and dread of the Apocalypse. When the world comes to an end and we can begin again. We're not so clear about the fact that it is we who are going to come to an end. God is often invoked to reinforce the reality in our minds of an unreal past. We rummage through the past as if ransacking an attic for treasures that can be used to prove the rightness of what we believe. What we don't know, we make up. There's a story of tourists going through one of the California missions. A noisy kid, pointing to the font in the church, yelled, "Mom, what's that?" "That's where the Indians cooked their food," replied the mom. Improvising.

Because Americans have been such successful improvisers (or so the myth goes), we've become the most powerful nation on the planet. And naturally we take that to prove that God endorses the American way.

In a talk a few years ago, the actor Kirk Douglas told a story about his fellow actor John Wayne, who severely criticized him for accepting the part of Vincent van Gogh in the movie *Lust for Life*. Wayne suggested that he and actors like Douglas had the obligation to play manly men—tough guys—on the screen, not wusses like that crazy Dutch painter. Kirk Douglas commented, "The trouble with John Wayne was that he thought he was John Wayne!" Wayne had fallen into the trap of believing his own propaganda. In the same way, we might say, "The trouble with those who indulge in God-is-on-our-sidism in our country is that they really think that God is a kind of domestic chaplain to the American agenda."

When we try to get behind our beliefs to see how they function, we realize that a lot of what we believe is made up so that we can make sense of the world. When Winston Churchill used the metaphor of "the Iron Curtain" at the end of World War II, he helped to create the kind of world we all lived in up until we heard of *glasnost* and *perestroika*. It wasn't that the emerging reality of the Soviet Union wasn't threatening, it's simply that Churchill helped us make sense of it by coming up with an image, a myth. Words can galvanize a nation into action. They are the myths nations and individuals live by. The myth "Greater Serbia" has cost the lives of many, as has that of "Palestine."

Rival stories abound in this country—some of them cruel and contradictory. America, after all, was founded by people who had a chip on their shoulder about religion—and with good cause. Many came clutching the Bible. In its pages they thought they found clear principles for governing themselves and their society. They had no doubt about why. For our forebears, religion was not a hobby or a trivial pursuit. The New England Puritans had been treated with a heavy hand in the old country, and they were equally if not more heavy-handed with their fellow citizens in their new homeland. Sociologist Peter Berger reminds us that "They fined, whipped, jailed, cropped, maimed and hanged in an effort to maintain a pure social order and to erect a *true* Church of Christ!" Cotton Mather in Massachusetts saw Rhode Island as the latrine of New England because that tiny and despised colony gave safe harbor to "Antinomians, Familists, Anabaptists, Antisabbatarians, Arminians, Socinians, Quakers, Ranters—everything in the world except Roman Catholics and real Christians."

Our forebears were scandalized by the horrors of diversity. No wonder Thomas Paine responded: "The most detestable wickedness, the most horrid cruelties, and the greatest miseries that have afflicted the human race, have had their origin in this thing called revelation, or revealed religion." Wouldn't it be better to leave our longings to silence? How awful to tell a story about them and then force others to accept the story as dogma. Yet this is what generations of ordained ministers thought was their vocation. Many of us thought of ourselves as a kind of spiritual police force.

The choice we have is of either being dangerously focused or fatuously vague about words such as *God*. In 1890 the U.S. Supreme Court spoke of Americans as a Christian nation, a Christian people. In 1952 the Court was content to call Americans a religious people whose institutions presuppose a Supreme Being. It seemed prudent to be as vague as possible. Nevertheless, religion, when banished from one area, crops up somewhere else. The problem of religion intruding in government hasn't gone away.

Religion has always been exploited for political or cultural purposes. Religious symbols are used to justify class interests and class culture. Each class calls in the clergy to bless its troops. Priests, ministers, and academics sometimes prostitute their profession by being chaplains to those in power, court jesters to the ruling oligarchy.

The New Christian right, for example, is on a crusade to change American society with highly specific programs about which there is no shadow of doubt. But the same can be said of some left-wing Christians. There is a belligerent and excommunicating "liberalism" in the mainline churches—excommunicating because we tend to anathematize those who don't agree with us. Both sides seek changes in society by means of government-sponsored social engineering. "God is for lower taxes; God is against them. God is for a large defense budget; God is against it. God is prolife; God is pro-choice; God loves you; God's gonna get you."

Those who would like to impose a one-size-fits-all state religion are up against an impressive diversity of faith practice in this country, however. In much of the southern United States, everyone's a "Baptist," even the atheists, because it's a Baptist culture. New England Congregationalism colors everything there. People outside of California think of Californians as a tribe of laid-back hedonists. I was brought up to make little or no distinction between a Christian and an English gentleman.

Recently I came across what I can only describe as Methodist Buddhism in Hawaii. I visited a temple modeled on a Methodist chapel. The Buddhist bishop acknowledged the sect's debt to American Protestantism when he knowingly and with a smile summed up Buddhism in the phrase "Buddha loves me, this I know, For the *gathas* tell me so." One of the hymns written by a former Anglican priest went like this:

> Ever onward, Ever upward,
> Gently held by Love's embrace
> Till we reach Nirvana's summit
> And behold Truth face to face.

There's more cross-pollination between and among religious traditions than we realize. Those who want to call America a Christian nation cannot stand the idea of a Great Story (with many chapters and translations) that insists that we are one human family. They tend not only to be racist and anti-Semitic but sexist and separatist, as well. Theirs is a form of Christian storytelling that is exclusive, individualistic, and coercive. The list of those of us who are definitely not included in this narrow "Christian" commonwealth is impressive. The motto "God is on our side" is exclusive by definition.

The Religion of the Marketplace

Among those who most confidently claim that God is on their side are the capitalists. Although God's blessing is still invoked, however, the magic story of material success has grown so powerful that it hardly needs sanctioning anymore. The global economy shapes our imagination and turns every human being into a potential consumer. Friends of mine have the first three words of the U.S. Constitution—*We, the People*—framed on their wall. The word *People* has a line drawn through it and is replaced by the word *consumers*.

The American Myth of becoming rich, which is now wearing a bit thin, is nevertheless still very strong. According to former senator Bill Bradley, the argument runs something like this:

> Religious impulses cannot compete with people's desire to have more material things. Some argue that the economic myth of open economics and markets is also the only one that is truly egalitarian. Either you make it or you don't. That myth is truly global. It accepts the premise of interdependence, and rewards not individualism but a systems approach. Thinking systemically, according to that view, is the only way to succeed in a world of highly competitive individuals and units.

We can see how this view of the world is crowned with the aura of religious approval. It is the "theology" of the dominant version of Christianity in America.

Charles Handy, a mentor of business leaders, describes the dying myth of our culture, of unlimited growth that will "provide the wherewithal for all our wants, and technology [will] somehow deal with any unwanted consequences." Our shopping malls "stacked high with trivia, with all the detritus of a throwaway society where growth depends on persuading more and more people to buy more and more things that they may want but can hardly need. . . . We need our economies of glitz and sleaze to provide work of a sort for many of our people."

There are political and social consequences when the possibility of meaningful work is eroded. You can't talk about religion without bumping into politics. Handy goes on, "The American freedom to live where you choose, and to choose whom you live with . . . results in ghettoes of the rich, ghettoes of the old, and, inevitably, ghettoes of the underclass." The situation is like that of the city-states of medieval Europe, with their thick and well-defended walls. It's great if you're on the inside, if you belong to the club. But even the insider knows that no matter how thick the walls, they are not impregnable. That's why even the rich are insecure and have a mentality of scarcity. Because the walls are not as well defended as we think, we will have to alter the rules of membership of some of the clubs we belong to and let down our defenses.

Handy points out another American myth cultivated by popular American religion: Make the rich richer, and the wealth will trickle down. Riches don't tickle down. "Paradoxically, it works the other way round—you make the rich richer by making the poor rich, because then they have more money to spend. To start the cycle, however, you have to invest in the poor, enlarging their capabilities, enhancing their skills, underwriting their initiatives. . . . but it always calls for short-term sacrifice by the rich in the beginning."

Religion itself has taken on the characteristics of a commodity. The new century has seen the explosion of religion in both intensity and variety, with new religions springing up and old ones mutating in a free-market religious economy. The religious landscape is unstable, and people are changing brands and suppliers. There are nearly ten thousand distinct and separate religions in the world, and it's no longer politically correct to call them "cults." They are "new religious movements." Theodiversity is on the rise. God is being decentralized.

Ian Suttie suggests in *The Origins of Love and Hate* that our major repression is not of sexual or aggressive impulses, but of affection and openness. You cannot get enough of what you don't really want—*things*. What is needed and wanted (but our culture denies), Suttie argues, is emotional closeness. "Not sex, nor food, nor power, nor any other surrogate can satisfy that need."

When humans are seen chiefly as consumers, the dominant version of reality becomes oppression and violence. The narrative of violence—from sexual and racial abuse to military macho to the imprisonment of deviants—needs to be contradicted. Walter Brueggemann identifies the great taboo of our age as the sacredness of the marketplace. Hidden and not so hidden is the *"economic violence* embedded in free-market ideology that denies an obligation to openness to the neighbor who is in truth a deep inconvenience and drain on resources."

The dominant narrative of violence tears at the social fabric by reducing life to a contest to see who can have the most, who can have it first, and who can have the best. The biblical revelation is about trust, about a covenant that binds the haves and the have-nots in one community. Truth in the end is about kinship. We are members one of another. These are the dominant motifs of Judaism and Christianity and are found in other religious traditions, as well.

What is the dominant version of reality for you? I feel out of tune in a culture in which the dominant view is that persons are commodities that can be bought and sold. This isolating mechanism brings with it a loss of connection and an epidemic of depression. It's important to take note of the background of our lives. Is the backdrop of life the sacred canopy or the marketplace? Are we primarily neighbors or consumers?

Religion tries to analyze and name our longings. Today those longings are plastered over by an unending parade of entertainments, obsessions, addictions, and distractions of every sort. But there are cracks and gaping holes in this stultifying fabric, and I want to widen them to let in life.

The Scary Clash of Consumerist and Fundamentalist Religion

However murderous or mindless fundamentalists are, they are reacting, in part, to the soullessness of the materialistic culture and its global takeover. In turn, their actions make us even more fearful and defensive. The walls of separation get taller and thicker.

It has been suggested that a religious revival in the Northern Hemisphere will be lead by clear-eyed and, some fear, fanatical missionaries from the Southern. The rogue religion of the future will be Christianity, not Islam. The next few decades will be no picnic as we experience a shakedown of all the world's religious traditions and the emergence of some new ones. The post-Christian nations of the West are not clear about their beliefs or values. They lack a coherent story. We are so liberal and plural that we fail to appreciate the fact that other peoples live from a deep level of longing that expresses itself in what are to us bizarre beliefs. But our beliefs seem crazy to them. We believe in the marketplace, in consumerism, in the autonomy of the isolated individual—crazy things like that— things that bear little or no relation to the limitless mystery to which or to whom we are oriented and related.

Shusako Endo, a Japanese novelist and a Roman Catholic, thinks Christianity in Japan is a problem because it is too much a Western religion. It is dogmatic, uncompromising, and patriarchal. It sees reality in terms of black and white. Its history is full of "I am right and you are wrong," bringing inquisitions, intolerance, punishment of dissidents, and downright lack of compassion.

When I look at Christianity, I find it surprisingly future-oriented. It looks forward to something—some fulfillment or consummation. It is concerned with time. History is going someplace. Where? Martin Luther King suggested that the trajectory of history is toward justice. And Walter Brueggemann, teacher of the Hebrew Bible, suggests that the trajectory of the Gospel is toward inclusion. Justice and inclusion are signs that we're going in the right direction in our believing and in our belonging. In the language of the story I know best, they are signs of the Kingdom.

8

God Unbound

Mysteries at the Heart of Faith

Unfortunately mysticism is true.

—Walter Bagehot

A visitor asked one of the old monks on Mount Athos what they did all day. "We have died and are in love with everything."

When the British economist Walter Bagehot (1826–1877) wrote "Unfortunately mysticism is true," he meant that mere self-interest and opportunism lead to a dead end. "Realism" isn't enough. He also wrote of the isolating power of the impoverished imagination: "Poverty is an anomaly to rich people. It is very difficult to make out why people who want dinner do not ring the bell." How do we break down confining and excluding views of the world? How do we storm the ramparts of privilege and exclusion without creating another nightmare? Mysticism isn't escapism. It's seeing connections, which make a social and political difference.

The monk on Mount Athos makes a similar connection in his statement. It brings together two things that the modern consciousness finds contradictory: the inevitability of death and our being called to be in love. "Unfortunately mysticism is true" is a way of saying that no matter how "rational" or "scientific" our approach to life, there are things that can't be fixed—things such as death and love. We live in and are bound by mystery. But that's not all. Seeing the connections between and among things (which is what mysticism is) has moral bite. There are implications for our behavior. Mystics are rebellious and subversive. That's why the Church has tended to honor them only after they are dead.

For mystics, the world is a sacred place—a view we are only just recovering. The shared life of a monastery, for example, meets the needs men and women have for a moral compass, community formation, and food and shelter—all within the context of a romantic venture of life as the School of Love. Come to think of it, such a place would be ideal for an adventure of human conversation. Conversation and true conversion go together. Monastics live in an obedient community—one where the members *listen to* each other. Life, according to this tradition, is the *peregrinatio pro Christo*—exile for Christ's sake—an ongoing process of conversion. Conversion means having the heart open to and sometimes broken by new possibilities.

Mystics also are open to two texts *other than* the Bible: the Book of Nature and the Book of Experience. St. Bernard begins his analysis of the Song of Songs with these words: "Today let us read in the Book of Experience." Every day the world offers itself to us for our contemplation. Every day we experience that world afresh and always can learn something. The boundlessness is inside us as well as outside. The mystical tradition tells us of a threefold method for living on the boundary of mystery. Living "on the boundary" is a way of being free, of being "already dead" to the pettinesses and the worries that enslave us.

- Be attentive and awake.
- Be open to new possibilities because the spiritual journey is alive and dynamic.
- Learn to discern the movements of your own psychology because the book of the human heart is very complex and knowledge of God and knowledge of self go together.

The question of why is always worth asking, as it leads eventually to wonder. But we lose a lot if we try to bypass difficult questions. Our wonder is deepened only after struggling with the hard realities of the world.

Biblical and Mystical Rebellion

The Hebrew Bible helps to make us rebellious. The Bible and the mystical tradition challenge us with the inexhaustibility of God and the mystery of being. What do we need to rebel against? Against anything that reduces human beings to things. The Bible keeps before our eyes the great unfixables of love, death, and time.

Mystics have a particular take on the Bible. They understand the continuities and discontinuities of *process* that are significant for our transformation. They acknowledge that, according to scholar Bernard McGinn, "*some* biblical texts could not be read literally and [that] *all* biblical texts were capable of many meanings." If the Bible is the "Word of God" and God is an inexhaustible mystery, we shouldn't expect easy one-meaning-fits-all kind of reading.

One early medieval mystic, John Scotus Erigena (c. 810–c. 877), for example, elucidated three principles of interpretation that speak to our contemporary situation:

1. God's infinity and essential unknowability require that revelation in the Bible and Creation must contain an infinite multiplicity of meanings.
2. The priority of negation in all interpretation, because God is better known by *not* knowing.
3. The distinction between *mysterium* (something that actually happened) and a *symbolum* (which is for instruction—such as the Genesis account of Paradise or the opening of the Fourth Gospel).

There are, then, layers of meaning that require an endless conversation to plumb their depths. The deeper we go, the more aware we become of our ignorance—our "*not* knowing." At the heart of the spiritual quest is the art of discernment—the ability to discriminate with discretion between facts and meanings.

Coming from the ninth century, this sounds to me revolutionary and contemporary. John Scotus Erigena's distinction between *mysterium* and *symbolum* gets less confusing if we think of the latter as something like what we mean by myth (in the positive sense, of a story that gives our lives meaning).

The point of reading the Bible is for mystical transformation, not for defending a particular position or to punish those we regard as deviant. This makes one realize how recent biblical fundamentalism is and how it betrays God's boundless mystery. At the end of the conclusion of his *Periphysion,* Erigena generously states, "Let everyone hold to what opinion he will until that Light shall come which makes the light of the false philosophers a darkness and converts the darkness of those who truly know the light."

The Power of Myth

Flat, literalistic, one-dimensional religious thinking kills the spirit, starves the soul, and renders it incapable of learning anything new. Finding a generous, unsentimental, and inclusive story in which to locate ourselves instead of relying on narrow definitions to help us make sense of ourselves is the task of the new generation of seekers. Seekers see themselves as mysteries that are both open and complex. We have, for too long, been dominated by the kind of mentality that likes to measure and quantify everything. What cannot be counted doesn't count. We love to define things and discern their boundaries. Good stories introduce us to the immeasurable and the unquantifiable. They can be judged but they can never be measured because they are capable of endless interpretation. Being human on a full-time basis invites us to recover our lives as myths rather than as scientific studies, to move out of the prison house of "scientific" definition and into the open space of narrative.

Psychologist James Hillman writes about the priority of myth over definition. "Instead of reducing meaning to a definition, myths amplify and complicate. They are the path of richness. Myths add information to phenomena and offer insights. They provide images, puzzles, humor." We need myths to make us wonder, question, and imagine, so that we move from being part-time humans to being full-time ones.

Whether we believe it or not, the great myths are still being played out in the world—in individuals, in societies, and in nations. I sense great stories being played out in us whether we know it or not. Each of us is the hero of some story or other.

Hugh McWearie is a character in Robertson Davies's novel *Murther and Walking Spirits*. McWearie castigates a friend for not taking the spiritual journey seriously, for not realizing that his psyche is the stage of a great drama. He complains that we talk glibly about such things as the Oedipus complex, about the guy who wants to possess his mom. There's also the Hercules complex, about the guy who must grapple with his twelve labors while his wife and kids are neglected. What about the Apollo complex, about the guy who thinks you can have all light and no releasing darkness?

> And women—our towns and villages are jammed with Medeas and Persephones and Antigones and God knows who, pushing their wire carts in the supermarkets unrecognized by anyone but themselves, and then probably only in their dreams. All engaged in the Hero Struggle.

When the Symbols and Myths Change, We Change

Being a human being is to be summoned to participate in a great myth because our lives need interpreting. Our interpretation of life will depend on the particular myth to which we are captive. Not all myths are equal. Many of them are destructive. Our liberation from the limiting and tyrannical and into the liberating and loving depends on how awake we are or want to be. Our way of escape is in our being willing to learn new "languages" such as music, art, and drama—the things that open the heart to the mysteries of faith. In fact, that's our job. We are interpreters and translators of stories that began before we came on the scene and will still be being played out long after we're gone. Everything that happens to us relies on something that was there before. When we say "I love you" for the first time—even that is a quotation! Goethe's dictum was *"Alles ist*

Symbol" (Everything is symbol). Life, therefore, isn't about winning arguments but about reconnecting and reeducating the soul via symbols, myths, and rituals. This doesn't mean that they are fixed forever in an endless cycle of repetition; myths are more versatile than that. The new is always breaking in, and fresh versions are always being minted. New languages have to be learned and new material incorporated into the stories being played out in the world.

What happens when something new occurs and we haven't the word or words for it? What do you do when you see something new but have no vocabulary for it? Isaac Newton in the seventeenth century believed that science is about measuring things. He also noticed that things never stood still. He wondered how you measure things in perpetual motion and flux. When he began his work, there weren't even the concepts to quantify motion. Earlier, Galileo faced the same problem when he observed sunspots through his telescope in 1611. How could he tell anyone without getting into the quagmire of language? Why was it a problem? Because "everyone" believed that the sun was pure and lucid, with no shadows or impurities. That's what people thought they saw, but the telescope changed that.

Galileo and Newton changed the way people saw the world and therefore changed to stories they told themselves about what their lives meant. They forced those who took any notice to reframe what they meant by being a human being on a full-time basis. What Galileo and Newton perhaps failed to understand was that such changes were so profound that they would be resisted. Their discoveries required a new way to look at the myths and rituals by which people interpreted and negotiated their lives. In Berthold Brecht's play *Galileo* there is a scene of orgiastic social chaos after Galileo's announcement that the earth isn't at the center of the universe but moves around the sun. If the earth isn't at the center, perhaps other things can be questioned? Perhaps the king isn't at the center of society? Perhaps the pope doesn't have the authority he thinks he has? Newton and Galileo started a revolution, but they didn't do away with our need for myths and rituals. Their discoveries challenged the old way of telling stories.

Darwin, in his day, effected a similar revolution, as did Freud and Marx. Even today, many religious people deny scientific discoveries because they cannot imagine another and different version of the story from the one they were taught. When we recover religion as a work of the imagination and are able to play with it in stories and myths, we wake up to the liberating fact that dogma isn't "eternal" but, like everything else, has a history. The constant evolving image of God in our consciousness over the centuries is bound to have an effect on the way we articulate our hopes. Those who affirm that Jesus is the same today, yesterday, and forever tend to forget that we aren't. Human consciousness changes. Moreover, it is impossible to get into the minds of those who have gone before us (even if we need to try). That's why history keeps on being rewritten.

Rules for Talking about God

We have forgotten some very simple rules for talking about God. The irony is that it is often rigid conservatives who know little of the tradition and have forgotten the rules for doing theology. Fundamental principles of theological discourse tell us that God is a mystery beyond all our imaginings, and therefore no expression of God can be taken literally. That's why we need thousands of names. And still, thank God, God remains elusive. An Augustinian principle is "If you have understood, what you have understood is not God." The late Jesuit theologian Henri de Lubac suggested that people who seek to know God are rather like "swimmers who can only keep afloat by moving, by cleaving a new wave at each stroke. They are forever brushing aside the representations that are continually re-forming, knowing full well that these support them, but that if they were to rest for a single moment they would sink." We are being challenged, once again, to entertain the belief that God really is. The fact that we are contingent and mortal, that we have no choice but to live in this particular time and not in another, should come as no surprise. Being human means the here and now, not some other place and time.

Our resistance to interrogate reality is understandable because when we do, we experience radical powerlessness. We're opened up to the need for a continuous exodus from our tiny, frightened selves.

We need to recover our capacity to be surprised. Our culture tends to think of life as a debate, an argument, rather than as a mess and a mystery.

According to the Talmud, Adam and Eve spent only twelve hours in the Garden of Eden. They hardly had time to unpack. This is a reminder that human beings have always been on the move. Permanence is an illusion. "Here we have no abiding city"(Hebrews 13:4). So where are we going? Are we not searching for a place that will take us in and give us shelter? If the best we can expect is only twelve hours in Paradise, we'd better look for permanent shelter elsewhere—either after death, or via some divine intervention.

This doesn't stop us from longing for Paradise in one form or another (although we shouldn't underestimate our efforts to delay our arrival). Our basic drive seems to be to stay alive here on earth. "Better to be a live dog than a dead lion"(Ecclesiastes 9:4). This basic instinct to stay alive should not be despised. It is better to be looking at a Tuscan sunset than to be dead; to hug a child, to weep with the sorrowful, to visit the sick, than to be dead. But this longing to stay alive and to be safe isn't exactly Christian hope. What makes Christian hope Christian? It would help if we looked at what makes us dread the future. What makes us not want to be human beings on a full-time basis? What renders life desperate—without hope—for millions of people? We know the answers: poverty, injustice, indifference, frustration, violence, technology, and depression. Let's look at the last two.

Seen steadily and whole, life is hard to bear. Being human can be hell. No wonder millions turn to religion for relief. Religion is the opium of the people. But nihilism is no less an opium. The poet Czeslaw Milosz writes of the discreet charm of nihilism.

> Religion, opium of the people. To those suffering pain, humiliation, illness and serfdom, it promised the reward of an afterlife. And *now* we are witnessing a transformation. A true opium for the people is a belief in nothingness after death—the huge solace of thinking that for our betrayals, greed, cowardice, murders we are not going to be judged.

The Power to Choose

How do we recover the basic mystery of our existing at all? What makes you get up in the morning? A friend of mine told me that PTC—the power to choose—was the constant mantra used by his mother during his childhood. With every human eventuality—the bad as well as the good—we have a choice about how we'll go through what life throws at us. The life of the will—how and what we choose to do with our lives—is at the center of the spiritual life. And our choices matter. We also have choice in being consciously aware of our choices. Our choices, over time, build up character. We become their sum total.

Mystics see that the real wonder of the world is not *what* it is but *that* it is. When we are confronted every day with the wonder that there is anything at all and not just nothing, our minds try to get around the mystery. We come up with contradictory explanations. One is "Since I am caught in the middle of life, I can't know anything for sure. I'll just have to muddle through." This is why the view that "everything is equally true and equally false" is attractive to some of us. It gives us the illusion that we are dogma-free.

Others can't stand the uncertainty and need to explain everything either scientifically or religiously: "I have the truth and I know exactly what it is." The scientific mind likes this as much as the religious one and thinks that its descriptions are somehow explanations. Science explains nothing, but its commitment to more and more accurate descriptions of the universe is important and has an impact on the way we *imagine* meaning and purpose in life. But both the religious and the scientific "fundamentalist" tends to short-circuit the issue of wonder and amazement.

We value the power to choose because our freedom depends on it. *"Je suis Catholique. Je suis un homme libre!* (I am Catholic. I am a free man!") claims my friend Father François Legaux, rector emeritus of Chartres Cathedral. He means that standing in the mystical tradition places him always on the boundary where death is always present and love is always possible. Such it is to be free.

Humanity Unbound

Christians find it hard to believe their own message of freedom. As the grand inquisitor in Dostoyevsky's *The Brothers Karamazov* knew, human beings long for certainties; they want miracle, mystery, and authority. They don't want actual experience. They don't want doubts and questions. The grand inquisitor saw the Church—in supplying all the answers—as more merciful than God. Religious establishments (churches, temples, and synagogues) can't resist the temptation to clean up the messes that God leaves behind when the divine has been at work. God can't have gotten it quite right. We need to correct God's work. After all, you can't have *both* freedom and security. God needs domesticating, tidying up, bringing into line. But freedom, God, mystery (whatever you want to call it) won't be domesticated. Most people will conform to the prevailing power, but (thank God) there will always be those who rebel.

In the story of the grand inquisitor Jesus comes back to earth—to Seville. He is seen raising someone from the dead outside the cathedral. The grand inquisitor has him arrested and thrown into prison and comes to visit Jesus at night.

> "Know that I'm not afraid of you. Know that I too have been in the wilderness. I too have lived on roots and locusts, I too prized the freedom with which you have blessed the human race, and I too was striving to stand among your elect, among the strong and powerful, thirsting 'to make up the number.' But I woke up and would not serve madness. I turned back and joined the ranks of those *who have corrected your work*. I left the proud and went back to the humble. What I say to you will come to pass, and our dominion will be built up. I repeat, tomorrow you shall see that obedient flock who at a sign from me will hurry to heap up the hot cinders about the pile on which I shall burn you for coming to hinder us. For if one has ever deserved our fires it is you. Tomorrow I shall burn you."
>
> When the Inquisitor ceased speaking he waited some time for his Prisoner to answer him. His silence weighed down upon him. He saw that the Prisoner had listened intently all the time,

looking gently in his face and evidently not wishing to reply. The old man longed for him to say something, however bitter and terrible. But he suddenly approached the old man in silence and softly kissed him on his bloodless aged lips. That was all his answer. The old man shuddered. His lips moved. He went to the door, opened it, and said to him: "Go, and come no more . . . come not at all, never, never!" And he let him out into the dark alleys of the town. The Prisoner went away.

And the old man?
The kiss glows in his heart.

The silence of the prisoner says it all. The kiss promises revolution and freedom—the love of God unbound.

Forms of Diminishment

Imaginative religious commitment helps us not to make what spiritual leader Deepak Chopra calls "premature cognitive commitment." Research biologists took a collection of flies and put them in a sealed container for a long period—so long that the insects accepted that container as their world. When the lid was taken off, the majority of the flies remained within the jar, even though they could escape. They made a "commitment" to their closed environment. There was a similar experiment with fish. Scientists placed a clear partition inside an aquarium. Later the partition was removed, but the fish behaved as if it were still there. Given enough reinforcement, various species will commit themselves to what they know but go no farther. We get imprisoned in what we take to be reality. Our world remains small and our allegiances petty when we refuse to use our imagination. To be fully human is to commit ourselves to what we do not fully know.

The narrow way in which some people interpret the Bible and the diminished reality they inhabit have parallels in other texts and authorities. There is *The Diagnostic and Statistical Manual of Mental Disorders* (*DSM*, 4th ed.), published by the American Psychiatric

Association. This "bible" of psychiatry contains definitions that diminish us. There are nine hundred pages defining three hundred "disorders" covering everything a human being might do—from smoking too much to simply getting old. There are disorders for everything people do, including reading, mathematics, and writing. For anyone suffering from age-related cognitive decline (780.90), there is caffeine intoxication (305.90) as long as you do not succumb to caffeine-induced sleep disorder (292.8). Narcissistic personality disorder was eliminated in 1968 and restored in 1980. The one I like the best is borderline personality disorder—a wastebasket diagnosis that therapists often give to patients who are unlikable, troublesome, and difficult to treat. There are a lot of these people in our churches, synagogues, and temples! It would be funny—a parody of psychiatric pretentiousness—if it weren't for the wholesale mislabeling of poor people, blacks, and women on often shabby scientific evidence.

This is not to trash psychiatry but to point out that our descriptions of our mental and spiritual states fit a particular cultural situation, and the descriptions whither away when times change. Our descriptions/stories matter. Who is Lord over us? Who gets to say who you are? We have the tendency of always wanting to surrender our sovereignty to someone else. The power to diagnose is enormous and potentially dangerous. Those who claim to define our ills and label us deficient in some way have great influence. They are, in some ways, the true sovereigns of the culture. It is interesting that psychiatrists still vote on what constitutes "mental illness," and definitions of mental illness reflect the prejudices and special interests of those in power. Before the Civil War, a physician in the South argued that slaves were suffering from two forms of mental illness: drapetomania (an uncontrollable urge to escape) and dysathesia aethiopica (as evidenced by destroying property on the plantation, disobedience, and refusal to work). Slaveowners were thereby reassured that mental disorder, not the intolerable condition of slavery, made blacks seek freedom.

Carol Tavris point to the imperialistic tendency "to medicalize problems that are not medical, to find pathologies where there is only pathos, and to pretend to understand phenomena by merely giving them a label and a code number."

There's a story of a mental disorder that was in fashion for twenty-three years at the end of the nineteenth century. It described a condition that seems very much alive today. It was called fugue, ambulatoire, and dromomania. Another name for it was pathological tourism. It described an aimless wandering about. People were driven by irresistible impulses, and yet they conducted themselves in a seemingly purposeful way and gave an appearance of competence and normalcy. The first case was diagnosed in 1887 and the last in 1909. Both cases were in France. The condition of pathological tourism fitted with the world people were imagining then. *What do we do with experiences for which there is yet no language?* We live by parables and symbols, and sometimes we need our world to be broken open because we are trapped inside a relentlessly unchanging prison. Today it seems that we suffer from pathological tourism of an interior sort. We are desperately looking for a good story.

The story I try to live in and that lives in me has at its heart a banquet to which everyone is invited and at which there is enough for everyone. It calls me out of my tiny world and my petty allegiances and unmasks me and everyone around me as creatures of great dignity called to a caring and joyful solidarity. So the primary metaphor is that life is a banquet. It is outrageously generous, and the bread and wine are freely given away. We gather around God's table, and (as theologian Harvey Cox reminds us) the bread and wine tell us that we depend on the earth and the rain and the sun for sustenance. "It reminds us, each time, just how fragile all this is." Fortunately mysticism is true.

9

Missing Each Other and Missing Ourselves

In Christianity, the church is the crown of the path of practice, the true teaching authority. When a church manifests understanding, tolerance, and love, Jesus is there.

—Thich Nhat Hanh

Ubi caritas et amor, Deus ibi est. (Where love and charity are, God is there.)

In 2001 the *Washington Post* ran a report about a little village in Mexico where the church is dedicated to Mary Magdalen. A man had tried to steal the statue of the saint, and four hundred of the faithful made him pay. "Men beat him with their fists; women and children kicked him. The mob took its revenge for two hours, until the thief was dead, hanging limp in the glow of neon-lit crucifixes." Talk about being unclear on the concept. My faith is tested when I read of such barbarism in the name of God. The only way I can begin to understand it is to think that Christianity hasn't happened yet.

It's easy to resist religion when we concentrate on its bad record in history and the terrible behavior of some of its adherents. But our resistance only gets stronger when we set aside those objections and see the profound kind of changes the best of religion would demand of us. For one thing, we are brought uncomfortably close to others. Everyone becomes a neighbor.

Being brought close to others can initiate an inner struggle with a self we may have long neglected. It brings suffering in the form of painful consciousness of the evil in the world, and knowledge that we are called to stand against it. And it asks us to wait in impenetrable darkness until there's enough light by which to see a little of the way ahead. We would rather be up and doing. But in a true spirituality, there's a lot of waiting and watching.

I've never been convinced by the argument that religion is essentially a form of escapism. It hasn't been my experience, and it certainly is not the experience of its greatest followers. Religion at a very low level might be escapism, but at its highest it is risk and adventure. It is movement into the unknown.

Human Solidarity or Turf Wars?

The deeper we go in any particular religion, the more likely we are to bump into practices of prayer and compassion and come out into a shared place of respect. Father Bede Griffiths (1906–1993), a Benedictine monk deeply influenced by Hinduism, often used the image of the human hand to illustrate what the great religious traditions had in common. The tips of the fingers represented the religions of Islam, Hinduism, Christianity, Judaism, and Buddhism. As you go deeper (by moving down from the tips of the fingers to the palm), you move closer together and enjoy an underlying unity of love and compassion.

Father Griffiths also loved the Jesus Prayer—the repeated prayer of "Lord Jesus Christ, Son of God, have mercy on me." He saw all humanity being embraced by the same love while expressing awe and appreciation in different ways and giving different shape to the experience. This love, this energy, is present in every human being. Beyond word and thought, beyond all signs and symbols, this Word, he believed, is being secretly spoken in every heart in every place and at every time. This reminds me of what St. Augustine of Hippo told his people:

> Do not think you must speak the truth to a Christian but can lie to a pagan. You are speaking to your brother or sister, born like you from Adam and Eve: realize all the people you meet are your neighbors even before they are Christians; you have no idea how

God sees them. The ones you mock for worshiping stones may be converted, and may worship God more fervently than you who laughed at them. . . . You cannot see into the future, so let every one be your neighbor.

Claiming that we all live in "the web of life" has become a cliché, but this affirmation of basic connectedness is the dominant version of reality put forth by the best in all religious traditions. When we wake up to that vision of human solidarity, it's as if we become spies from another country. Being willing to take on and contradict the dominant version of reality of the world requires cunning and subversion, because we are all infected by the world's view, which breeds violence and division. Taking a religious point of view in favor of a world where everyone is a neighbor is revolutionary.

This is where we find the real resistance to religion. The conflict, deep down, is not one about beliefs but about sharing resources—about being neighbors. Religion often gives people their identity, but it does not follow that the differences in identity *cause* the conflict. Religion provides the conditions or the justification for violence but not necessarily the cause, which often is land and water. We easily become a threat to others, especially where there is a real or perceived scarcity of resources.

The other chief fuel of much of the world's conflict is vendetta—not "You must be wiped out because of what you believe" but "You must die because of what you or your forebears did." Perceived atrocities that have festered unavenged fuel the fires. In the Bosnian tragedy, most Serbs could not care less what Muslims *believed*. The cry was "Look what they did to us!" not "Look what they believe! Their God is false!"

It's possible to fake being neighbors. I might say, "I'm willing to put up with a lot from you as long as you stay clear of me and make no demands." This is tempting, but it doesn't get us very far. Neighborliness can come into conflict with individual freedom. Yet without freedom there can be no true neighborliness, only a restricting tribalism. True neighborliness can never be coerced. Exchange between neighbors must be freely given. "Good fences make good neighbors" is a proverb that needs examining. It's popular in psychology today to talk about "boundary issues." Establishing boundaries can be important, but it's a matter of balance. For some of us it wouldn't hurt if a wall or two fell down so we could see the world afresh as a place we share with others.

Learning the Language of the Other

Across the divide, people look at each other in tragic mutual incomprehension (as Pope John Paul II put it with regard to the Galileo controversy). We don't speak each other's language—sometimes literally, but even among English-speakers, differences in cultural background, economics, gender, education, and countless other varieties of experience can render us unable to communicate. Some of us hide in ancient forms and styles of communication. In the "religious club" people converse in shorthand about heaven and hell, using code words such as *redemption, damnation, sin,* and *repentance,* and leaving everyone else in the dark. There are "languages" such as Mormon and cybernetics that I don't speak at all; and others, such as accounting and physics, that I stumble over.

So one of the tasks of the spiritually awake is to listen to and learn each other's language. We live in a world in which we need to be multilingual; survival depends on our being able to speak a variety of languages. I'm not being quite literal (although it wouldn't hurt if everyone in the United States were fluent in English and Spanish or English and Chinese). Think of "language" as simply a way of communicating. "Computer" then becomes a language, as does "economics." Add to this the speed at which we "talk" and the levels at which we communicate, and we see how disadvantaged some of us are.

There is also a language we all might unlearn: the language of contempt or insult. An Englishman who was an expert on Eastern thought was touring Grace Cathedral in San Francisco a few years ago. On looking at the Spanish crucifix near the south doors, he unthinkingly said to me, "Why would anyone worship *that?*" The crucifix is late thirteenth century and is very beautiful, a picture of poignant and deep love and sadness. I don't think he meant to offend, but I wanted to react with an equally crass question: "Why do Buddhists revere that grinning little fat guy?" Statements as thoughtless as these are declarations of war.

Here's an example of tragicomic mutual incomprehension from my own tradition. As reported in "Episcopal Turf Wars" in *Time* magazine in July 2001, in a Denver church, Thaddeus Rockwell Barnum (a great name for the circus of religion) was consecrated, along with three others, as a missionary bishop to the United States by the archbishop of Rwanda. They were leaving the mainstream Episcopal Church because it had failed to censure "firebrand bishop John Shelby Spong," and the American Anglicans were deemed "incapable of self-correction." *Time* described the service as "the exodus of disaffected traditionalists." Church spokespersons were asked to comment, and one anonymous source unhelpfully called the participants assholes. The dialogue of insults between these factions has continued, most recently in the intensive media coverage of Bishop Gene Robinson's confirmation as the first openly gay Episcopal bishop. But is it really about beliefs or about insults endured and turf won or lost?

Think of the genuine great intractables of religion and politics: in the Middle East, in Northern Ireland, in the former Yugoslavia, in "the war on terrorism." We cannot truly communicate with each other. We don't speak the same language, or the languages we do speak are simply not up to the depths we wish to communicate or are hopelessly corrupted. God gets confused with all sorts of things: real estate, tribe, mental constructs. We need to learn more languages. We need to stretch our understanding to see everyone as a neighbor.

Becoming Multilingual

Once when visiting Quaker friends in Chicago, my wife and I shared a weekly ritual at 6:30 A.M., along with two friends linked on a conference call. We prayerfully affirmed the five mindfulness trainings from the Buddhist tradition: the cultivation of compassion (including the commitment not to kill), loving kindness (working for the well-being of all creatures), personal responsibility (including sexual behavior), loving speech (being agents of reconciliation), and sound physical and mental health. This simple practice requires no formal belief in God and isn't the possession of one tradition. It is open to all.

Most of my mentors of fifty years ago couldn't have imagined a world in which such friendships were possible or even desirable. But it's more than friendship, and certainly more than easygoing tolerance. It's a willingness to be open to other languages. It's seeing everyone as a neighbor. It's being able to argue passionately about the truth without having to demonize each other.

Learning another language means learning a new way of thinking. This is what happened to me when I tried to learn Hebrew (I passed an exam in it but wasn't very good at it). I entered a whole new world of understanding. When you learn a new language you don't just learn the words, you learn a whole new way of thinking and looking at the world. That's why translation is almost impossible. Something is always lost, always betrayed.

Language has to do with how we know what we know. Anthropologist Claude Levi-Strauss believed that the deepest difference between our way of knowing and that of traditional peoples is that "primitives" believe that you couldn't understand anything unless you understand *everything*. I think there's great truth to this. It's not our task to understand everything intellectually. What is required is a web or framework that can act as a container for knowledge. Communion is built into the fabric of things. We are neighbors. We were made for love by love to love each other. That is the backdrop, the overarching image of religion at its deepest and best.

What makes us real? Doesn't it have something to do with the level of consciousness and our appreciation of the possibility for communion? That's why dealing with multiple consciousnesses and their complex languages may be the biggest issue of our time. Different levels of consciousness live within each of us, often unaware of each other or even at war with each other. A person might be a sophisticate in business and a troglodyte in religion. I'm told that at some deep level within us we recapitulate the whole history of evolution. If this is so, each of us has quite a psychic zoo to care for.

I am on the side of communion and want to be able to speak and be at home in many languages. Yet I have my preferred ways of communicating, too. Huston Smith suggests that the three prevailing "languages" of the traditional, the modern, and the postmodern all have their value, but he has a preference for the "language" of the traditional worldview because it allows for the fulfillment of the basic longing that lies in the depths of the human heart. I agree with him, and this is where I part company with many of my progressive and liberal friends.

In the quest to break through whatever keeps us from seeing others as neighbors, language often breaks down, and we need other ways to communicate. We say, "A picture is worth a thousand words," and it is; pictures can go where propositions cannot. One task in reimagining religion is learning skills that enable us to distinguish between the images and the reality to which they point. We come to see that images lie and tell the truth at the same time. They lie when we get stuck on them. We call getting stuck on an image *idolatry*. They tell the truth when they become a window through which to see a larger and more generous world. The window through which we see reality needs constant attention.

We need art to bring us into that larger world.

Christian Images: Making or Mending Fences?

When it comes to seeing the world as neighbors, Christianity (like most religions) doesn't make a very good window. The words and images are, for the most part, opaque and don't let in the light. They don't lead the believer into that more generous reality where everyone is a neighbor and everything is connected.

Christians need to look at the way they express themselves and their deepest convictions. They forget how they come across. Rowan Williams, archbishop of Canterbury, suggests that all too often what is preached and taught sounds like an expression of the male urge to shake off the threatening and humiliating ties that bind spirit to body, to the earth, to the cycle of reproduction. Woman is imaged as a sign of fallenness, of "unspiritual" nature. We have forced a split between flesh and spirit with tragic consequences.

Are there parts of the Christian language and vocabulary that should be revised or even abandoned? The Roman Catholic writer James Carroll certainly thinks so. He believes that we have made the sacred mistake of putting the cross at the center of Christianity in the wrong way. Carroll insists that Catholics must not only "reverently and silently" remove the cross from Auschwitz but, far more fundamentally, must remove the cross from the center of Christianity. The Church's fixation on the death of Jesus as the universal saving act must end, and the place of the cross must be reimagined in Christian faith. Why? Because of the cult of suffering and the vindictive God behind it.

Such writing disturbs our inherited certainties and, for some, seems to mean the total dismantling of traditional Christianity. It also invites us to learn a new language. Many Christians have come to see that the very foundational documents of Christianity are polluted (St. John's gospel in particular, with its insistent mantra of the Jews, the Jews, the Jews as responsible for opposing and killing Jesus). This language must go. Believers are being challenged in their understanding of who and what Jesus thought he was. This is good. This doesn't mean that I agree with Carroll in every particular, but I do think that basic beliefs should always be open to reimagining.

The historian Eamonn Duffy joins the conversation by pointing out that the actual situation of the centrality of the cross in the early Church was more complicated than Carroll allows. It took some time before a public Christian art evolved. So "it is not in fact the case that the cross ever dominated Catholic symbolism in the way Carroll thinks it came to." There was another image, that of the Madonna and Child, which, while preserved by the Catholic and Orthodox Churches (albeit often in a frozen form) has been lost or sentimentalized. "The figure of the Virgin and Child has always been important, and has exercised a fundamental modifying role on the dominance of the crucifix." "Mary and her baby" is a language that needs to be learned if there is to be wholeness and balance to the image of suffering love.

Duffy is right when he insists:

> The cross is not some arbitrary demand of God imposed on a hapless victim . . . but a marker where human beings find themselves, at the intersection of justice and mercy, time and eternity, death and life. All of which, of course, is the language of myth: but myth is the coin of religion, which makes sense of our world by telling such stories.

Violence under the Skin

In the late 1990s, violence between Muslims and Christians in Indonesia cost nearly 5,000 lives. More than 200 million people in 350 ethnic groups inhabit the 13,677 islands of this troubled country; 90 percent are Muslim, but there are strong Christian communities. The worst of the bloodshed was in the Moluccas, the famed Spice Islands of eastern Indonesia, with a Christian community founded by St. Francis Xavier.

In January 1999, a terrible cycle of violence began, with a petty criminal demanding protection money from a bus driver. Unwilling to comply, the driver (a Christian) went for the extortionist (a Muslim) with a machete. "The Christians are after me!" shouted the extortionist. Within two hours, a Christian mob had appeared, wearing red headbands, and a Muslim one, wearing white. One incident led to another, and the violence spread. A Protestant crowd occupied a mosque and turned it into a billiard hall, placing a wooden cross on the roof. Enraged Muslims caught a Christian and murdered him, dragging his corpse in triumph through the town behind a car. Christians then caught a Muslim and chopped him to pieces.

In November 2000, an army of Muslims (against the orders of the president) arrived to convert Christians by force on one of the islands. There was forcible circumcision of both sexes without painkillers or antiseptics. One teacher who refused to convert died. Such forced conversions ran into the thousands. Elements in the army supported the Muslims, and elements in the police supported the Christians. Within two years, thousands were dead and thousands of houses, workplaces, shops, markets, hospitals, clinics, schools, convents, mosques, and churches were destroyed.

At base this was not a Christian-Muslim conflict. It was a battle over money and power by those hiding behind ethnic and religious strife, which they stirred up to gain a political end. But the fact that religion is so easily exploitable is a scandal. Why bring all this up? Because what Christianity and Islam are really about lies somewhere else.

The deeper truth is found with Sister Brigitta, who, with a Protestant pastor and a leading Muslim, founded the Movement of Concerned Women. There were just fifteen members, who would walk into conflict areas demanding a cessation of violence. They gave medical aid and helped the victims. They called for reconciliation. They were trying to penetrate the fog of tragic mutual incomprehension.

Everyone Is Your Neighbor

Is it really possible to have both freedom and security? The grand inquisitor's worry is genuine. How much personal freedom are we willing to give up to feel "secure" from terrorist acts? It is possible in a community that requires full forgiveness and full responsibility. We begin by hearing and heeding each other in silent listening. Communion happens when we attend to each other, when we adore each other, when we allow the pictures we have of each other to dissolve and continually re-form. We make sure that we have a plurality of windows to see the world.

Our dominant reality today is a world of ultimate responsibility but no forgiveness. We live in a society where everything is permitted and yet nothing is forgiven. Yet to be fully human and not despair, we need to be fully accountable and fully forgiven. Holding these two together is very difficult, but without forgiveness, accountability would be too hard to bear, and without accountability, being human has no moral content.

In *The Brothers Karamazov* Dostoyevsky reminds us of the evil and terror of isolating individualism:

> Until you have become really, in actual fact, a brother or sister to everyone, brotherhood, sisterhood, community will not come to pass. No sort of scientific teaching, no kind of common interest, will ever teach humankind to share property and privileges with equal consideration for all. Everyone will think his or her share too small and they will always be envying, complaining, and attacking one another.

Note what Dostoyevsky finds unnatural: separation and isolation. We need one another to be ourselves. Individual independence is an illusion, and the isolated self is a nonentity. I cannot be me without you. I may not like it, but it's true. I can exist and survive without you, but I cannot become who I am meant to be without you. Let everyone be your neighbor. Let's not miss each other.

10

Recovering the Sacred

The Really Real

Religion resides in our eyes rather than in our minds. We see;
then we love.

—Alun Lewis

When I was a student I read a great deal of the work of Mircea
Eliade—the leading expert on what used to be called comparative religion. He defined the sacred and "the really real." Because
of this, the life of the imagination is serious business. What we think
of as real is determined by the way we imagine the world. Secularism is as much a way of imagining our shared world (thought to be
liberating humanity from the shackles of religion) as is the image of
the sacred. And insofar as popular religion was imprisoning, secularism was an important corrective. It was needed and it worked for a
while, but there was something good in what it rejected. However,
our longing for depth wouldn't go away, and as *the* way of understanding and celebrating the human project, secularism has proved
inadequate. In fact, it is discredited and dying. Some of us feel ready
for a breakthrough into something new. We're pregnant.

There are also political and social implications involved in the
direction the world (or that affluent part of it) is moving. We are told
that there's a meltdown of "the real" coming, if not already upon us,
in favor of the virtual, the projected, the made up. The popularity of

the *Matrix* movies has made the most of the philosophical commonplace that the world is something we make up. Something "big" is
happening in the world. What is it? The new and deepening world of
cyberspace, with its ever-expanding and complex forms of delivering
information, is available to everyone with the money and the education to buy it and understand it. Professor Neil Postman reminds us,
"New technologies alter the structure of our interests: the things we
think *about*. They alter the character of our symbols: the things we
think *with*. And they alter the nature of community: the arena in
which thoughts develop."

We are in the middle of a world revolution in which old boundaries are breaking down. A new world order? Or a new world chaos?
What stories and metaphors will help us live with what's coming?
We will have to choose our metaphors carefully, or they will choose
us. Will we be so unconscious that the myths (perhaps savage ones)
will play out in us, like some manic mass psychosis? Or will we be
sufficiently awake to choose the myths and metaphors by which we
live? We need ways of discerning the difference between crazy and
repressive stories and those that are liberating and loving. We are in
a war of images about the fate and dignity of the human.

The images we choose to interpret our experience have implications for the way we think and feel about ourselves, about our "soul."
Is spirituality a commodity? Can it be? In cyberspace nothing is
actually produced, but everything is marketed and up for sale, so
spirituality *appears* to be a commodity. We go shopping for meaning
in rather the same way that we pick out a shirt or buy a stereo. If we
treat the life of the spirit as if it could be bought and sold, glory,
meaning *being in all its fullness,* fades or becomes fake. When cultural options are presented as consumer goods, passion drains
away—becomes virtual. More of us are feeling trapped in a world of
consumer pluralism in which we are *handled* and *managed* rather
than truly governed.

We have lost something. What is it? A sense of the sacred. The
sacred is important for human freedom because it signifies what
cannot be bought or sold. The hope for the world lies in recovering
its sacred identity. The sacred, in the end, won't be controlled or

manipulated and certainly can't be co-opted by the consumer culture. It is the guarantor of true freedom.

But there is danger here. If the chosen or imposed metaphor for being human is that of a consumer rather than of a neighbor, why not market the sacred and use it as a profitable means of social control? As the secular project is dying, there are those who believe it must be replaced with a theocratic totalitarianism. One side denies the sacred; the other makes a grab for it. This totalitarian grabbing for the sacred as a possession is present in all the great religious traditions. In Christianity, it is found in fundamentalist Protestantism and in Vatican-dominated Catholicism. I like John Dominic Crossan's vision of the Third Vatican Council: "In a solemn public ceremony in St. Peter's Basilica, they all implore God to take back the gift of infallibility and grant them instead the gift of accuracy." The same could be said of Protestant conventions and Orthodox synods.

Theocracy *imagines* that there can be an end to dialogue and discovery. We must come to closure. *No more questions!* That's why it's so attractive. Believers, once in power, would have the right to outlaw unbelief. According to Rowan Williams, archbishop of Canterbury, "It assumes that there could be a situation in which believers in effect had nothing to learn."

Pregnancy, Suffering, and Communion

But there's another path toward recovering the sacred than the grim ones just outlined, and in it lies my hope. It can be found by searching the Christian tradition, but a similar path can be gained from many starting points in other traditions.

I was fortunate to learn about the best and the most attractive aspects of my tradition from some remarkable human beings. The monks who prepared me for priesthood taught me that the life of faith was like falling in love. We were in the school of love, and the Holy Spirit was breathtakingly attractive and attracting. We were told that God is madly in love with us and wants us to come "home." I learned that the world was a sacred place and that the sacred was an encounter with "the really real." Because of its sacred character, the monks told us that the life of faith is risky, challenging, revelatory. It is full of surprise and risk—an ongoing revelation of human possibility and ruin. The sheer beauty of it all swept us away.

Above all, we were told to look at the basic images of Christianity not as dogmas, in the first instance, but as pictures—pictures of the really real. Pictures of the sacred. When we asked questions about the divinity of Christ and the status of Mary, we were told that such inquiries led only to a dead end. Instead we were told to *look,* to open our eyes. "Allow those pictures to work their transforming magic on you," they said. What happens when, for example, we look lovingly at a woman with a baby (any woman with any baby)? How should we respond and behave in the light of that image? We were told to look, not to worry about interpretations and definitions, with eyes wide open, at a woman with a baby in her arms or at her breast, and ask ourselves, "In the light of this image, how should I be in the world? How should I behave? How should I treat others and myself?"

What about Jesus? We were told to forget Jesus for a moment and look at the face of suffering humanity. Use your imagination to enter, however briefly, into the sufferings of others. There you will find both God and your neighbor. Finally we were told that whenever we delighted in good company, we were catching a glimpse of the meaning of the Holy Trinity. The monks told us that three experiences would be ours: pregnancy, suffering, and communion. These three gave life its dramatic structure. The experiences were somehow present in the images, and out of the experiences and the images came the teachings and doctrines of Christianity. The advice was to start from experience, not doctrine. Doctrine is there to help you question and probe your experience. What should we expect? Love. This love would come in three forms: pregnancy, suffering, and communion. We would always be laboring with new life and, while there would be struggle and pain sometimes, we would be part of a movement of mutual love building a new community. It was all very idealistic and perhaps naive. On the other hand, the monks were no fools and had labored and loved for justice in the then apartheid South Africa. They were authentic. They also told us that these images of pregnancy, suffering, and communion, acknowledged or not, played themselves out in every human life. You didn't have to be a believer to experience the drama of life.

The images of pregnancy, suffering, and communion spring from what Rowan Williams describes as "a truthfulness that exposes the deepest human fears and evasions and makes possible the kind of human existence that can pass beyond these fears into a new liberty."

In the Image of God:
The Shared Human Story

Although Christianity is the religion in which I am rooted, I have a deepening interest in the other great religious traditions. All the great religious stories are about the relationship or covenant with God and with each other. I get the impression from my friends who follow a spiritual path other than mine (Jews and Buddhists in particular) that they share the same struggles as I do and see the terrible consequences of the gap between faith and practice. They know about pregnancy, suffering, and communion as basic experiences of being human.

Lionel Blue is a retired English rabbi who is on British radio from time to time. He sees the need for a movement to rebuild a new working image of God. As a Jew he wants an image of God that "respects the experience of the Holocaust and its unanswered prayers, and the enormous Jewish contribution to inner knowledge, from Freud onwards." This is an exhilarating and great spiritual challenge, and our three basic images invite revision, review, and innovation.

We're all caught up in the radical openness of human identity. Its mystery is always unfolding and is never finished. This openness and mystery of being humanly human lead me to slip into God-talk, push my imagination to the limit, and force me into poetry and storytelling. This openness and mystery also undermine literal interpretations. This open and unfinished quality of human life is expressed in the idea that we are made in the image of God. And the two things we

"know" about God are that the divine is unknowable and inexhaustible. If this is the case and we are made in this God's image,
what does the doctrine say about us? If God is a mystery, then so are
we. There's something unknowable and inexhaustible about us.

The philosopher Voltaire was amused that human beings got it
the other way around. We like to make God in our image. Voltaire
said, "In the beginning God created us in the image of God and ever
since we've been returning the compliment." The poet Rupert
Brooke pointed out in a satirical poem that if fish could speak they
would tell us that God is a great fish and heaven a mighty ocean—
"And under that almighty fin, the littlest fish may enter in." It is
important to begin with God so that we are drawn into mystery. If
we begin with ourselves, God becomes strangely like us and is
reduced to our size.

Christians also claim that this never-ending mystery is "illumi-
nated" for us in Jesus, who shows us that at the center of the mystery is a love that turns the idea of power upside down. We call Jesus
divine because he makes visible the mystery in his living, dying, and
rising to new life. He shows us that we exist only in relationship with
each other and that the secret of life is found in our giving it away.
He uncovers the secret of true power coming from a self-giving and
self-emptying center. Jesus shows us that the pregnancy, suffering,
and communion we experience are part of the very life of God. Saying "Jesus is God" is a way of saying that humanity and divinity, while
radically separate, are so connected in Jesus that they will never be
parted. We dare talk of the humanity of God and the divinity of
humanity. It's a way of expressing the inexpressible open and unfinished nature of being human. This is why Christian teaching has a
poetic structure.

One of the old creeds (the Athanasian) struggled to put this mystery into words and claimed that God became one of us "not by the
conversion of the Godhead into flesh but by the taking of humanity
up into God." The creed was trying to say that God is not just a bigger and better version of us. Rather, who we are is linked with the
unknowable and inexhaustible God. This means that to be human
is to be open to an unfolding and never-ending mystery. There is no
unchanging human nature.

At the same time, to be human is to live in the mess of history. We are flesh and blood, and we are going to die. We are called into a pilgrim community to celebrate joyfully God's hospitality, in which the unqualified and the rejected are especially welcome. This means that we are in an endless conversation with the mystery of what it is to be human in the context of thrilling images of pregnancy, suffering, and communion in a community centered on a table from which no one is excluded. These three images and that of the banqueting table set the political and social agenda for our being in the world. They also can stimulate endless and fruitful conversations about human meaning and purpose.

What does this say about other spiritual teachings and paths? A woman with her baby, a picture of suffering humanity, and a community of loving people—these images are hardly threatening, and to use them to dominate and coerce others would be to abuse them. This approach to the Christian tradition through the doors of the poetic imagination allows for receptivity and respect when it comes to people on other journeys. The pilgrim who is open to mystery has no need to be either defensive or offensive. In fact, he may discover that there is only one destination after all.

Dogma: The First Word, Not the Last

It will be up to the reader to judge how far my view of Christianity is off-track: revisionist and idiosyncratic. When I say to the non- or ex-Christian (open-minded or despising), "You've got it all wrong about Christianity. This is how it really is! Tell me what it's like for you to be human. Tell me about your experiences of pregnancy, suffering, and communion," at what point do I so redefine Christianity that it becomes almost unrecognizable? Do the primordial and lovely images override the dreadful witness of history? What is the essence of Christianity, anyway? Can the essence of anything be distilled absolutely from its cultural manifestations? We are beginning to learn that Christianity isn't simply one thing and that there are many voices. Each of us has to make up his own mind as to its essence.

Some years ago a friend and I went to see the movie *The Last of the Mohicans*. As the Hurons were massacring everyone in sight, I mischievously whispered, "Don't you just love this Native American spirituality?" My friend got back at me later that week when she whispered in my ear, during the burning of the heretics in full ecclesiastical splendor in Verdi's opera *Don Carlo,* "Don't you just love this Catholic spirituality?" What is the essence of Native American spirituality? It has been romanticized into a version of pure ecology—before the European settlers the American continent was a peaceable kingdom. What is the essence of Catholic spirituality? The repressive policies of the Vatican? The prayer life of the Spanish mystics? The glories of Catholic universities and hospitals? What is the essence of Protestant Christianity? The myopia of fundamentalists? The radical freedom of the Reformation? Heroic witness under persecution?

I ask you to consider the *best* of the Christian tradition (we have, after all, spent a lot of time looking at the worst) and see it through its three basic images of pregnancy (Mary), suffering (Jesus), and communion (Trinity). It means leaving behind the world of dogma as something fixed and forever—the last word—and entering the world of dogma as the *first* word to help us move into mystery, with dogma seen as metaphor, poetry, and myth. To steal an image from the poet Rainer Maria Rilke, dogma, rightly understood, should be like an ice ax breaking up the frozen sea inside us. It will open the floodgates of the imagination. It will liberate the mind and heart, not imprison them. So try a little dogma! The monks (following G. K. Chesterton) told me that there were only two kinds of people: those who believe in dogma and know it, and those who believe in dogma and don't know it.

The test of dogma is in the character and life it builds. I suppose there would be few objections to hoping that human beings would be more Christ-like, and it wouldn't hurt if the human family embodied more of the spirit of the compassionate Buddha. If we think of Christianity as a story rather than as an argument, we might avoid the trap of spiritual-empire–building and allow other traditions to be in conversation with our own.

Remember that the only way to talk about the sacred is by metaphor. Metaphor's power lies in bringing two disparate things together for us to move forward in our feeling and thinking to a place where we could not go before. This is how we construct or invent new ways of thinking and feeling. No wonder we're frightened of poetry, myth, and metaphor. They bring in the new (pregnancy). The invite change (suffering). They promise connection (communion).

There's often a stern voice inside us telling us that we are not supposed to think beyond our means. We should be satisfied with flat, one-dimensional thinking, with a kind of nine-to-five inner life. But there are already analogies, metaphors, and poems buried in our feelings and thoughts. Sometimes these treasures and mysteries trapped inside us are liberated when we read a book, see a movie, or fall in love. This is how we move forward in our lives, by engaging in images, often strange ones. They bring us to places we wouldn't have reached otherwise.

But even metaphors and myths aren't adequate. When someone asks me, "Do you *really* believe in the Virgin Birth? Do you *really* believe in the Resurrection?" they want a simple yes-or-no answer. Usually they're not open to a long conversation. They don't like the idea that there may be a hundred questions that need to be asked in preparation for the final "Do you *really* believe in X (or Y)?" They assume that there are answers based on an objective knowledge we simply don't have. With theologian John Millbank I would answer, "'Yes, of course we believe.' But what we're saying is that the story of the Virgin Birth is a complex theological statement that none of us fully understands. The idea that it's nonsense, that it doesn't fit secular principles, is in itself a secular form of knowledge. The Virgin Birth is not just a metaphor."

"Wait a minute," you might be saying to yourself, "I thought you said it *was* a metaphor." Yes it is, but it's not *just* or *only* a metaphor. It's something more than that. It uncovers the mystery of language. John Millbank writes, "Jesus is essentially a linguistic and poetic reality." What can that mean? It means that language is a lot stranger than we think. It has the power to take us by surprise.

We live by images, and while we cannot step outside that imaged world, nothing is just a metaphor. The poetic is the only way we can get at certain truths, and its function is ceaselessly to retell and reframe the story we keep telling ourselves about our world and ourselves. It involves the constant retelling of human history by breaking it down into particularities (including the mystery of the particular, unique, and unrepeatable you) in the light of the three images—especially the shocking image of the cross.

How do you know the truth about yourself? We know that we're missing the mark when we say things like "Susan is just an alcoholic" or "Brian is merely a loser." Those little words *just* and *merely* reduce people to categories—in this case alcoholics and losers, respectively. Of course, we need to organize our thinking to get things done. That's why we make lists and sort things into groups: dogs, cats, humans, and birds. Then we further break those down into Irish setters, Burmese, Asians, and finches. But no matter how often we refine these lists, we never do justice to the particulars— dog, cat, human, and bird. My dog Tuppence was particular. There was no other dog like her. Christianity is, among other things, the celebration of particularity. Mary and Jesus are characters in a particular story about how love moves in the world.

The cross—however misunderstood—is one of Christianity's peculiar particularities and is central. It throws everything off balance. It undermines our social and political routines. A medieval maxim was *Crux probat omnia* (The cross tests everything). Actual Christians have pondered this with mixed results. How could a public execution liberate the human race? And does it *really*?

The Gifts of Other Traditions

As spiritual pilgrims in a wide-open world, some of us have not only learned to trust people on paths other than our own but also have discovered that we cannot go forward on our journey without their help. The central images of Christianity elicit a spirit of hospitality and openness. The pregnancy of new possibilities, the vulnerability of suffering love, the free gift of communion—none of these images bullies or coerces. Each invites conversation. Christ and Buddha are not antithetical. They are not at cross-purposes. Neither are they identical. The man on the cross and the princely contemplative are different images telling different stories. But they are not at war. They can be in conversation. There is grace in both.

Buddha has brought many back home to Christ, and Buddhism enables many to go on calling themselves Christians because the *form* of Christianity they experienced earlier in their lives had become a suffocating tomb. One of the reasons why Buddhism has helped many Christians is that Buddhism seems uninterested in history or, better, has a very different sense of history than is usually found in the West. Aren't the meanings of historical events more important than the details of the events? As Karen Armstrong points out, the Buddhist scriptures "give little information about matters that most modern Western people would consider indispensable. We cannot even be certain what century the Buddha lived in." Christians take history very seriously, but they often have a very narrow view of it.

George is a card-carrying Roman Catholic and a friend. Last summer he totaled his car and didn't exactly walk away. He broke a lot of bones. During a long period of rehab he rediscovered his inner life through meeting a young American Buddhist who was recovering in the bed next to him. George took up yoga, which speeded his recovery. Later he stayed for several weeks at a Tibetan monastery in northern California. He still calls himself a Christian but the disciplines of yoga and Eastern meditation are part of his life now and have helped him go deeper into his own tradition. For example, he now experiences the Eucharist and the Mass, in a wholly new way, as signs of God's radical hospitality. Before, he was a tribal Roman Catholic. Because of his encounter with Buddhist practice he's more grounded in his own tradition, yet more open to others. He's become a "Here comes everybody" Catholic.

I'm always searching for versions of the great story that reflect neither received Christian versions nor secularized liberal ones. The novelist Bruce Chatwin provided one in his novel *The Songlines,* which centers on Australian aborigine myths. Alien to both popular Christian stories and their secular counterparts, these speak across cultural lines about how a community of trust is maintained by stories, dreams, and songs. In this version of the story, the world is held together by songlines or dreaming-tracks:

Aboriginal Creation myths tell of legendary totemic beings who wandered over the continent in the Dreamtime, singing out the name of everything that crossed their path—birds, animals, plants, rocks, water-holes—and so singing the world into existence.

Arkady, a character in the book, explains

> how each Ancestor, while travelling through the country, was thought to have scattered a trail of words and musical notes along the line of his footprints, and how these Dreaming-tracks lay over the land as "ways" of communication between the most far-flung tribes. "A song" he said, "was both map and direction-finder. Providing you knew the song, you could always find your way across country."

"To them, the whole of bloody Australia is sacred," comments the Westerner in the novel. We might expand that to "For us, the whole of the bloody world is sacred!" The sacredness of the world is a meeting place for many stories.

Each child, according to one myth, is born with a fragment of the Song. The suggestion is that if we all were in touch with the music that is our birthright, we would not only be bound together in one community but also would be free to move about as we please because we would know our way. We would have at our fingertips a musical map, the songlines crisscrossing our history and experience. The word *sacred* implies such profound connections.

Each generation needs to sing and tell the stories to keep the lines deep and clear. They must be celebrated, acted out so that the reality of which they speak can be sustained. That is why we have to be in constant conversation about our own myths and stories. For them to be truly alive, we must be free to question them, collide with them, argue over their true meaning, and struggle with others about where they are leading us.

To do this I must be able to trust you and you to trust me. If reality really is genuinely sacred, as the aboriginal myth claims, then true life for the self involves commitment to others in ways that will require acts of both sacrifice and delight.

On Sacred Ground

A human being is sacred ground. Our exploration is not that of the heroic and solitary individual. We are on a spiritual journey with many companions throughout history. We do not have to start from scratch.

I stand very much in the Catholic tradition, with its education in classical theology. We were taught not so much *what* to think as *how* to think. We were taught to be unafraid of the conversation with the world and all it had to offer. John Dominic Crossan gives this example: Thomas Aquinas got up each morning, as it were, studied a pagan philosopher named Aristotle, and found his thought absolutely congenial and appropriate for creating and structuring Christian theology. Why was he never afraid of the conjunction? He was never afraid because truth *from whatever source* is of the Holy Spirit. The Christian images are meant to initiate a conversa-tion, not to cut it off. They launch us into mystery. They do not abort the spiritual journey.

The three primordial images of Christianity stare at us out of the tradition, and each of them has technical theological words attached: the broken and ruined man (Creation and Redemption); the woman and her baby (Incarnation and Presence); and the com-munity of persons (the Holy and Undivided Trinity). But we get off on the wrong foot if we think talking about God is like doing a sci-entific study. The question "Is Jesus God?" is not like questions such as "Was Abraham Lincoln from Illinois?" The questions *sound* the same, but the latter question is easily settled by making a few inquiries. The question about Christ's divinity is a far larger one, about how we interpret the world. We don't know what life means until we have learned how to turn it into a story—a myth. A myth, in this sense, is not something untrue, but a story without which the truth could not be told.

Isn't this what you've done with your life? This is what I have done with mine over and over again. In the act of writing things down I have written a mythology—I have tried to stop the camera of my life to get an occasional still photograph. When I read a novel, or see a play or a movie, I am given myth material to look at the story of my life from another point of view. When I look at the cathedral where I work, or wander, as I have often done, through the body of Chartres Cathedral, with its vast empty spaces, its silence, the light refracted through the stained glass, I am introduced to a new vocabulary pointing to new and unexpected worlds. In such spaces lives a Stranger, a truly Other—and when this Strange Other speaks, I resonate with the unknown. I can hear bells tolling in the soul. I am more than I can possibly know. "Is Jesus God?" is as much a question about humanity as it is about divinity. It is as much a question about you as it is about Jesus.

Underneath is the question "Who do you think you are?" We are on holy ground. The sacred is the air we breathe. It's the really real.

11

Healing the Wounded Imagination

Ideologies and the mutual hatreds they generate are territories of the mind.

—George Steiner

It is the task of art to undo the work of our vanity, our passions, our spirit of imitation, our abstract intelligence, our habits . . . making us travel back in the direction from which we have come to the depths where what has really existed lies unknown within us.

—Marcel Proust

We interpret the world and understand ourselves via images and stories. When the faculty to imagine gets wounded or diseased, we find ourselves caught in destructive fantasies from which there appears no escape. Fear of the unknown or unfamiliar takes over, with destructive and malevolent results. To make matters worse, the culture bombards us with ready-made images falsely promising fulfillment and happiness. No wonder so many of us are depressed. The basic image of our culture is that we are consumers. The basic image of the great religious traditions is that we are related—connected to each other, to the world, and to God.

Only Connect—Only We Can't

Central to the task of reimagining Christianity—or imagining how any faith can begin to live up to its promise—is putting the creative energy of the imagination to work discovering and building bonds between neighbors. We need to bring every watt of imaginative power we possess to this task, because the barriers to overcome are so formidable and the stakes are so high.

Part of the challenge in this is that we tend not to trust the power of our imagination. And our imaginations are often wounded, crippled by personal experience and/or cultural damage. We like the controlled fantasy of the movies, but we don't trust the freewheeling imagination because it gets out of hand, and we like to be in control. It's one thing to be scared out of you skull sitting on a sofa with a couple of friends watching a horror movie. It's quite another to reel in terror when you realize that the imagination can build or destroy the world where you live. That's why we tend to disable the imagination and sabotage its subversive healing work. We think of it as a monster lurking in our depths that must be kept in chains. That's why some fundamentalists want to burn books or ban fantasy. Fantasy is not literally true, such thinking goes, and what isn't literally true is a lie and should be labeled as such. The imagination survives such attempts at self-crippling, but it often reasserts itself in violent ways. Something we had long suppressed and forgotten erupts from our depths. The beast escapes; images emerge that frighten us or that do incalculable harm in the hands of unscrupulous or unconscious people.

Being open to the imagination is an art. How do we deal with the monsters and mysteries that come up, unbidden, from the depths and learn to treat them as images and not as directives? They should be neither suppressed nor acted on. We are to consider them with an artist's judgment and not an idolater's compliance.

Fear Poisons the Imagination

The imagination isn't always benign. It needs healing and regulating. It can be seductive and destructive. The imagination gets diseased when fear of outsiders takes over. History has many examples of political leaders who used metaphors such as "cancer" or "vermin" to describe elements in society they wished to suppress or eliminate.

In September 1899 there was the notorious case of a Jewish officer in the French army, Alfred Dreyfus, falsely convicted of treason. He was an outsider, and in a wave of Catholic prejudice the cause of race, nation, and religion were unjustly served.

If we go to Germany in the 1930s, we find Christian scholars hailing the rise of the Nazi Party as an act of God. The success of the party with almost no violence (at the beginning) and being spared civil war was a wondrous achievement. It was a work of the imagination—but one diseased by resentment and humiliation. Rather than talk of the nation, Hitler preferred the term *ein Volk* (one people), with a common faith marching toward the same promise. The vote for Hitler was an act of faith. He gave millions hope by capturing their imaginations. You have only to see old newsreels of the Nuremberg rallies to get some idea of Hitler's imaginative genius.

The Nazis called the Jews vermin. When that metaphor got lodged in the brain and the Jews ceased to be considered human, it was easier to exterminate them. The Nazi mentality was incapable of metaphor. The images became concrete, real. Jews were *literally* considered the equivalents of disease-bearing rats and therefore *should* be exterminated. Images are dangerous because they demand a kind of obedience from us, but images need to be confronted with questions, with the possibility of revision—rather in the way the stories we tell ourselves about ourselves need constant questioning and retelling. Images, like fairy tales, are to be believed and disbelieved at the same time.

Slobodan Milosevic conjured up ghosts from the late fourteenth century to justify his cry for Serbian nationalism. The protagonists fought an old and scorching story. In June 1398, Turks routed Serb knights under Prince Lazar in the Field of Blackbirds at Kosovo. It is said that a child at the breast is still greeted with "Hail, little avenger of Kosovo!" In 1987 Milosevic declared before cheering crowds, "They'll never do this again. Never will anyone defeat you!" The story from 1398 still had power—at least in the hands of a manipulative leader. Thus myth plays itself out on the bloody stage of history in the name of nationalism. There's an old expression, "Patriots love their country; nationalists hate everyone else's."

Poverty of Imagination and Its Price

The spiritual life of the Western world (at least) could be viewed as a neurotic and depressed system caused by poverty of imagination. One of the things we've learned from studying clinical depression, the biochemical kind, is that while it's not possible to avoid pain, it is possible to have our pain in deeper and more fruitful places. The experiential can be used to affect the physical. James Ballenger of the University of South Carolina Medical School writes, "Psychotherapy changes biology. Behavior therapy changes the biology of the brain—probably in the same way the medicines do." But therapy, insofar as it removes a stumbling block to creativity, doesn't always strike us as good news. Why? Because after you've removed a disability, people still have to live their lives, and the world is a hazardous place.

According to Ballenger, when asked a question about drugs as a way of helping relieve depression—"Don't they blank out your life?"—the answer is "No. What they do is to allow you to have your pain in more important places, in better places, for richer reasons." A well-developed imagination allows us to have our pain in depths we didn't know existed—in better places, for richer reasons.

The other huge cost of impoverished imaginations is violence. When we try, and fail, to edit out any discomfort and unpleasantness in our lives, we tend to turn on others. We look for someone or something to blame for our distress. We see that violence coming up again and again in many children who have been rendered flat-souled by the boredom of a bland life. We witness suburban youths killing each other.

Children, like all of us, need ways of negotiating their anxieties and joys. Those killer children from the suburbs lacked imagination and affect. For them, as the critic David Hickey points out, there is no sublimation of anxiety into dance, drama, music, into ecstasy and joy. He says that their poverty of imagination enabled them to wipe out "a million hopes, dreams, and memories by squeezing a tiny metal trigger"; they couldn't imagine the empty space they were making in succeeding generations; they couldn't even imagine their own futures. They couldn't connect.

Imagination as Empathy

The work of the imagination is serious business because through it we build or destroy the world. We've already *imagined* that everyone on the planet is a neighbor rather then merely a rival consumer. Imagining that we are guests and hosts of each other, not rivals or vandals, would mean working for a more just and genuine neighborly society in which each person was truly valued and therefore not open to becoming a vandal or a terrorist. Even those who surrender to a destructive imagination are guests in this house of being they have not personally built.

It takes real imaginative work to see others not merely as unthreatening but also as possible sources of celebration and revelation. George Steiner reminds me of the importance of sheer hospitality and respect in many traditions:

> Trees have roots, men and women have legs, with which to traverse the barbed-wire idiocy of frontiers, with which to visit, to dwell among mankind as guests. There is a fundamental implication to the legends, numerous in the Bible, but also in Greek and other mythologies, of the stranger at the door, of the visitor who knocks at the gate at sundown after his or her journey. In fables, this knock is often that of a concealed god or divine emissary testing our welcome. I would want to think of these visitors as the truly human beings we must try to become if we are to survive at all.

The truly human is the stranger at the door—a divine emissary, an angel—our neighbor. The guest master at a monastery in Egypt once greeted me "as an angel of God—just in case!" It's not a bad image to help us greet everyone we meet—just in case they have something to teach us, or a message we need to hear. Without such an act of imagination we miss the risk and the hope of being connected to others.

Andrew Solomon sees an analogy between the epidemic of depression and the environmental movement. In some way we are doing to ourselves what we're doing to the ozone layer. One neighborly act would be to "start doing small things now to lower the level of socioemotional pollution." Solomon writes, "We must look for faith (in anything: God or the self or other people or politics or beauty or just about anything else) and structure." Faith in *anything*? Solomon qualifies this by implying that he means anything that calls us to imaginative acts of love and compassion. We are to "help the disenfranchised whose suffering undermines the world's joy." And saving the ozone layer and the rain forests is directly connected with saving ourselves.

The Imagination Gap in Religion

We should expect our religious institutions to have trouble with the life of the imagination. We can say on one hand that religion relies completely on the imagination—but in practice it tends to set limits, to discourage fresh interpretation. In old-fashioned language this limiting of the imagination is called *idolatry*. Our allegiance to race, nation, and religion must be provisional if we are to avoid it. The imagination, after all, is not to be trusted. I may be an angel but only *may be*. And even if I was, on a particular occasion, an angel, the status wouldn't be permanent! We hallucinate reality, yet the imagination is all we have. For this reason some of us have to opt for voluntary exile because we should always be prepared to leave a community when its life becomes toxic. For this reason the life of the imagination keeps us humble. It keeps us from fixating on images rather than on the thing to which they point. That's why Christianity and Judaism have protocols against idolatry. We can get fixated on the images.

In Graham Greene's novel *Monsignor Quixote,* the priest has a dream: Christ had been saved from the cross. There was no final agony, no stone to be rolled away. He just stepped down from the cross, to the cheering crowd. A happy ending. Idolatry is a way of fixing things so that the ending, if not entirely happy, at least maintains our view of the universe. In the priest's dream,

> There was no ambiguity, no room for doubt and no room for faith at all. The whole world knew for certainty that Christ was the Son of God. It was only a dream, of course, only a dream but nonetheless Father Quixote has felt on waking the chill of despair felt by a man . . . who must continue to live in a kind of Saharan desert without doubt or faith, where everyone is certain that the same belief is true. He had found himself whispering, "God save me from such a belief."

God save us from idolatry—from mistaking the image for the reality; from confusing certainty with faith.

Another danger is the depression and sadness we experience when the images that used to nourish us become dry and stale. Julian, the hero of A. N. Wilson's novel *Daughters of Albion*, reflects on the sadness of his own incurable agnosticism. He isn't concerned about conventional belief. "But," he reflects, "it had begun to sadden me that I could put all this religious inheritance to no good or imaginative use. It lay around like lumber in my mind, but it did not quicken the heart."

I think that's where many intelligent modern people find themselves. They would like to find a place for the narratives of the Bible, with all the music, art, and architecture it has inspired. It gave millions of people a great story to help them interpret their lives, negotiate their passions, and deepen their loves. Julian says:

> I regretted my unbelief, my failure to respond imaginatively to the Old Story. The great majority of Europeans for the last 1,900 years had lived with this story as a background to their lives and somehow made use of it. Imaginatively, I was cut off from them, and from it, unable to find the mental or emotional equipment with which to respond to it.

What do we make of this dilemma? Why can't people connect imaginatively with the Judeo-Christian story? One reason, of course, is that the story has fallen into the hands of the literalists. Another is that the story has been presented in a closed way. D. H. Lawrence wrote, "Now a book lives as long as it is unfathomed. Once it is fathomed, once it is known and its meaning is fixed or established it is dead." Meaning and wonder get sucked out of a text once it is "understood." Religion disconnected from wonder is either dried-up ritual or moralism. The poetic imagination allows the wonder of the world to be unfathomable.

Seeing the connection between wonder and the web of life (*neighborliness* is too weak a word) might help us recover the poetic imagination. The novelist Margaret Atwood writes, "Long ago, we are told, images were worshipped as gods, and were thought to have powers of gods; so were certain words—holy names." Images pointed to the sacred, and the dominant way of interpreting the great text of the Bible was by way of allegory. Atwood maintains that later, at the beginning of what we think of as the "modern" world, God, if not visible, was at least inferred, "lurking somewhere behind the Newtonian scenery." Even this assumption faded. There was no Real Presence. "But," she writes, "in the West, as religion lost ground in society at large, the Real Presence crept back in the realm of art." I think she's right. The world is full of things waiting to be seen. We don't notice things.

Art Shapes and Heals the Imagination

The poet Dante Alighieri did much to heal the wounded imagination of his time, during which the prevailing image of life was *contemptus mundi* (contempt for the world). The world was a wretched place. This story illustrates the tormented imagination of the period: a holy monk died at the same time as St. Bernard and appeared in a dream to a bishop to tell him the fate of the 30,000 souls who had died at that instant. Only the monk and St. Bernard made it to heaven. Three managed to get to purgatory. The remaining

29,995 went straight to hell. Such stories have a potent effect on the imagination.

Dante took these terrible images and made them part of a journey of hope. He put the doctrine that we could be lost forever (eternal damnation) in the context of freedom and love. He gave it new meaning and helped rid the European imagination of its worst fears and of its mindless acceptance of cruelty. He did it by writing a poem, the *Divine Comedy*, which has penetrated and changed the consciousness of millions. Dante transformed the imagination of his day, making it less cruel and more human. We need poets and artists to do the same in our day. We need a "poetic" project to heal our imaginations from the three great wounds of race, nation, and religion.

The arts are essential because they provide a container, an interpreter for our passions. We need to order our desires and long-ings and to negotiate our fears and anxieties, our hopes and aspira-tions. We need ways to find meanings in new situations, or new meanings in old situations. Above all, we need an antidote to both violence and authoritarianism.

Art is an area where we may, in relative safety, face our fears, confusions, and longings and see the world generously, if sometimes threateningly. The arts help us mitigate our narcissism and fuel our imaginative grasp of what is beyond ourselves, to transform our anx-ious discomfort at not knowing into a kind of wild pleasure and joy. They withhold information so we have to stretch to enter the real-ity into which they invite us.

Theologian Gil Bailie uses Aeschylus' play *Agamemnon* as an example of the way art lays bare the terrifying impulses that lurk just beneath the surface of our lives. The goddess Artemis, cursing Agamemnon, has stranded his fleet at Aulis due to lack of wind. The way out is to sacrifice his daughter Iphegenia, who is gagged in preparation for sacrifice because the victim's voice must not be heard. Greek tragedy brilliantly portrays the underlying mechanism of sacrificial violence. The tragedy is that there is no alternative voice. The chorus intones: "The rest I did not see,/Nor do I speak of it."

The cycle of blood went on in the House of Atreus because the victims cannot be totally silenced nor the evidence efficiently hidden. This is art as a cry for justice. Justice will not come, nor will our depression be lifted, until everyone has been heard. In personal as well as in communal life, help can come only when the truth is told.

"Take notes and the pain goes away," wrote Virginia Woolf in *The Years*. For me, my therapy is in the writing and the preaching. I make no apologies. That's how God works. Naming helps. Just learning to make the distinction between what actually happens and my ideas about what happens helps. Artistic expression is vital therapy.

The Three Functions of Art and Imagination

Alan de Botton describes three ways in which contact with the arts is beneficial to the human spirit, and I think that can be extended to encompass any serious exercise of the imagination.

Feeling at Home Everywhere

Our imagination is stretched and our sympathies enlarged in our appreciation of art. We are connected to a larger universe. When we "recognize" someone we know in a portrait painted four hundred years ago, our world is transformed. Art can expand the number of places where we can feel at home and widen the range of human experience. "It means," de Botton writes, "we can open the zoo gates and release a set of trapped creatures from the Trojan War who we had previously considered with unwarranted provincial suspicion, because they had names like . . . Telemachus or had never sent a fax." He goes on to observe that the mind, once activated, is "like a radar newly attuned to pick up certain objects floating through consciousness." Imagine that we have dormant antennae that need to be reactivated. If we are truly awake to those other frequencies that are always present, "Our attention will be drawn to the shades of the sky, to the changeability of a face, to the hypocrisy of a friend or to a submerged sadness about a situation which we had previously not even known we could feel sad about."

A Cure for Loneliness

When we open the gates of that inner zoo we might let *ourselves* out, too, by allowing fictional characters to widen our vision of human experience and show us that in both our joy and our pain we may be joined with others. Or we may find images and words that help keep us from feeling estranged from life.

I think of the agonies of adolescent love, and how the power of literature helped me weather them, as well as feeding my nascent love for poetry and symbol. At high school, I was assigned nineteenth-century French poetry and wallowed in it. Instead of the flattened-out emotions dished out by contemporary culture, such literature can furnish the mind and help it imagine what it would be like to receive "the last word, touch, glance, exchanged between two human beings totally in love." Adolescence is more than raging hormones. It is the initiation into passion, and if it doesn't have a creative outlet, it turns rancid. We may turn on others and even shed blood, or turn on ourselves and become depressed and flat-souled.

New Insights on Reality

De Botton calls this the "finger-placing ability" of art. There are moments when we can't quite put our finger on something—a feeling, an emotion, an intuition—and a work of art does it for us. When we read a novel, see a play, or look at a piece of sculpture, we say to ourselves, "Ah! That's who I am!" or "That's what that's about!" A work of art is able to describe what is going on inside us better than we can on our own. Art helps me to see things I would never see on my own and enables me to hold contradictions together. De Botton uses the French Impressionists as an example of our discovering new vision. In 1872 Claude Monet's painting *Sunrise* went on exhibit—a scene of Le Havre Harbor at dawn. Viewers found it bewildering, and irritated critics gave its creator and his cohorts the intentionally unflattering name "Impressionists," implying that Monet could not accurately depict what dawn in Le Havre really looked like. But in painting a dimension of visual reality never before captured, Monet shows that our notion of reality is often at variance with reality itself. Think how we domesticate religion and bring God down to our size. We cannot see the difference between our idea of God and the reality of God. We have clichéd ideas about God as small, domesticated, and manageable. Art helps us see what we actually see rather than what we think we ought to see.

The poet W. H. Auden pointed out that the purpose of poetry (and all art) is not to enchant but to disenchant. It delivers a dose of reality never yet noticed until the revelation of the poem, the piece of music, the painting. The genius of the artist, said de Botton, is "to hang on to the original muddle" as he looks at the world and waits until a new pattern manifests itself, and thus "restore to our sight a distorted or neglected aspect of reality."

Hang on to the original muddle and you will never see the harbor at Le Havre in the same way. Hang on to the original muddle, and an image of God that enables us to be humanly human will emerge. This is the only way we recover the strangeness and wonder of things and escape from the clichéd life of convention.

Art is central to human flourishing. It is not an option. And this, in spite of people wanting to invest in it, control it, or clean it up, in spite of schools dropping art programs because they are too-expensive extras. When we catch a glimpse of the immensity of the commonplace, we suddenly take notice of people and things. We cease to be sedated and pay attention. Think of what a poem, a piece of music, can do to us. Think how ordinary experiences shape our sense of the future. "To be 'indwelt' by music, art, literature," says George Steiner, "is to be made responsible, answerable to such habitation as a host is to a guest—perhaps unknown and unexpected—at evening." It is to experience what he calls "the commonplace mystery of a real presence."

Into a Larger World

Liberating and healing the imagination save us from settling too easily for a shallow reading of life and thinking we have arrived. When we discover an image that nourishes us and speaks to us, we are brought to the end of our rope—to the limits of language. The new becomes possible.

Several years ago we had to have our lovely Irish setter, Tuppence, put to sleep. She was getting old, her back legs were giving out, and she was incontinent. I was the one designated to take her to the vet, who, to his credit, interrogated me thoroughly as to the wisdom and necessity of killing the dog. Once he was satisfied, we went ahead with the first injection, to relax her. With the second Tuppence looked at me, and in that look I became part of the long history of close relations between humans and other animals. I was in a long tradition of such partings. There is no such thing as just "putting an old dog down." The death of Tuppence made me wary of expressions like "It's just a sunset." "It's only your imagination." "It's only symbolic." The death of our dog resonated with layers of meaning, with Presence.

When I stand with a much-loved dog at her death, or read a brilliant novel, or hear certain pieces of music, I am placed in a larger world. I realize not only that I am not deep enough on my own, but also that there are depths in me yet to be explored. The work probes me, reads me, asks me questions, makes demands. If we see and acknowledge this connection between ourselves and works of art, art isn't merely a distraction, it is a means by which we begin to understand ourselves. Marcel Proust wrote, "In reality, every reader is, while he is reading, the reader of his own self."

Art also is unnerving, because while it helps me decode my life, it is always subject to error and revision. This is its genius, and it's why art and fundamentalism do not go together. Watching movies such as *The Lord of the Rings, Harry Potter and the Sorcerer's Stone,* or the *Star Trek* series—all fantasies about the future, or a distant past, or a new kind of present—remind us of our need for fantasy. Religious people tend to take their fantasies and make them concrete. Stories about a Muslim or Christian heaven are great works of the imagination but are diminished when taken to exclude others and as literally true. They banish other equally valid fantasies about a realm that can never be described.

Art doesn't, as many fear, push us into relativistic chaos. Art deepens and brings us to see levels of meaning and possibility hitherto hidden from us. Art makes the invisible visible and yet reveals the very inexhaustibility of the things we hear and see and touch. As Steiner reminds us, "The bush burned brighter because its interpreter was not allowed too near." God is the artist or poet of the world, and the divine creation cannot be corraled or contained. We can only admire and be changed. We cannot possess. We cannot buy or sell.

A Creative Connection
to the Future

Katherine Anne Porter wrote of the calling and power of art in June 1940, ten days after the fall of Paris. She was no artist in an ivory tower, and her insights of more than sixty years ago are relevant today. We, too, live under the threat of world catastrophe. We, too, try to grasp the meaning of those threats. She confesses that "most of the energies of my mind and spirit have been spent in the effort to trace them to their sources and to understand the logic of this majestic and terrible failure of the life of man in the Western world." She goes on:

> In the face of such shape and weight of present misfortune, the voice of an individual artist may seem perhaps of no more consequence than the whirring of cricket in the grass; but the arts do live continuously and they live literally by faith; their names and their shapes and their uses and their basic meanings survive unchanged through times of interruption, diminishment, neglect; they outlive governments and creeds and societies, even the very civilization that produced them. They cannot be destroyed altogether because they represent the substance of faith and the

only reality. They are what we find again when the ruins are cleared away.

She had something in 1940 that, I think, we lack right now: a creative connection to the future. Her art was an affirmation that Hitler and his sort never have the last word. But it seems as if many of us have a crippled relationship to the future. So we might use our imaginations and take one more look at the old, old story, with its formative and regulating images of pregnancy, suffering, and communion—the stories of the Mother and Child, the broken and ruined man, and the loving community. We might encounter Christianity again for the first time.

12

Jesus the Broken Man

The cross is not some arbitrary demand of God imposed on a hapless victim . . . but a marker where human beings find themselves, at the intersection of justice and mercy, time and eternity, death and life.

—Eamon Duffy

The image of the crucified Christ is one of the central images of Christianity—some would say *the* central image. It has been portrayed so often in paintings, icons, and sculptures that we may have become a little numb to it—at least when we don't shy away in distaste or horror. There is also a lot of annoying and even repellent talk about "redemptive suffering," about how suffering is good for us.

When I look at the thirteenth-century Spanish crucifix in Grace Cathedral, San Francisco, I am deeply moved. It's hard to put into words, but this depiction of the suffering of Christ is not one that emphasizes the horror of the event. Rather there is a deep sadness about the way human beings treat each other. This crucifix invites us into the world's sorrows without any kind of explanation.

To some, the cross is an unwelcome symbol of where Christians have gone off track. Many Jews see it as a grating reminder of the blame for Jesus' death visited on them (sometimes violently) by centuries of Christians. The Roman Catholic Church has gone some distance to repudiate and apologize for that view, but there is still some way to go.

The other thread of just criticism addresses the suggestion implicit in the cross that Jesus' sacrifice was to appease an angry God. Penal substitution was the name of this vile doctrine. I don't doubt for one moment the power of sin and evil in the world or the power of sacrificial love as their antidote and the peculiar power of the cross as sign of forgiveness and restoration, but making God vengeful, all in the name of justice, has left thousands of souls deeply wounded and lost to the Church forever.

What does the image of the cross mean to me? It is a sign of the necessary crucifixion of ideologies in the face of concrete human experience—the crucifixion of power plays, the crucifixion of a god we think we can conceptually control. It also is a sign of humanity's need to find someone to blame for its ills. When we suffer or are threatened, we look for scapegoats. Scholar René Girard suggests that scapegoating is the idée fixe at the heart of our culture. It is, for him, the mechanism on which society, culture, and religion are based. The murder of the innocent and our ability to make acts of scapegoating violence sacred seem to be built into us. The cross speaks directly to this dark issue of scapegoating.

In the tradition, Christ is both victim and victor. In calling the victim Lord, Christianity is weird, and we have lost touch with the strangeness of it. In the sacrificial language in which it is couched, the doctrine tries to do the impossible. Love surrenders itself for Love's sake. Christ is both the sacrifice and the One to whom the sacrifice is made. This has a troubling effect on cultures that depend on occasional episodes of solemnly sanctioned righteous violence (rituals of sacrifice) for the sake of social solidarity. The story of the crucifixion challenges society's primary illusion: that the killing of victims is a noble act. Its address hits us when we realize that the sacrificial victim is God. The divine to whom sacrifice is owed breaks the cycle of violence.

That's why the appropriation of religious wisdom by spiritual dabblers is such a tricky thing. We like the easy stuff. We don't mind a Buddha, a Moses, or a Jesus we could take home as a friend and kindly mentor. But what about the one who would turn your world upside down by identifying with victims everywhere? How about being overwhelmed and embarrassed by a fierce and unconditional love? In the final chorale in Bach's motet "Christ lag in Todesbanden," there's an unnerving image:

> Hier ist das rechte Osterlamm,
> davon Gott hat geboten, das ist
> hoch an des Kreuzes Stamm
> in heißer Lieb gebraten

The literal translation is: "Here is the true Easter Lamb, whereof God has commanded, which is high on the cross's stem, in hot love roasted." You can't get much odder than that, yet such images permeate the Bible. Abraham was willing to bind his son Isaac on the altar of sacrifice. The prophets equated idolatry with adultery. Jesus said, "This is my body, this is my blood."

These images of God's involvement with us are too hot for some, but scholars Catherine Madsen and Scott Holland insist, "Such images arise wherever religion touches the whole personality. They cannot be suppressed without arising in a new place. Their very outrageousness breaks the bounds of decorum; beyond those bounds there remains only intimacy with the divine."

There's no getting away from the sacrificial language, and it's the only language I know that matches the violence of history and the slaughter of the innocent. Christians call this stopping the cycle of violence the Atonement.

The revelation of the cross (in spite of some of Christ's followers) is an irrepressible cultural force. Theologian Gil Bailie points out that however poorly Christians have followed Christ, the world would be an even more brutal place without it. But even as the Gospel won't allow us to make violence respectable and sacred, it is still hard to break its relentless cycle. That's why repentance and contrition are central to Christian practice. They afford a necessary form of lucidity—of seeing through our illusions and evasions.

In the cross we see a God who chooses to suffer violence rather than sponsor it. This isn't a God I could have thought up. Mine would look a little more imperial, like Caesar Augustus. The late Anthony Bloom, the Russian Orthodox bishop in London when I was growing up, said on a British TV program, "Of course the Christian God exists. He is so absurd, no one could have invented him."

The Hebrew Scriptures (in Isaiah) speak of the Suffering Servant and contradict any "normal" view of an all-powerful God. The cross turns our ideas of power upside down. People yelling for revenge and thinking themselves righteous are deluded. Imagine a mob running after someone to lynch him. He has offended rules of society and he is a scapegoat. Just as they are about to string him up, there is a revelation. The very one they are about to hang is the chosen one of God. He, the victim, turns out to be the one who shows us who God is and what God is like. Imagine the confusion and the anxiety of the mob. They would be torn between two necessities. The first is that their chosen victim is, after all, innocent, and that they were wrong to hound him and start to string him up. Second, what were they going to do with the feeling in the gut that victimizing others is necessary for the good of society? What were they to do when the act, which they believed brought the community peace, was taken away from them?

In light of all this, it's easy to see why the Church insists on the need for repentance as a lifelong process. Conversion is not an option. Why? Because the tendency to violence is in our blood. What's worse is that random violence is becoming recreational. At the end of William Golding's *The Lord of the Flies,* Ralph runs away from the boys who want to sacrifice him. "A naval officer stood on the sand . . . " The boys begin to come to their senses. "It has been humanity's recurrent dream that it would eventually be able to do just that, come to its senses." Golding commented that the naval officer rescued the children from their own terrible violence— "And who will rescue the adult and his cruiser?"

The broken and ruined man asks me the awful question that lurks under our fear and ignorance. It's a question hiding behind every act of violence. What will you do, what sort of human being will you be when you realize that you are not in control and that you are marked for death? What kind of life will you choose to live while you still have time? Our destiny is to possess nothing—every last bit of it. This is the secret of Jesus—the secret of the only true power, the power that gives itself away—the meeting place not only of all the great traditions but also of all those who long for a new humanity.

13

Mary, the Pregnant Life

Indeed I often think that maybe half our heritage is transmitted to children around the crib at Christmastime—and especially in the wonderfully mysterious explanation of the Incarnation to little kids that Mary is God's mommy.

—Andrew Greeley

I visit the Cathedral of Our Lady of Chartres every year. It is a place on the boundary or borderland of the strange and the familiar—with a great focus on Mary. At first old Protestant suspicions made me skeptical about her role in the Christian story. But the building won me over. It reminds me of a great cave that lets in light through its stained-glass, storytelling windows. It reminds me of something I have lost, a sense of connection with mystery, with the mystery of birth and death. Mary is everywhere. In nearly all of the images she is holding the infant Jesus. The empty cathedral, with its lights and shadows, points to her as a sign of pregnancy, of new possibilities.

Archbishop Rowan Williams puts it well: "After all, it is she who literally makes a home for the Creator of all things, the strangest reality we can conceive, in her own body and in her own house, she whom we meet again in the Gospels struggling with the strangeness of her son, from the finding in the temple to the station at the cross."

The boundary I am invited to cross on this annual pilgrimage is the boundary of myself, or better, of that image of myself that relies on some external validation and on my being in control of my life. Mary and her Son are signs to me that I am free to choose to cross that boundary or, as Rowan Williams puts it, "I can be unceremoniously bundled over it by the realities of my life. If the latter happens, I may want to deny it and retreat, but the image before us of Mary pointing the way reminds me that I can do that only at the cost of truth and, ultimately, of any life that matters."

What is this boundary? For me, the boundary is between the human and the divine. The images of Mary show just how porous the boundary is not only between God and us but also between one human being and another. She looks out at me from icon and stained glass and silently asks, "So you thought you knew what a human being is? Look. Here is a wonder. The awesome humility and availability of God." The pictures and stories about Mary bring me to the boundary, and I meet people who also are on a boundary-crossing journey who tell different and wonderful stories about the journey. I don't have to judge them. They may tell different stories, but they are my companions. What do we have in common—the motley crowd that shows up at Chartres and other places of pilgrimage? We share a common vulnerability in that we're not always sure we're in the right place at the right time. Being human has become something of a mystery. Yet we have an instinct that the most fruitful place for crossing the boundary is "in those areas of our life where we feel at sea, not understanding, not succeeding." The mystical traditions all agree that in our honest helplessness we come closer to the real well of life deep within us. Mary, then, reminds me of and connects me to my own mystery and invites me to respect the mystery of others. The image of Mary giving birth to Jesus stirs up in me the mystery of my own birth and the subsequent "births" of my own development as a person.

St. Simeon, the New Theologian (c. 949–1022), speaks of two births. "The ineffable birth of the Word of God in the flesh from his mother is one thing, his spiritual birth in us in another. For the first, in giving birth to the Son and Word of God, gave birth to the reforming of the human race and the salvation of the whole world. While the second, in giving birth in the Holy Spirit and to the Word of knowledge of God, continually accomplishes in our hearts the mystery of the renewal of human souls. Thus anyone, married or unmarried, who lives with integrity toward God in the deeper level of their being may not, like Mary, bear the Son of God in the flesh, but they can and do become like her, and will be God-bearers to humankind."

The Vulnerability of the Word

We begin and end in mystery, which turns our ideas of power and control upside down. Jesus is God's Word to us, and this communication comes to us in the form of a baby who cannot speak. The Word waits in silence. The imagery is stunning. You can hold the Word (God's communication to you) in your arms. You can suckle the Word at your breast. The Word—the communication—is as vulnerable as that. In the New Testament stories of the Nativity there are other key players besides Mary and her baby, including an old man (Simeon) and an old woman (Anna). They hold the Word in their arms and remind us that our view of power is false. It is not centered in Rome or Washington, seats of empire. True power is to be seen in a helpless baby, held in the arms of two old people as good as dead. These images teach us that what we share in common is our peculiar vulnerability. But it's a pregnant vulnerability, full of possibility and power.

Mary's Sacred Silence

La Madonna del Parto was painted by Piero della Francesca on the wall of the Church of Santa Maria di Momentana at Monterchi in about 1460. Mary is standing, wearing a blue robe. Her right hand points downward at a long split in the dress, indicating her pregnancy. Her left hand is on her hip and her face exhibits . . . what? Boredom, serenity, indifference, resignation, acceptance?

Above her is a canopy being held open by two angels—a reminder of the Ark of the Old Covenant, a sign of God's dwelling among us. Mary is the Ark of the New Covenant, protecting in her womb the Son of God. In this way Mary is a sign of the Church, the

Body of Christ, the place where God dwells. She is also a sign for every human being—male and female—as the place where God chooses to make a home.

It is said that the artist meditated on the sacred silence of Mary when he painted this picture. Catholic tradition speaks of the contemplation of the *silentium Virginis circa secretum Dei* (the silence of the Virgin concerning the secret of God) and of the *Verbi silentis muta mater* (the mute mother of the silent Word). This concept is echoed in these words St. John of the Cross: "The Father utters one Word and he utters him forever in everlasting silence, and in silence the soul has to hear him."

The Word that erupts out of silence and returns to silence is a key to the true understanding of theology and, by extension, to our self-understanding. We cannot do without words, and yet words fail us. "The Word who cannot speak" points to the radical way of knowing by "not knowing," of which our culture is ignorant. This way of "not knowing," of "learned ignorance," is of the utmost importance in the spiritual life. It provides protocols against the tyranny of narrow definitions. The truth is that we can only *imagine*—but our imagination is all we have, and it is notoriously unreliable and always needs reforming and healing.

What informs the architecture of our thoughts? This image of the silent Mary could be liberating to those of us caught in destructive definitions and narratives—those we have taken on our own or those imposed on us by others.

Renewal and transformation could begin by our waiting for our own secret to reveal itself in the pregnant silence—the silence of the Virgin concerning the secret of God—in whose image, it is said, we are made. One of the words used for the life of contemplative prayer is *parturire* (to give birth). So in the silence we, too, by the grace of the Spirit, give birth to ourselves—to the true self that is both secret and known, the self-in-God. Loved and in communion with all things, the soul is born in and out of the secret silence of God. This silence at the heart of mysticism is not only the meeting point of the great traditions but also where all hearts might meet.

The picture of the woman with her baby stands alongside that of Jesus on the cross. In one sense, it's all one picture. Pregnancy is a kind of suffering that brings to birth in us the communion of all things, which is our destiny.

Leaving Doctrine Aside

I haven't mentioned Mary's virginity (perpetual or otherwise). Nor have I taken on the Roman Catholic doctrines of the Immaculate Conception or the Assumption. You can't talk about Mary without mentioning these, can you? Well, you can. They are best left to one side at the beginning of the conversation.

While these doctrines (or better, devotions) can be occasions of fruitful meditation, they are, on the whole, distractions and allow people to miss the point of Mary's true role in the story. She reveals the awesome humility and availability of God. For my part, I won't allow those who insist on a literal interpretations of these myths and doctrines to deprive me of my devotion to her. Was she literally a virgin? I don't know. I do know that in the old stories and commentaries about her, *virginity* was often a code word for absolute dedication. Christ, in this regard, was even referred to as the archvirgin. But much of the emphasis on virginity arose from a negative and destructive view of sexuality. So I doubt very much whether Mary was literally a virgin, but I know many who sincerely believe that she was.

What we have in common is the conviction that when we look at her image with the baby at her breast or on her lap, we see something of the heart of God. We are drawn into the awesome mystery of intimacy with God. It is all deceptively simple. Andrew Greeley celebrates "the wonderfully mysterious explanation of the Incarnation to little kids that Mary is God's mommy." The clever and sophisticated consider this too naive and simple-minded, but that's why the merely clever and the sophisticated miss a lot. There is a deep truth in the story of the mother and her baby for those who are willing to open their hearts.

St. Catherine of Siena (1347–1380) wrote:

Today, O Mary, you have become a book in which our rule is written. . . . In you is manifested the strength and freedom of human beings. I say that the dignity of human beings is manifested because when I look at you, O Mary, I see that the hand of the Holy Spirit has written the Trinity in you, forming in you the incarnate Word.

We look at a pregnant young woman and see a rule in which is set out a picture of our strength, freedom, and dignity. Mary is a book we can read. The Holy Spirit has written the Word in us. This is how we tick. This is how we are wired. Don't get caught in the sticky mess of doctrinal controversy. Just look.

14

Trinity Means Communion

Our duty to preserve the human person in his integrity, his
freedom and his individuality, and to arm him spiritually
against the evil of totalitarianism, is not just something it
would be nice for us to discuss and perhaps to study. It is an
urgent task which demands insistently to be acted out.

—Thomas Merton

The Holy Spirit has written the Trinity in you." The doctrine of
the holy and undivided Trinity is a doctrine about what it is to
be human. Since we are made in the image of God, and God,
according to Christians, is a communion of persons, what does that
say about us? We sense that on one hand, we want to stand alone
as free individuals, and on the other, we want to be in a freely chosen relationship with others. We want two things at once. We want
individuality without domination from another. But we also want
intimacy and community.

The doctrine of the Trinity—God as Father, Son, and Holy
Spirit—developed as a way of putting into words the experience of
the early Christians. They believed in *one* God, yet they experienced
this God in Jesus as an ongoing presence in their lives. At the same
time they were going through a change in the way they understood
themselves. Never before had anyone experienced what we now
take for granted—what it is to be an individual. In fact, much of
what we take as given about what it is to be human was hammered
out in the first four centuries of the Christian era, as people tried to
give voice to their experience both of Jesus as a lively presence still

among them and of themselves as beings made in the image of God. St. Augustine's *Confessions* are significant in that they reveal the beginnings of a new way of reflecting on the self, and not the self in isolation. This is the self who is both radically unique and yet in communion with others.

God was clearly God, and yet God came to them in three ways that were distinct but not separate. They knew God as Creator. They'd meet God in the flesh in Jesus. And after he was gone, they were aware of his all-pervasive Spirit; they encountered this living presence whenever they met together to break bread. At the same time, they reflected that they felt more truly themselves when they were in communion with God and with each other. They didn't feel less themselves but, like lovers, they felt more themselves when they were with people they loved. Out of this furnace of experience there emerged a dynamic and open understanding of God and of them-selves—a doctrine of God that was always capable of revision.

Their experience brought new problems because it set the Christians on an adventure that is still going on, in spite of efforts of authoritarians to close it down. Their own humanity was being shaped by forces beyond their control. The Holy Spirit is wind and fire, elements that cannot be controlled or subdued. Imagine what it was like to reflect on the fact that a human being was made up of such elements. If we are made in the image of God, there is some-thing about us that cannot be controlled, subdued, or enslaved. That's why questions about the Holy Spirit (in fact, questions about religion in general) are often questions about authority. Who gets to say what's what? Whose version of reality is the most accurate, and what are the consequences of our false choices? The name of the game is freedom, but we don't really want to be free. We want to control or be controlled, but the Spirit blows where it will.

Perhaps that's why the Church has been somewhat weak with regard to the life of the Spirit. It cannot and will not be controlled by synods, canons, and rubrics. The Church organizationally has often preferred to control rather than attract, dominate rather than invite, compel rather than win over. Human beings don't like the messiness of history, and in the name of efficiency they tidy up what resists rigid reorganization. But Christianity is based on a lot of uncertainty about what can be known and controlled. All we have are pictures, and the mystery of wind and fire cannot be contained in them. This is nowhere more true than in our talking about God as Trinity. We are not dealing with definitions but with mysteries, and a dogma, properly understood, isn't the last word on a subject but the first—a starting point.

To Be Human Is to Be Trinitarian

In Genesis 18, Abraham is visited by three young men, angels who bring the news that Sarah, his wife, in her old age, will bear a son. Abraham invites the messengers to a meal. This image of the three figures seated around a table on which there is a chalice became known as the Old Testament Trinity and was made famous by Rublev's icon. It's hard to tell who the figures are. Are they men? Are they women? Are they angels?

This image of God tells us that we are human—truly ourselves—insofar as we are lovingly inclined toward each other, concentrated on the chalice of love. The icon of the Trinity teaches us how to be human. To be human is to be in a communion of love. Think of the three figures around the table as an image of divine hospitality. As the Eastern Church teaches, the world is a wedding, and everyone is invited.

The opening of the Fourth Gospel has been translated, "In the beginning was the conversation and the conversation was God and in the fullness of time that conversation entered into our flesh." If I had to sum up the theological method of my faith commitment, it would be to affirm my trust in that conversation—which is not superficial chat but the belief that, according to theologian John Millbank, "the Christian Church is best understood as schooling in conversation." And any conversation about Jesus, Mary, and the Trinity comes down to the nature of true power and how it is to be exercised.

Knowledge, as expressed in the Hebrew word *yada,* is an act of love, not an act of domination. When someone has understood, he says: "I see it. I love you. I behold God." The result is pure theory and pure good pleasure. "Theory" in this sense is not "mere theory" but has something godly (*theos*) about it. It suggests a vision of life for its own sake. It connotes service, not mastery. Today we know in order to master our object. If someone thinks he understands something, he says: "Yes. I grasp that. I've got it. I understand it." The result is a kind of domination. But when we *know* someone or something as an act of love, we are in communion and escape from one being enslaved by the other.

Novelist D. H. Lawrence was saying much the same thing when he wrote, "Now, a book lives as long as it is unfathomed. Once it is fathomed, once it is known and its meaning is fixed or established it is dead." So it is with doctrine. Words are all we have, and words won't do.

I heard something very much like this in remarks by the Tibetan Buddhist scholar Robert Thurman at a reception a couple of years ago. He said, in effect, that speech was the primary act in Buddhism. I thought, "Wait a minute. You're poaching on Christianity!" But then I realized that no one and everyone owns the truth. For Buddhists, too, the Word spoken and received is primary. Any conversation, if it is to be true, requires not only the recognition of the one who speaks but also the acknowledgment of the one who listens. In fact, my sense of myself requires that I be listened to, attended to. I need others to be myself. When people aren't listened or attended to, when they are rendered invisible, they become depressed or violent. We depend on each other. Without each other, the self is wounded. For me, this is pure Trinitarianism. I cannot be me without you. You cannot be you without me. But it's more important to live the doctrine than to define it. If Buddhists call it something else, that only makes the conversation more interesting.

Something similar happened when I heard a Chinese American journalist claim (quite rightly) that his tradition had much to teach contemporary Americans about eating and family life. "We sit at a round table and the food is placed in the middle and we all share from the same platter. In the West, we have our own plates and don't know how to share in the same way." I heard echoes in this of what I had been taught about Holy Communion. There's one table and we all share the same bread. If we look and listen, we have more in common with each other than could possibly divide us.

Stuck with Each Other

So the Trinity is an image of a communal God, and since we are made in the divine image, the collective precedes the individual. The mystics saw in the holy and undivided Trinity the mystery of their loving made visible—the mystery of complete unity and radical identity. Love is structured on patterns of mutuality, identity, and solidarity; it unites and differentiates at the same time. In your love, I am more myself, not less. This is echoed in Dante's vision of heaven as complete unity in unimaginable diversity. With this God, there is no permanent flight of the alone to the Alone. With this God, we are stuck with one another.

I come back to the issue of freedom. We become truly free if we open our lives for other people and share life with them, and if other people open their lives for us and share them with us. Then others are not to be dreaded. They are no longer limitations of our freedom but its extensions. According to John Millbank, "As long as freedom means domination, everything has to be divided, isolated, singled out, and differentiated, so that it can be ruled." Our freedom isn't like that. We are freed *for* each other, and we experience God in and through each other. There is no freedom without justice and mutuality. Mutuality establishes human society, and justice "consists of the mutual recognition and acceptance of other people. Mutual recognition of human dignity, and mutual acceptance, create a humane and just community." In this sense, true Trinitarian spirituality is intensely political.

We need shared rituals—feasts and ceremonies of the future— that bind us together. It's not accidental that as we live at the beginning of this new millennium, we ache for a new vision of society that understands the human race as a single family. It is the "heavenly" vision of planetary consciousness with a divine "ecology" of sacredness and reverence, of a way of being human that involves longing

for the other to be free and being able to accept the other's difference without fear, of a politics of a just society of only one ethnic
group of infinite variety—the whole human family. Is this naively
Utopian or simply an accurate description of who we really are as a
people? A holy family, we might say?

Communion Is Political

The adventure and possibility of communion excite me, but sometimes it seems harder and harder to find it actually manifested in the
life of the Church. The last thing we want is excitement, risk, challenge, and revelation. Thomas Merton's call to action (in the epi-
graph) only hardens our resistance. If we were serious about the
human family being called into communion, we'd fight for it. The
principle in "Being *is* communion" may be true, but it isn't easy.

The world of our experience—dominated by pluralism, diversity,
and confusion—seems rarely in communion. We're able to experience this even on a cosmic level, thanks to the work of astronomi-
cal science. When Edwin Hubble in the early 1920s discovered
galaxies beyond the Milky Way, the universe as we know it expanded
by a factor of 100 billion. We live in a reality without boundaries or
a center. How far has this penetrated our consciousness? Is it any
wonder that we look for something to hang on to at a time when
there is more fragmentation than communion?

This immensity and our apparent insignificance in the face of it
only serve to heighten the issue of choice. We're invited—no, challenged—to take sides, to be on the side of all that protects and hon-
ors the human spirit. This is Merton's urgent challenge.

We're not only stuck with each other, we're also stuck with the
world we helped to create, and its polluted ecosystems. In this sense
human solidarity—willed or not—is becoming more and more of a
reality. We are united by AIDS, SARS, and ecological imbalance. The
upside of the inevitability of solidarity is that we—all of us—have a
choice to move from seeing ourselves stuck with one another to cul-
tivating and celebrating our communion with each other. We have
obligations to each other and to the planet. And there is no greater

perversion of religion than the false piety of insisting on the separation of the political from the spiritual. Since the principle is "Being *is* communion, " how we arrange our common life is central to a healthy spirituality. Politics is simply the means we use to organize our shared lives. It is how we express responsible solidarity. Moreover, politics responds to spiritual needs, not just economic needs.

Ironically, the religious folk who deny the connection between religion and politics in our society are also the most adept at exploiting it. The religious right is better organized politically than the religious left. I admire the tactics of the religious right because they at least take evil seriously—although I'm not sure they always identify it accurately or are aware of their own capacity for it. They miss the aspect of evil that hates differences. Philosopher William Irwin Thompson writes, "Evil is destruction of differences; good is the creation of ever new differences. The good emphasized diversity, individuation . . . and the participation in the universal through the unique." This echoes the philosophical notion that the "good" see reality as an integrated whole, an interconnected web, whereas the "bad" divide reality up into unrelated little lumps. The "good" make connections, the "bad" fragment. True communion celebrates differences—a principle not usually honored by the religious right.

Passionate Engagement

Those monks who taught me to fight apartheid in South Africa were driven by a passion for the humanly human. This kind of passion for the beauty of communion led to social action. They believed that we are called to be in love with the world and with each other, and that loving in this way could get you into trouble.

How do you prepare for this passionate engagement with the world? By prayer. Besides expressing sheer amazement at the miracle of being, prayer, for the monks, was a way of concentrating love so that action would spring not from anger, but from a clarity about the call to communion that left no one out. It also involved a commitment to self-knowledge. The twin prerequisites for prayer, they said, are an acknowledgment of our own fragility and a sense of wonder. These help us be more generous to people of other faiths and to "those whose faith is known to God alone." The monks didn't recommend the way of safety.

So compelled were they by the vision of God's hospitality toward the unqualified and rejected that they broke the law by breaking bread with dishonored people of another race. When I visited these monks in Johannesburg in the early 1980s, I had lunch with then Bishop Desmond Tutu and I drove, without permission, out to see some friends in Soweto Township. When it was pointed out that I was breaking the law, it was a wake-up call to me. Simple acts of friendship, in some parts of the world, are considered illegal.

The monks encouraged me to be subversive for the sake of communion, and I have tried to be ever since. The theater of the Spirit is peopled with thrilling images of love and mercy in a community centered around a table from which no one is excluded. The images of a subversive Eucharistic table set the political and social agenda for our being in the world.

Communion of Body, Mind, and Spirit

We are beginning to understand ourselves in a holistic way. The sense of solidarity—both negative and positive—is beginning to take hold. We live in a networked world not only economically but also spiritually. And there have been new breakthroughs in modern medicine, for example, that have corroborated the ancient wisdom that told us that the integration of body, mind, and spirit is essential for human flourishing and for understanding how life works.

It turns out, for example, that all kinds of physical ills, from cold sores to herpes to mononucleosis, can be aggravated by chronic unhappiness or anxiety. Caretakers of Alzheimer's patients have been found to manifest stress by a reduced number of disease-fighting T cells in their blood. We compromise the communion of body, mind, and spirit to our detriment.

Through taking part in scientific study of men with prostate cancer, I learned that stress reduction was as important as diet and exercise. Stress reduction implicitly recognizes the importance of prayer and meditation in healing. The relationship to mind and body is complementary and complex. It is designed for communion. There is no separate mind detached from the material matter of the brain.

Science writer Matt Ridley notes that we "instinctively assume that bodily biochemistry is cause whereas behavior is effect," but he demonstrates that this need not be true. The psychological can precede the physical, and the spiritual precedes both. So when you are stressed by a life event, you become more vulnerable to infection, cancer, and heart disease, but the reverse also is true. When you are part of a loving community, able to laugh and experience joy, your immune system is in better shape. There are some good side effects of going to Mass or practicing mindfulness!

The January 2000 issue of the *Harvard Women's Health Watch* provided twenty suggestions for healthy living. Here's the final one:

> *Keep the faith.* One practice that has emerged as healthful is attending religious services. Several observational studies indicate that people who belong to religious groups of any faith, sect, or denomination tend to be less vulnerable to a host of conditions—from colds to depression to death. That doesn't mean immortality is the reward of going to services. But it does suggest that during periods in which people were surveyed, the death rate tended to be lower among people in religious congregations than in the population as a whole.

This isn't to reduce spiritual disciplines to the useful and pragmatic. It's simply affirming that body, mind, and spirit are meant to be in communion. You might get the same benefits if you went bowling or had a dog.

Our task, as we wake up to ourselves as integrated beings in a living system, is to find the means of "defrosting" ourselves for the sake of wholeness and community. The old name for this is conversion—but conversion in the sense of a radical turning, a new course that changes everything, including what we do to our bodies and what we put in them. The slow and committed path of integrating body, mind, and spirit will change the way we operate, behave, think, and feel.

Caught in a Living System:
How Communion Works

The business mentor Richard Pascale and his associates have written the book *Surfing the Edge of Chaos: The Laws of Nature and the Laws of Business,* which deserves attention beyond the field of business management. They describe principles of living systems that could well be applied to religious communities and the search for communion. We are part of a living system whether we like it or not, and it's enlightening to learn how it functions.

Pascale outlines four principles of living systems that can be applied to the Trinitarian quest for freedom in communion:

1. Equilibrium is death.
2. Innovation usually takes place on the edge of chaos.
3. Self-organization and emergence occur naturally.
4. Organizations cannot be directed, only disturbed.

Without going into a lot of detail, we can glimpse what these ideas might mean in practice as we seek to reform religious institutions. These ideas can shake up our ideas of authority and hierarchy: since innovation usually takes place on the edge of chaos, the solution to a problem and/or the source of a bold new initiative can originate anywhere in the system. We should be prepared for surprises, since innovation can come from any source.

In my own life, for example, healthy change came from a signal from the body when I was diagnosed with prostate cancer. Unexpectedly, it was something biological, not psychological or spiritual, that shook up my whole system and pushed me into a deeper commitment to wholeness. I also found out that I couldn't seek healing just for the cancer. The system itself was demanding attention and integrity.

What are some of the implications of living systems theory for religious institutions? If social engineering from the top is obsolete, what could this mean for the papacy or the Southern Baptist Convention, for ecclesiastical authority in general? Imagine the

Roman Catholic Church unleashing its considerable and wonderful distributed intelligence throughout the world.

Another Pascale principle is "the power of positive deviance." Its basic tenet is that the wisdom to solve problems exists and needs to be discovered within each community. It is a way of looking at something that works when the "evidence" says it shouldn't.

He gives the example of undernourished children in a village in Vietnam. Against the evidence, there were exceptional families in which the children appeared to be reasonably nourished. Why? They discovered that the exceptional families were feeding their children more frequently and adding freshwater shrimp and crab and sweet-potato leaves to the basic rice diet. "Positive Deviance has the feel of a dance and a courtship, as opposed to a march and an invasion. Essential to the approach is first, respect for, and second, alliance with the intelligence and capacities residing within the village." Here, in a nutshell, is a little parable of how authority is distributed throughout a system and how true communion is thereby fostered.

Pascale also voices a maxim that is pregnant with possibility and hope: "When you begin to talk about the future in a creative way, the future begins to alter the present." A vision of communion that respects the principles of living systems—that upsets the status quo, braves chaos, asks leadership of all, and disturbs the peace—could start to make a difference quickly.

The Radical Hospitality of a Transformed Community

I am struck over and over again how churches protect the Tradition instead of letting it loose. The Catholic theologian and Jesuit Karl Rahner taught that Christianity is permanently growing and in process. Being a faithful Christian is not simply a matter of preserving the past, but rather it is a courageous engagement with what is new, with what seems strange. Christian maturity is coming to love the subversive freedom of a God who will not be pinned down. Like most institutions, we at Grace Cathedral in San Francisco resist the Spirit and avoid risk as much as possible. But we live in one of the great crossroads of the world, like it or not. I have the privilege of being part of a community dedicated to daily prayer. This ground bass of prayer coupled with the lively glory and tragedy of living in a modern city bring together two aspects of the work of the Spirit— the still, small voice and its wind and fire. We catch glimpses of what true communion might look like, a communion that transcends the confines of one tradition or tribe.

Our risk lies in choosing each other over and over again in the face of failure and disappointment. This is what being in love means. The Church is a dangerous place because it calls out the best in us—the desire to do right and to be good (not in a goody-goody way but in the deep sense of being true to who we are in God). It is dangerous because we forget that the adventure originates with God and that it is beautiful. When we forget that our longing for the good and the true is grounded in the beautiful, the spiritual life degenerates into moralism and perfectionism. A cruel idealism overtakes us. Resentments are mobilized, and we become harsh in our judgments. Living in the Spirit is a matter of choice not to live from our resentments and disappointments but from our new life in communion.

What would a community open to the Spirit look like? One way the Spirit works on us to build community is through repentance (saying sorry) and compunction (having the heart punctured, being cut to the quick). They provide protocols against abuse and manipulation. The capacity to feel sorry for what we have done and the grace to admit it give public debate the lucidity it needs to go forward. So one way to move ahead is to understand that community is not an end in itself but a by-product of a vision of what human beings are that stretches us beyond our limits and continually introduces us to new possibilities.

The work of the Spirit is to unsettle us through love by opening us to positive deviance. We don't build community by building community. We build it by having our eye on something else. What is that something? Christians see it in God's great risk of communion, manifested in the Eucharistic table, from which no one is excluded.

The Spirit also is practical, pushing issues at us in the democratic experiment, in the confusion and challenge of everyday life. A democratic society requires citizens who can repent—admit their mistakes and not gloss over their shameful acts. A democratic society needs citizens who are committed to telling the truth even if they seldom get it quite right. It is our seldom getting it right that necessitates ongoing conversation and our ongoing conversion.

In short, the Spirit calls us to be a compassionate and critical community with clear values. A strenuous form of spiritual maturity is demanded of us if we are to meet Thomas Merton's challenge to protect and defend human freedom, integrity, and individuality. Being is communion. This is what the Trinity is trying to teach us.

15

The Challenge of Christ
Christian Life and Practice

Jesus, the Son of God

Over lunch one Sunday, John Dominic Crossan and a group of us talked. "Imagine," Dominic said, "a conversation taking place in the first century between a Roman citizen and one of these new Christians. The Roman asks, 'What's all this about Jesus?' The Christian replies, 'We believe he is the Son of God.' 'Oh really?' replies the Roman, not overly surprised because 'Sons of God' were not uncommon. 'We have a Son of God, too. Emperor Augustus.'" In other words, they wouldn't get caught in an argument about whether somebody was the Son of God—that was a given.

What was really at stake is the true nature of power. Is it to be seen in the Imperium of Rome or in a Jewish itinerant preacher who ends up on a cross? As Dominic put it, it is much easier and safer to discuss whether God exists, whether Jesus is the Son of God, whether mother Mary is a virgin than to discuss the demands of justice in light of what is revealed about the true nature of power. We're back to the necessity of bringing together "What would Jesus do?" with "What does justice demand?" Those competing parables about power (does it reside in Jesus or in Augustus?) present a far more dangerous choice: Does God exist as justice or as naked power? Is that justice incarnate in Jesus or incarnate in Augustus? If God creates the world as a communion of all beings in covenant with one another, think of the implications for how we are to be in the world. We have the power to choose which path to follow. Are you a neighbor or a consumer? Are everyone you meet rivals or companions? Do we build up a community or are we always at war?

God's Word to Us about Ourselves

Christians follow a strange path of faith. We have some good news to share, but we are always open to new information. We hold these two texts together: "We declare to you what was from the beginning," and "In their joy they were disbelieving." These words come from a couple of verses from the New Testament. The first is I John 1:1–2:2: "We declare to you what was from the beginning, what we have heard and what we have seen with our eyes, what we have looked at and touched with our hands, concerning the word of life." The second is in the "Peace be with you" section in Luke 24:36b–48. The disciples were startled and terrified at the appearance of Jesus after the crucifixion. He says to them, "Look at my hands and my feet; see that it is myself. Touch me and see." Luke goes on, "In their joy they were disbelieving."

St. John's gospel begins, "In the beginning was the Word . . ." In the beginning was the communication, the conversation, the act that created the world as a covenanted reality. Christianity, from the beginning, was a great dialogue—a *conversation*. The first conversation was when Hebrew Christianity met the culture of the Greeks. And what a meeting. What an explosion! The Jesuit theologian William Johnston suggests that we are in a unique position today to appreciate what it was like when Christianity launched out into the deep of the surrounding cultures in the first century. The Mediterranean world was a supermarket of beliefs—the California of the ancient world. We, too, are in the middle of a cultural revolution that is causing enormous spiritual dislocation.

The big task of inculturation began with Paul—a Jew from Tarsus who could speak Greek, a mystic and an intellectual. He realized that the Gentiles didn't need to be circumcised to enjoy the communion God willed for them. There was a great fight about whether to include the Gentiles, and Paul won the day. Then Peter saw a vision telling him that nothing was unclean—everyone could be included. Yet telling a story about God coming as one of us and dying on a cross as a way of showing that life is a party and everyone's invited was a scandal to some and downright daft to others. It still is.

There emerged a mystical tradition that took communion with God and with each other as the prime project of Christianity. Communion, relationship, is *prior to* belief. It is a mistake to think that you have to swallow a few correct beliefs before you can embark on the spiritual journey. This mistake, in part, is what can make religion such a dried-up, miserable affair. You are *already* on the journey.

I once asked the spiritual mentor Ram Dass what game we were in. "Being at one with the Beloved," he said. That's not particularly Hindu. That's not exclusively Christian. It is simply true. The Word of God—Jesus—isn't the property of Christians. Thich Nhat Hanh, a Buddhist monk who has touched the lives of millions in the West, isn't in the business of "converting" people to Buddhism. He encourages them to deepen their commitment to their own roots and join with others in practicing compassion and love in action.

Since we're living in a world where God is being decentralized and democratized, people want direct experience and resist all forms of authority, even when it is legitimate. Buddhism is attractive in the West because of this appeal to direct experience. The Buddha says, "He who sees me, sees the *dhamma* (the teaching), and he who sees the *dhamma* sees me." He *is* the teaching. This may help some to understand Jesus as the Word of God. Think about Jesus and how we understand Christ. "He who has seen me has seen the Father. He who sees me, sees the Word and he who sees the *Word* sees me."

On one hand, we know a lot less about the historical figure of Jesus than we thought we did. On the other, we are discovering more variety in the Christian tradition as we discover new voices from the past. This is the result of well over a hundred years of New Testament scholarship. Karen Armstrong points out that "this has not prevented millions of people from modeling their lives on Jesus and seeing his path of compassion and suffering as leading to a new kind of life. Jesus certainly existed, but his story has been presented in the Gospels as a paradigm."

Jesus *is* the Way to a new kind of life. Jesus and Buddha have this in common with all great spiritual teachers—to make human beings more conscious of themselves, to get to be more real. What attracts me to Jesus is that he has a distinct personality, in contrast to the Buddha, although wonderful stories about the Buddha's life have been written.

The Snare of Experience: Making Jesus in Our Image

When it comes to Jesus, we begin with finding ways to experience his presence. It's tricky because experience is an odd thing. It's a hybrid—something caught between an event and its interpretation. A monk friend used to say, "Just because you've experienced it doesn't mean it really happened!" To which another friend responded, "Just because it happened doesn't mean you experienced it!" Both statements are true. Something happens to us and we look at it through the prism of our beliefs and assumptions, and we have an "experience." We need two skills: one, accuracy in stating what happened; and two, self-knowledge about the lens through which we look at life. A friend of mine often used to say, "I know it's true. I know it happened this way. It's in my journal." When she said this, her family rolled their eyes in disbelief. My friend's journals were often a device for her to make sense of her reality and more often than not had little relationship to how her husband or children experienced those same events.

In short, if we start with experience (and I think we should), we're in for a rough ride. We're wedded to poetry, myth, metaphor, and the dangers of subjectivity. That's why we need each other to keep testing for reality. We make Jesus in our own image. He has been made into the pale Galilean of late Victorian piety, the Marxist of the shallow end of left-wing politics, the individualist of free enterprise. The Irish

Jesuit George Tyrrell—excommunicated for accepting the findings of the then new biblical criticism—made the point a hundred years ago that in any search for the historical Jesus, we end up seeing our own reflection in the bottom of a deep well.

When I was growing up, Jesus was very much an English gentleman, a good sport, and would have loved a game of cricket. And when Scripture was read on Sunday morning, the Hebrew prophets all sounded as if they went to minor public (private in Britain) schools. Texts change radically, depending on who's reading them. A. N. Wilson comments in *God's Funeral* (referring to the Jesus of classical scholar and clergyman Benjamin Jowett), "he might very well have been to Rugby and won a scholarship to Balliol." When I hear a Texas evangelist speak about Jesus, it's no wonder Jesus comes across as someone born in Lubbock. We can never step out of our culture. Each of us lives in a particular place at a particular time.

But even when we have taken into account the dangers, inaccuracies, and pitfalls of religion based on experience (with its violent behavior, repellent doctrines, and thin moralism), there's a discernible Spirit of Jesus that is healing and compassionate in the New Testament, in the Fathers and Mothers of the Church, in the sacraments (particularly the Eucharist), and in the experience of Christians through time. It is a Spirit that is dynamic, loving; it invites others into being; and it does not bully or coerce. It is the Spirit of Jesus.

The Challenge of Being Christlike

What does it mean to follow Jesus? What was he like? What do his followers do, and what are their distinguishing characteristics? It seems as if there are as many answers as there are Christians. There is a tendency to identify Christianity with a single set of authorized beliefs. Not only is there no such single set of beliefs, neither is there an absolute path to being Christlike. This is partly because the subject of Christian life is a place where many of the historical, theological, and psychological challenges of being a Christian come home to roost. Christian life has been played out in different ways throughout its history, and over the centuries Christians have argued about many issues, including grace, free will, sexuality, and social justice. There also are distinctive pieties in the various traditions, and sometimes the differences are radical, particularly around issues about who is included and who is excluded from the community of faith.

One has to have a sense of humor and irony to have a vigorous spiritual life because of its apparently hypocritical nature. We say one thing and do another. Comedian George Burns came up with a piece of advice for aspiring actors: "The most important thing about acting is honesty. If you can fake that, you've got it made." This isn't as cynical as it sounds. Human beings grow into the roles they eventually play in the world by acting *as if* they were already familiar with and proficient in them. The authentic life begins with acting as if something were the case. Act as if justice mattered, even in the most corrupt situations, and justice will then have a chance.

Often what trips up both people of faith and those who criticize them is a crippling idealism. Because of the high idealism involved, all forms of piety and practice are easily caricatured, and a sense of humor and irony is essential for the life of faith.

In spite of differences, common patterns emerge. On the whole, Christians are for peacemaking over war and for reconciliation over retaliation. The practical morality of giving a cup of cold water to someone in need is central. "And whoever in the name of a disciple gives to one of these little ones even a cup of cold water to drink, truly I say to you, he shall not lose his reward" (Matthew 10:42). And because self-righteousness and moralism are traps into which believers fall, penitence also is essential: "The sacrifice of God is troubled spirit; a broken and contrite heart, O God, you will not despise" (Psalm 51).

The Vision of Humans in Community

What then is a human being from the point of view of Christian life? What kind of people are Christians? The mystical tradition defined a human being as made in the image of God (and therefore free). A human being is a *capax Dei* and *Deo congruens* (a capacity for God and God-shaped). Therefore Christian life is a matter of sharing in the divine life—actually participating in it—as a way of transformation. In the Eastern Church the process is called *theosis*: "God became one of us so we might share in the divine life." In fact, one early writer could talk of the "humanity of God." Christian life is nothing less than sharing in God's life primarily through contact with the community and by sharing in the sacraments.

Therefore, two characteristics of Christian life are freedom and joy. Freedom requires that the question of being human remains open. Joy naturally flows from the experience of being truly free. The ancient formula to describe human purpose was "The glory of God is a human being fully alive." This suggests an open vision of human nature that finds its fulfillment in being orientated toward God. We are what we do with our attention. We are to attend to God and to each other, and this loving attention gives rise to the fully human community.

The poet Dante's vision of heaven is a place of radical mutuality—complete unity in unimaginable diversity. How, then, are we to behave? The fourteenth-century mystic, Lady Julian of Norwich, wrote, "God is kind in his being." And we are to be kind, too—not simply in acts of benevolence but also by being the kind of people who are loving and compassionate. Kindness also suggests family relationship, as in "kindred."

Prayer and Sacraments

The way, then, in which we participate in and/or imitate the life of God-in-Christ is through prayer, both private and corporate, and through sacramental participation (baptism and the Eucharist).

Christian life is much more than behaving in a certain way. It is becoming a certain kind of person through a process of allowing the images to work on us in a long process of transformation. In fact, one image is that of our being pregnant with ourselves. We are midwives to each other in a process of formation. There is suffering, too. Above all, there is communion. The dominant image is that of a banquet to which everyone is invited. We don't live in isolation. The impulse toward society is in our nature.

Don't forget. The principle is "Being *is* communion." Participation in society is necessary for our becoming fully human. St. Thomas Aquinas wrote, "God is not solitary," and neither are we. In fact, Christian life is a kind of love affair in which we all seek to love and be loved in one communion. The ancient mystics believed that Eros is natural to us. We long for God. That's the way we are built, and a Christian life that tries to bypass the passions is no life at all. We were made by love, for love.

Christian life is expressed in certain disciplines that reinforce the narrative structure of that life. Most Christians would agree that reading the Bible (in private prayer and study as well as in communal worship) is central, as is sharing in Holy Communion. Both practices build the Christian character by giving it shape and direction. The Bible provides the architecture of the way Christians think about themselves and the world.

The Embodied Life

Although the Church has a poor history with regard to its understanding of and teaching about the body and sexuality, the body is of central importance to Christian life and to understanding the work of Christ. It is a sacrament of God's presence among us. As obvious as it sounds, it is the way we relate to each other. As the tradition has it, the body is the place where God chooses to dwell. The basic goodness of sexuality and its enjoyment is affirmed, as are the use of food and drink and the disposition of wealth. The traditional monastic vows of poverty, chastity, and obedience express one way of living the embodied life, as does marriage and other committed relationships.

There is risk and hope in human connectedness, and the Christian life is a *connected* life and has been defined as "the art of making connections." These connections are manifested physically by water (baptism), bread and wine (Eucharist), oil (healing), and sexual intercourse (marriage). There is a connection between receiving the bread and wine in the Eucharist and action in the world (social justice).

The fully embodied life is a connected and integrated life of body, mind, and spirit requiring our paying attention to the narrative structure of our lives. They are going somewhere and will come to an end. That's why preparing for death is important and why practices of self-simplification are central. The three traditional disciplines of prayer, almsgiving, and fasting express three basic relationships: prayer in respect to God, almsgiving in respect to others, and fasting in respect to ourselves.

The primary narratives of Christian freedom are enacted in the rituals of baptism (the crossing of the Red Sea) and the Eucharist—the banquet to whom everyone is invited, *without exception.*

The sacramental vision of life is central for me, hence my devotion to the Eucharist. It is the drama of God being with us, being one of us, being on our side. God places himself in our hands as absolute gift. Jesus surrenders himself entirely into our hands. And what about God? Friendship is at the heart of the divine life, according to St. Thomas Aquinas—a friendship that we are called to share. St. Augustine thought of the history of the human family as a vast musical score in which all the wrong notes and bad rhythms were led into harmonic resolution. In *De Musica* he wrote, "Dissonance can be redeemed without being obliterated."

The story of redemption is like a great symphony that embraces all our errors, our bum notes, and in which beauty finally triumphs. The victory is not that God wipes out our wrong notes, or pretends that they never happened, but that He finds a place for them in the musical score that redeems them. This happens above all in the Eucharist.

There's a statement by the parish of St. Gregory Nyssen in San Francisco that captures the spirit of this *shared spiritual* journey I have tried to illuminate through the primordial images of Christianity. St. Gregory of Nyssa, who lived in the fourth century, saw life as an unending process of discovering how God is at work among us and in the world. Sin is the refusal to keep on growing in this discovery of the most important truth of all.

"This is true perfection: not to avoid a wicked life because we fear punishment, like slaves; not to do good because we expect repayment, as cashing in on the virtuous life by enforcing some business deal. On the contrary, disregarding all those good things we hope for and that God has promised us, we regard falling from God's friendship as the only thing dreadful, and we consider becoming God's friend the only thing truly worthwhile."

It's matter of falling in love, and falling in love gets you pregnant, introduces you to peculiar form of suffering, and invites you into the adventure of communion.

The Converted Life

The goal of the converted life is to find God in all things and is based on the conviction of the unity of reality. Everything is connected. St. Ignatius Loyola (1491–1556) tells us that those advanced in the spiritual life constantly contemplate God in every creature. This life is based on trusting the immediate relationship we have with God, since a human being is, by definition, the place where God chooses to dwell. Human beings aren't meant to be solitary, and we find out who we are and what we are about in the company of others, through a constant process of conversion. The traditional Benedictine greeting is "Please pray for my conversion, as I pray for yours."

Christians claim that something happens to us when we follow Jesus and see him in everyone we meet, just as something happened to the followers of Jesus in his own day. What did they see in Jesus? New Testament scholar Walter Wink puts it this way: They saw a human being fully alive, and for them, such life carried divine power and authority. But more important, this way of being fully and freely human "had now entered the heart of reality as a catalyst in human transformation. Like a bell that reverberates to the core of our being [Jesus, the incarnate Word of God], the Human Being is, as it were, an invitation to become the fullness of who we are. And with the invitation comes the power to do it." Being a Christian and following Jesus, then, is a way of becoming pregnant with ourselves. We are to be born again, and not just once, but many times.

16

Revising the Great Story

"I don't see clouds and water like that," a woman once said to the painter Turner. "Don't you wish you could, madam?" he replied.

I believe our task is to develop a moral and aesthetic imagination deep enough and wide enough to encompass the contradictions of our time and history, the tremendous loss and tragedy as well as greatness and nobility, an imagination capable of recognizing that where there is light there is shadow, that out of hubris and fall can come moral regeneration, out of suffering and death, resurrection and rebirth.

—Richard Tarnas

Human beings cannot live without a story, and some of the stories they have told themselves are horrendous. These stories have reinforced lesser solidarities at the expense of greater ones. A lesser communion has been paid for by excluding or even killing others. But the principle behind the story is that "Being *is* communion, reality *is* relationship." Our myths are about how we relate to each other and the world (either as allies or enemies) and how we understand our place in the scheme of things. Another principle is, "How a thing shows itself depends on the relationship." The work of the late mythologist Joseph Campbell was largely to point out the fourfold relational function of all our mythmaking. Its purpose is to forge a relationship between us and the mystery of being (which some call God), the physical world, others, and our deepest selves. We can do that by exclusion or inclusion. The choice is always ours.

What makes it all wondrous is that there is no exact repetition in the storyteller. The text of the story may never change, but its texture changes in the telling. There have been millions of human beings, even millions of your particular tribe, but there has never been anyone quite like you. This fact—that each of us is radically unique—has implications for the story and the way we are to tell it. It will not be a generic story of a species but the great adventure (sometimes lonely) of becoming a person in the company of other persons. It will not be simply *our* story, but it will uniquely yours, too. So we look for a story (in which we uniquely take part) that celebrates our differences (our becoming free persons) in the deepest possible way for the sake of communion.

The Troubling Stories of the Bible

The Bible is central for Christians and speaks through its many and various stories, myths, and poems to the miracle of becoming a person, but the Bible is a difficult book for me. It is always being appropriated for partisan purposes, and I find that its great messages can best be received indirectly through, for example, poetry. I wish people who quote the Bible admitted that they were puzzled by it. Anyone reading it today should be mystified by it. As Robert Carroll puts it: "If reading the Bible does *not* raise profound problems for you as a modern reader, then check with your doctor and inquire about the symptoms of brain-death." I have found my way back into the Bible—into a Bible of depth, difficulty, and diversity. I find it disturbing and puzzling. It is always challenging my interpretation of things.

I find that treating the Bible literally kills its ability to probe me with disturbing questions. Literalism kills argument, and what's great about the Bible is that it invites dispute and conversation. The ancient rabbis went in for *endless* interpretation. That's why I can believe it could be the Word of God. Its meaning is elusive and leads to more and more questions. The philosopher Nietzsche described the Hebrew Bible as the best book in the world. It had this distinction because it is not just a system of worship and beliefs. The Bible is great because it is in constant *argument* with itself.

On December 21, 1613, Galileo wrote a letter to Benedetto Castelli Benedictine, his best and most beloved student, about the view that Holy Scripture cannot err and that the decrees in it are absolutely true and inviolable:

> I should only have added that, though Scripture cannot err, its expounders and interpreters are liable to err in many ways . . . when they would base themselves on the literal meaning of words. For in this wise not only many contradictions would be apparent, but even grave heresies and blasphemies, since then it would be necessary to give God hands and feet and eyes, and human and bodily emotions such as anger, regret, hatred, and sometimes forgetfulness of things past, and ignorance of the future.

Besides, there are other "stories" that call for our attention. In the Middle Ages, the mystics saw the necessity of reading from three books: the Bible, the Book of Nature, and the Book of Experience. One wasn't enough. The Bible, cut off from the other two books, becomes a self-authenticating collection of magic spells and incantations that are true because they are true. There is no way to test those truths. We no longer stone people (thank God) for breaking certain rules. At some point some sane scholar or rabbi protested and said, "The Bible cannot mean *that*! There must be a deeper meaning. Let's go find it." Yet gay people are condemned, based on a thin reading of Leviticus. Thus the spirit of the Bible (a great story of the breakdown of divisions and the celebration of communion) is betrayed by a narrow reading.

Think of what the United States has had to do to write the story about itself, which included all the immigrants from other lands. At the same time, it had to rework the story to make room for the dark chapters of slavery and the treatment of the indigenous peoples. Europe is going through a similar retelling of its story. Goethe observed that European unity was forged by pilgrimages on which Latins and Germans, Celts and Slavs, Angles and Saxons exchanged stories and songs. Now we are being forced to read from the Book of Nature in a way never before experienced. Father Thomas Berry describes Americans as "autistic" with respect to nature—"people so locked up in themselves that no one and nothing else can get in. We are talking to ourselves. We are not talking to the river, we are not listening to the river."

At this time in our history, we need to read more than one story. The Bible, as we have butchered it, isn't enough. Together we are working on an emerging global story, and even though we are a long way from realizing it, there is no human adventure to match it. The task of making our lives into a story involves the art of being able to see the same event from different perspectives. It may seem like a small step, but realizing that there is more than one point of view is crucial. Taking this small step is often difficult for those who only look to the Bible uncritically. They are unable to accept the generosity of God, who "speaks" to us in many voices. They unintentionally betray the deep stories of the Bible when they deny the possibility of a God who is alive and speaking to us in the stories of other tribes.

As the world looks for a new story, we have to admit that we have gone as far as we can with the old tribal narratives of the religious traditions. "My God is bigger and better than yours!" is a slogan that has to go. Yet the new story isn't strictly new. It's the old story of the cosmos. It strikes us as new because it is based on something we have forgotten—on a generous and inclusive vision of what it is to be human. Its stance is one of trembling with awe before mystery. Wonder is central, and wonder has been exiled. Cosmologist Brian Swimme and others insist that the universe itself is a story and we are part of it. "Every child can be told, 'You come out of the energy that gave birth to the universe; it is your beginning. You came out of the fire that fashioned the galaxies; it is alive within you.'" Now the cosmos itself has to be the context of our storytelling. Many of us already know the facts of cosmology, but we haven't incorporated them into our story. We also have failed to include the amazing story of our biology. We have failed to see the relevance of the miracle of the universe and the wonder of our bodies. What have they to do with storytelling?

How Large a World Are You Prepared to See?

In 1662 the Royal Society of London was established because (said its founders) people did not know what to look for or how. The eye refuses to accept what the mind does not know.

There's a story of a woman who had been blind since childhood. After she had radical surgery, she saw four brilliant shafts of light separated by dark valleys. Puzzled, she turned to a nurse, to be told that she was looking at her own fingers. There is evidence from early eye surgeries (when surgeons first learned to remove cataracts) that some patients who had their sight restored overnight were plunged into a mystery that overwhelmed them. They had no visual idea of form, size, or distance. Some even asked for the bandages to be replaced. When one was asked how big her mother was, she set her two index fingers a few inches apart. Some took months to tell the difference between a sheep and a tree. A comment of poet Gerard Manley Hopkins comes to mind: "When I look hard at something it seems to look hard at me *as if my eye were still growing*"(italics mine).

Our eyes need to grow if we are to tell a new story that calls us to communion. So we begin not with Adam and Eve, but 4 billion years ago, when life began in the seas. Life came ashore only 425 million years ago. Our immediate ancestors were relative newcomers, showing up 423 million years later. *Homo erectus* came on the scene 750,000 years ago, and *Homo sapiens* 150,000 years after that. Our crowd, *Homo sapiens sapiens,* has been around for only about 90,000 years. That's the background to our story, which celebrates our solidarity with the other animals. We are reminded that we share more than 98 percent of our DNA with the chimpanzee. And—wonder of wonders—this human creature began to speak and tell stories.

Why begin with the story of the planet and the emergence of language? It's important because it provides the context for all our storytelling and helps us get off the treadmill of a cyclical view of time as one damn thing after another repeating itself over and over—the same old mistakes and messes. And this brings me back to the Bible. The Hebrew Scriptures are a great gift to the human family in pushing for the kind of storytelling that moved us from the spatial to the developmental, from the cyclic to the view that we were going someplace. It helps us see that stories change over time. They need to—the stories of race, class, the stories of women and gay people. The stories of who's in and who's out.

The emerging story—to be true—will have elements of destruction and loss. In the Hebrew Scriptures we find key elements of the story in the narratives of Exodus and Exile. Neither will the story bypass the inevitability of death and the facing of emptiness. There will also be "shadow work," of which psychologist Carl Jung wrote so eloquently. The hidden, dark, and repressed parts of ourselves are ignored at our peril.

Storytelling Is Dangerous

Briony is the protagonist in Ian McEwan's novel *Atonement*. We follow her through her long life, beginning with her discovery at age thirteen that she is a budding writer. At the beginning of the book she watches her older sister strip down to her underwear and submerge herself into a fountain to retrieve pieces of a broken vase. She realizes that the scene could be written from three different points of view—hers, her sister's, and the young man watching. What's more, she experienced the freedom of being able to observe a scene without judgment—without having to look at what happens and decide whether it's good or bad and who the heroes and villains are.

> None of these three was bad, nor were they particularly good. She need not judge. There did not have to be a moral. She need only show separate minds, as alive as her own, struggling with the idea that other minds were equally alive. It wasn't only wickedness and scheming that made people unhappy, it was confusion and misunderstanding; above all, it was the failure to grasp the simple truth that other people are as real as you. And

only in story could you enter these different minds and show how they had an equal value. That was the only moral a story need have.

There is so much wisdom packed into these few lines that we might easily pass by it too quickly. The novel, in part, is about Briony's betrayal and struggle with these liberating principles, which she discerned as a teenager. A story well written is just that, and it becomes truly "moral" when it is free of moralizing. Stories exist in a strange middle ground. If they are good, they are true and not true at the same time. We cannot do without them, but they are notoriously unreliable. We are caught in our own interpretations and the interpretations of others, and those interpretations are often distorted, yet we cannot dispense with them. Convinced of their truth, we suppress the fact that they are necessary constructions, so we are caught between construction and deconstruction. Briony in the novel is trapped by her own hurt and inventiveness and causes a lie to unravel and damage lives. Her life is largely an attempt to tell a healing and atoning story.

The Bible is full of people doing immoral acts (King David lusts after Bathsheba and has her husband, Uriah, killed, to name just two). The power of the biblical stories is not so much in their ability to teach morality as in their brilliance in showing us how human beings make mistakes and become more fully human.

The failure to grasp the simple truth that other people are as real as you or I is perhaps the first false step on our journey through life. Just to know that people are genuinely "other" than oneself and not mere projections of our own egos is a major spiritual achievement and would help us be more accurate and compassionate in our storytelling. Storytelling also helps us understand the true nature of our believing. We don't actually *believe* things. We tell stories about people and things to place them in some relation to each other. Christian "belief" in the Trinity, for example, is a code word for a story about the nature of love as seeing and respecting the otherness of others. The Trinity is a "story" about love and the mystery of unity and identity being both preserved and honored without domination or confusion. A "doctrine" is not like a fact to be believed but rather a way of being in the world that is validated by experience. Theologians argue whether we ever could have found words for the experience of that kind of love without the controversies and the conversations about doctrine. Doctrine gives us the language to articulate something entirely new in our experience. Its structure is a conversation that never ends.

The Importance of Remorse

We need a story but we also need the discipline not to jump to conclusions, to come to the place of nakedness beyond all interpretations. Briony has to atone for her wild and premature hermeneutics—her narcissistic interpretations of things. Repentance—the ability to acknowledge that first false step and the willingness to begin again—is built into great storytelling, not least the telling of the story of our life.

The philosopher Richard Tarnas emphasizes the importance of remorse in our telling the human story because "The consensus is decisive; the world is in some essential sense a construct. Human knowledge is radically interpretive." This means that our constructs are penultimate, are sometimes wildly inaccurate, and can always be deepened. Tarnas goes on to quote Octavio Paz: "The examination of conscience, and the remorse that accompanies it, which is a legacy of Christianity, has been, and is, the single and most powerful remedy against the ills of our civilization." And what will this remorse look like? Tarnas comments:

> It will be a grief of the masculine for the feminine; of men for women; of adults for what has happened to children; of the West for what has happened to every other part of the world; of Judeo-Christianity for pagans and indigenous peoples; of Christians for Jews; of whites for people of color; of the wealthy for the poor; of human beings for animals and all other forms of life. It will take a fundamental metanoia, a self-overcoming, a radical sacrifice, to make this transition.

Remorse is essential because the story the planet needs now is one that isn't just from one tribe but from all tribes. There will be no peace or justice until everyone has been heard from. And insofar as our little narratives about ourselves render others invisible, we will be peddling lies.

Think of the competing interpretive myths of heroic progress and tragic fall. Greek tragedy still speaks to us because it rings true. Hubris brings us down. The myths are in our blood. However, we tend to construct stories from which the tragic has been eliminated. Contrast the actual life of a great artist such as Judy Garland with the character of Dorothy in *The Wizard of Oz*. The Judy Garland story cannot be told without an element of tragedy.

Tarnas changes H. G. Wells's dictum that "we are engaged in a race between education and catastrophe" to "we are engaged in a race between initiation and catastrophe." Religion is about initiation, and that's why it won't go away. Religion is about the kind of story-telling that initiates us into a larger reality. Repentance is part of the method because the story is always capable of revision. Participating in our own story with joy and remorse is important because if we don't wake up and live our story consciously, the story will go on without us. This is serious. There is an epidemic of depression in our culture, and I wonder if much of it is because we're cut off from any meaningful narrative in our lives. The stories live in us rather than us living in the stories.

The Story Is Never Fully Told

When it comes to Christianity, there's been something of crisis—to my mind, a false one—about the stories of the Bible. Are they to be trusted? If so, in what way? Are the words attributed to Jesus in the New Testament really his? My approach has always been skeptical with regard to the text and open with regard to the tradition. I don't believe that what we can know of Jesus is confined by the New Testament. We have two thousand years of experience and worship to draw on, and what emerges for me is a coherent and amazing personality. We can get to the truth only through inference—through myth and poetry, through metaphor and storytelling. There is no such thing as "what really happened." That's why history is always being rewritten.

In spite of its impossibility, we are always trying to rewrite history (our own personal story as well as national and international history) in the hope that we will be able to get to the bottom of what "really happened." It's our way of trying to understand our pain. Imagine what it would be like to have one's life revealed to the world through the distorted vision of someone else's prejudice and hurt. On a larger scale, this is what the powerful always have done to the weak. The rich (those who control the stories and the images) interpret the lives of the poor— as indolent or deserving, troublesome or to be pitied. The poor, of course, tell their own stories, but are not heard by those in power.

This raises the important question of the relationship between myth and reality. How are myths tested and regulated? How do we undermine destructive and harmful myths? How do we choose between or among conflicting stories? We are all in the business of mythologizing our lives. We cannot help it, but our mythologies need challenging and correcting from time to time in light of a great myth or story that has been tested over time.

I often wonder what has actually happened in my life and to my generation. I seem to be in a continual process of reassessment. Several years ago, over a meal, my son and I had one of those theological conversations that a father treasures. It was just the two of us. Edward was fourteen at the time and had left home to go away to school. He'd had "religion" up to his ears and was beginning to think for himself. "It's all in your head, Dad," he said with a certain amount of amused exasperation. I agreed with him, and we got into a discussion of exactly what is going on in our heads and how whatever is in them gets in and out. Edward's imagination was alive and probing. He was looking, as was appropriate, to the future. What was going to be the shape of the future for him? I, on the other hand, was more interested in the past (I hope not stuck in it) because, as a friend of mine puts it, "The present is what the past is doing now." Such musings were appropriate for a father who was old enough to be both shamed by and grateful for his past. Was I, I wondered, becoming an old fart, one of the great army of the faithful disillusioned? What began to intrigue me that evening was the way in which the past changes and shifts, and how we perceive it by the workings of the imagination. Life is a continual readjustment, which brings me back to the roving pain inside. It's a pain we need, a pain that calls us back to a life that cannot be controlled or manipulated. It calls us into the life of faith.

We Need a New Vocabulary

On reflection, I now realize that the people I knew when I was growing up and many of the people I meet now had and have no language for storytelling. They are starved of a particular vocabulary to describe what's going on inside them.

Journalist Andrew Solomon, who knows depression from the inside, writes, "Because the poor have limited access to the language of mental illness, their depression is not usually manifested cognitively." What does this mean? It means that people do not interpret their condition as psychological or spiritual. Intervention is required. When I was growing up, the words *therapy* and *psychological* were associated with going crazy or with psychotic outbursts. That was the only model then for mental illness. Besides, therapy and other psychological treatments were for the wealthy. Solomon writes of a Latina woman who, poor and depressed, was given a tonic (in this case, antidepressants) and felt better as a result, but "the idea of a debilitating mental illness that was not rendering her incoherent was outside her lexicon." She had no language to frame her experience, no way to tell her story.

I think that the Church, at its best, gives a new vocabulary for being more and more aware and alive. We are given a language of inclusion and hospitality, a lexicon of mutuality and community. We don't always use it well or speak it fluently, but it is available to us. And being able to speak the language of love helps us place our resources, our money, in the right context. Money becomes a sacrament rather than something that's simply our property. Why?

Because in the language of God's hospitality we know that we are all guests and hosts on this planet and here for only a short time. Everyone has heard the refrain "You can't take it with you!" The difference is that now we believe it. So if you can't take "it" with you, what are you going to do with "it"—with your time, with your talents, with your money, with you?

I now see the relationship between poverty and the absence of any meaningful story or history. Most people around me when I was growing up believed that they had nothing important to say to the world. Or if there was a story to tell, they had no vocabulary. Within the context of the family, my grandmother could spin a good yarn, but we didn't know how much was embellishment and how much was simply making it all up. Real history was the realm of kings, emperors, and popes. She always voted for the ruling class at the time (the Tories) because, as she said, "they were born to rule." If she had a story, it was shaped by fatalism. Others could influence the world and add their story. We couldn't. People like us were stuck. Others ruled the world. We had no say in it.

The Catholic Imagination

The life of faith provides us with both narrative and lexicon. Evangelical Protestants are good at storytelling, at witnessing to what God has done for them. "Tell me the old, old story" is the refrain. And within the context of the great story of God's love, their own story can be told. Roman Catholics have their own way of telling the story, which seems to have an easier relationship with the world than does that of Protestants.

Father Andrew Greeley writes of the decision of the early Church to make peace with the pagan nature religions in the way it proclaimed the gospel. This was no easy task and produced lots of tensions and some contradictions. Greeley uses the example of Ireland. There

> the intercourse symbol of male and female combined became
> the Celtic cross. God was pictured as rather like Dagda and

Jesus like Lug. The ancient goddess Brigid (Bride), goddess of poetry and spring and new life, was converted to the Christian saint of the same name who enjoyed similar responsibilities. . . . Her cross, a sun symbol, became the Brigid Cross of Catholic piety which, hanging over the doorway in west of Ireland cottages even today, asks Brigid's intercession till the warmth of spring returns. The Irish use the Analogical Imagination with a vengeance—and with the constant risk of corruption into folk religion and superstition which is always a danger for the Catholic imagination.

But the way of analogy (seeing connections between and among all things, between the inner and outer realities), as risky as it is, is the only way to go because it is the only way that makes room for the widest possible range of human experience. That's why it's better to tell stories than clobber people with dogmas. Why? Because religion is imaginative *before* it is propositional. Sacramental imagery always wins over propositional teaching. Greeley writes, "Jesus was a storyteller; the parables are the essential Jesus; they share with us Jesus' experience of the generous, hope-renewing love of the Father in heaven (who, be it noted, in the stories of Jesus loves with a mother's forgiving tenderness as much as She loves with a father's vigorous protection)."

Living between Stories

One way out of the mess of competing stories is simply to say "Relax. There is no story." This is the attraction of postmodernism, which claims that there is no great story after all, just a cacophony of rival stories. To those bullied and coerced by the great story as told by an institution or race, this is good news. But since the search for a great story is built into us, postmodernists find themselves saying that the great story is that there is no great story. At the very least, we are intuitively aware that the belief that someone else cares what happens to us is by itself sufficient to affect profoundly what we do. Isn't that why people attend church, synagogue, or temple regularly? But the value of postmodernism is to plant in us a healthy distrust of anyone who peddles a story as the one and only. We need to be reminded of just how tribal and local our little narratives are. We also might appreciate that we're at a vulnerable and frightening moment of living between stories—one dying and the other waiting to be born.

Margaret Drabble, in *Gates of Ivory*, writes about this in-between state as it is highlighted in the clashing narratives of the rich and the poor—what she calls "Good Time" and "Bad Time." It is worth quoting at length:

> Imagine yourself standing by a bridge over a river on the border between Thailand and Cambodia. Behind you, the little town of Aranyaprathet, bristling with aerials and stuffed with Good Time merchandise, connected by road and rail and telephone and post office and gossip and newspapers and banking systems with all the Good Times of the West. Before you the Bad Time of Cambodia. . . . Many are drawn to stare across this bridge. They come, and stare, and turn back. What else can they do?. . .
>
> Good Time and Bad Time coexist. We in Good Time receive messengers who stumble across the bridge or through the river, maimed and bleeding, shocked and starving. They try to tell us what it is like over there, and we try to listen. We invoke them with libations of aid, with barley and blood, with rice and water, and they flock to the dark trenches, moaning and fluttering in their thousands. We are seized with panic and pity and fear. Can we believe these stories from beyond the tomb? Can it be that these things happen in our world, our time?
>
> There is a relationship between Good Time and Bad Time. There are interpenetrations. Some cross the bridge into the Bad Time, into the Underworld, and return to tell the tale. So go deliberately. Some step into Bad Time suddenly. It may be waiting, there, in the next room.

Later in the novel, she goes on to comment on the triumphant narrative of capitalism and competition, there being "no longer any place in the West for self-sacrifice, dedication, brotherly love, compassion, community." Are we beginning to see, as we wait between stories, that whatever emerges as the new narrative must include self-sacrifice, compassion, and communion?

If religion is to be reimagined, we are going to have to retell the stories of how we came to be. Philosopher Alasdair MacIntyre points out that unlike the older cultures from which we all spring, "we have no institutions through which shared stories can be told dramatically or otherwise to the entire political community." We have few story-tellers who can address such an audience. We have very little sense of the kind of story we want or need to hear. Our audiences are privatized and dispersed—watching television and deciding who not to vote for.

What Stories Do We Need Now?

This question raises the issue of what it means to be a North American. As Americans we each have two identities, two stories going on at once. There is conflict and tension in our storytelling, which is wonderful when recognized, destructive when not. As Alasdair MacIntyre insists, some stories tell better in one language than in another. So we had better be aware of the kind of things English can do and what it can't as a language. "In this continent Spanish is not a foreign language, French is not a foreign language, Zuni and Navajo are not foreign languages, nor are some of the languages of West Africa. All these are *our* languages." We also have stories of conflict from which emerge new conflicting stories. So we have rival versions of the past. How would you have told the story of Columbus and 1492?

We also need to understand our narrative as it is understood by others and to tell it as it is told by others. If we don't, we wound our own self-knowledge. "Being unable to recognize how others understand us, we become blind to the relationships in which we stand to them and so obscure part of ourselves." Think how the Palestinians, the Israelis, the Serbs tell the North American story. It's no wonder that we tend to retreat from history.

What happens when we lose touch with the larger narrative of communion? There are three kinds of loss: first at the obvious level of everyday interchange, then at the level of politics and economics, and finally at the level of language itself. MacIntyre writes, "if we do not identify our everyday selves through our distinctive ethnic stories, then our ethnic particularity becomes mere nostalgia and sentimentality." And so does our religion. We shouldn't lose sight of our differences. When we do, we become bland, homogenized persons.

We also get into serious trouble in the realm of politics and economics. Without a narrative, we are diminished as persons and cannot debate or truly argue and come to a common mind. Without a people educated in storytelling, politics and economics are divinized. They become the story as told by those in power. We need a story about an ongoing *historical* community. Unless we have that, talk of rights and interests are abstract and arbitrary—just people shouting at each other, and the noisiest and/or the most powerful win.

Religion is about the stories we tell and the way we tell them. And the telling of these stories affects our political agenda. We are a depressed people made all the more so by what Karen Armstrong calls "a creeping new orthodoxy" of a sort of sentimental "positive thinking"—a shallow optimism that "allows us to bury our heads in the sand, deny the ubiquity of pain in ourselves and others and immure ourselves in a state of deliberate heartlessness to ensure our emotional survival." We can be indifferent to the poor and the oppressed because they are merely living out their karma. "A good deal of what passes for religion is often designed to prop up and endorse the ego that the founders of the faith told us to abandon."

The new story is already upon us, and it will be lived out by different people in different ways, from the comic to the tragic. We will either hang together or hang separately. The new story is about communion, and it will be up to us whether we experience it as a taste of heaven or a dose of the other place.

17

Here Comes Everybody

The best thing for being sad is to learn something. That is the only thing that never fails. You may grow old and trembling in your anatomies. You may lie awake at night listening to the disorder of your veins. You may miss your only love. You may see the world around you devastated by evil lunatics or know your honor trampled in the sewers of baser minds. There is only one thing for it, then: to learn. Learn why the world wags and what wags it. That is the only thing which the mind can never exhaust, never alienate, never be tortured by, never fear or distrust, and never dream of regretting. Learning is the thing for you.

— T. H. White, *Once and Future King*, Merlin
addressing the young Arthur

When we try to bring about change in our societies, we are treated first with indifference, then with ridicule, then with abuse and then with oppression. And finally, the greatest challenge is thrown at us: We are treated with respect. This is the most dangerous stage.

—A. T. Ariyaratne

Only the devil is tidy.

—Attributed to St. Augustine

Will, the "adult" hero in Nick Hornby's novel *About a Boy* (which was made into an excellent movie), finally grows up when he realizes that he can't opt out of being alive and being wrapped up in the lives of others. "Will couldn't recall ever having been caught up in this sort of messy, sprawling, chaotic web before;

it was almost as if he had been given a glimpse of what it was like to be human. It wasn't too bad, really; he wouldn't even mind being human on a full-time basis." The spiritual quest might be defined as our seeking ways to be human on a full-time basis. For me, this is what it means to be a Christian. It means being in a never-ending process of learning. This learning involves being pregnant with possibility and suffering the ups and downs of the human adventure. It involves our finding ways to live together in community.

Once you've caught a glimpse of what it might take to be human on a full-time basis, issues of inclusion and justice are bound to demand our attention. Being human on a full-time basis allows others in on the game, and these others are a messy lot. They leave the dishes in the sink and forget to turn out the lights. They sometimes lie and steal. They even, on occasion, hate and kill. Letting in the others on a full-time basis brings its share of grief. It could even get you killed.

Letting others in means giving up a sense of mastery and control. Anyone who thinks they're on top of things and has life all figured out must be either really unaware or asleep. We're all moving through time, which means we face the approach of certain death as well as the daily mystery of the unknown and untried. Most of the time we live with questions and not answers, and we look to some form of creativity not only to pass the time but also to make the most of it—to *redeem* it. We make up stories to pass the time and share these dreams, nightmares, and myths with others. Sometimes our anxiety takes over and we act out our nightmares in the real world. But the best of us (and the best part of each of us) tries to learn something, and (as Charles Dickens puts it in *A Christmas Carol*) "to think of other people as . . . fellow-passengers to the grave, and not another race of creatures bound on other journeys."

Each of us is called to leadership (even if it starts out as a leadership of one) in becoming human beings on a full-time basis. What kind of education for the soul is needed for those committed to being human on a full-time basis? Where can we get help to learn what we need to know? For example, how can we recover the symbolic life—the life of poetry, myth, and metaphor that feeds our souls, but not at the expense of others?

You Become a Leader When
You Face Reality

In an accelerated world of unsorted information, we cannot help but be learners and seekers—at least if we're awake. Just when we've figured something out, new information comes our way, and we have to rethink things. We have to move ahead even when we don't have the wit or the energy to sift through the piles of information lying all around us. We have to muddle through. It's no wonder that millions turn to ideology (in both religion and politics) as a cure for self-doubt, as a way to cut through the muddle. Others respond to ads such as "How to meditate deeper than a Zen monk . . . literally at the touch of a button." Just read magazine ads such as "What is enlightenment?" to get a feel for the spiritual supermarket. The consumerist mentality has infected everything, including our dying and death. We negotiate our way around death by buying things that make us look younger or move faster, when what we need is the patience and courage to look death in the face.

Those who manage to resist ideology and/or the promise of instant enlightenment find themselves in a situation of lifelong learning. Modern life requires us to learn new ways and new habits, not least to live with more uncertainty yet with more trust, with less control but with more openness to new possibilities. Those who resist being "managed" by ideology (theirs or somebody else's) must learn to think and act like a leader, but a different kind of leader than the ones we're used to. A leader is a person who isn't seduced by the "certainties" of ideologies or quick fixes and who doesn't surrender his or her will to someone else. In this sense, we're all called to be leaders.

What is leadership in this sense all about? Ronald Heifetz, a mentor of business leaders, tells us that the purpose of leadership is "to help people face reality," which is just what Will does in *About a Boy.* Some people are very good at facing the truth of a situation but are then paralyzed by it. There are others who can nail a situation but angrily or smugly sit on the sidelines. There has to be a connection between insight and action. There has to be a commitment to work for change, but change is, more often than not, painful. A friend of ours says, "The only person who likes change is a wet baby!" Commitment to link insight with action is the key be being fully human. Heifetz sums it up in this way: "Mustering courage to interrogate reality is a central function of the leader." "To interrogate reality" puts it well and brings us back to our earlier theme of the necessity of deepening and guarding questions rather than closing things down with quick answers. Will, Nick Hornby's hero, came alive when he started interrogating the reality of his aimless existence and began to respond to the people around him as genuinely other than himself, yet also linked to him in some kind of communion.

Institutions find lifelong learning as difficult as individuals do—perhaps more so. And religious institutions are often the most resistant to change, since they easily suffer from the illusion that they are the guardians of an unchanging truth. As a result, they find it difficult to repudiate actions in their past or admit that they were mistaken. That's why religious traditions have always bred rebels and subversives. The circle of control gets tighter and tighter and needs breaking from time to time.

Whether we like it or not, we now live in a free market when it comes to religion. While this has its downside in that it reinforces a consumerist world, isn't it basically a good thing? Ask yourself, Does a free market of religious options produce better "products" and vitality than one where there's a controlled religious marketplace? Isn't it better to be in a situation where no one religion has a monopoly? Isn't it better to live in a world where religious commitment is strictly voluntary? Isn't it better to be open to new learning than to think that we know it all? Autocracy might have been appropriate in another era, but now we're in a different version of the story.

The Democratic Experiment

The struggle for freedom and democracy is now part of the emerging world story. Are we up to this democratic experiment of being human on a full-time basis? It means taking on a peculiar form of suffering that sometimes involves our staying in the same room with people we find stupid or repellent. Intellectually and spiritually democracy is demanding because it asks us to be in two places at once: to look out for our self-interest and to imagine what it is like to be in someone else's shoes. It takes imagination and courage to divide our attention between two approaches to reality—that of the local and immediate, and that of "the big picture." Democracy asks of us the ability to hold on to a single vision and, at the same time, to be able to see many and even contradictory ends. Being a human being on a full-time basis means being light on your feet.

One of our weaknesses is the difficulty we have in imagining ourselves with any ongoing consistency. Liberals take refuge in relativism—truth is a matter of taste; and conservatives tend to look back to an idealized past—to, for example, Victorian "values" (forgetting child prostitution and the horrors of poverty in the wake of industrialization). We don't like history to be a mixed bag. We like the past to be neatly ordered. We are not in a national and international debate about the war between the absolute and the relative. The argument is about absolutes (since we all appeal to them), and this argument, if it is to be humane, requires the widest participation. Does anyone really want a relativist culture, in which anything goes? We need boundaries of some kind. Democracy is an ongoing debate about *which* boundaries we should draw. Total relativism is an absurdity, and a dangerous one at that. It is intellectually sleazy in that it gives people permission to espouse any cause—no matter how destructive—without having to give reasons for their choices. Critic Ernest Gellner reminds us, "Total permissiveness ends in arbitrary dogmatism." And it would be helpful for us to find out why we think the way we do. Psychology should not rule us, but it has a great deal to teach as we move through life by feeling as well as by thought. The fact that Adolf Hitler was beaten regularly by his father may have had something to do with the way in which Nazi philosophy developed. The human heart and mind—not always in sync—are forever forging ways to imagine new forms of faith.

When we look at the emerging community of Gen Xers and Gen Yers, the search for meaning is as strong as ever. They long for community as much as their predecessors and look for ways to "get out of themselves." Just attend any rock concert to see the need for ecstasy. Each new generation locates itself in stories and epics, and its members base their life choices on those stories. And when they have children, they wonder how they should bring them up. I find more and more that the problem isn't so much the content of religion (its stories and rituals) as it is the way the "doctrine" is expressed. That's why I am in sympathy with the founding of new postdenominational churches with their culturally "hip" music and their emphasis on direct experience. It's not my cup of tea, and it appears that the seeker-sensitive Church hasn't much of a future because it tends to underestimate the lure of tradition. There are signs that people (the Gen Yers) are longing to return to the tradition, even if they don't know what it is. Nevertheless, I have great respect for these new churches. They are willing to risk, and they have learned the knack of rejecting contemporary cultural values and yet use contemporary cultural forms. They are conservative but are impressive in helping people with destructive lifestyle changes. From a sociological point of view, they do a great deal of good. When people give up the slaveries of alcohol and drugs, sleeping around, and gambling, stability is created for building families and communities. At least they have a chance of becoming human on full-time basis.

Going Back to School

In the end, what is leadership for? What is it about? The Christian life was described by the mystics as the "school of love." Leadership in this context is about love, and, since we are poor lovers, we need to go back to school. Learning to love and not to hate is the adventure of becoming a person. My sense of who I am (my identity) requires others. I cannot be me without you. I have to be in conversation with others to come to a sense of who I am. I need others to listen, and I need to listen to others. Therefore trust is a big issue in learning how to love, as is learning to listen. For me to be me I need to be seen and heard and not rendered invisible. The reverse also is true. I have to be prepared to see and hear others. This makes us deeply dependent on each other. It has been said that the Church is best understood as schooling in conversation. And conversation requires that one speaks while the other listens.

Five Ways to Grow as a Leader

Psychologist James Hillman writes that there are five ways to grow as a leader: deepening, intensification, shedding, repetition, and emptying. He writes, "As in a garden or a marriage deepening brings ugly twisted things out of the soil. It's a work in the dirt." Deepening comes first, and it means going in and down, like the roots of a plant. It means acknowledging what's happening and not running away. In the mess and muddle, we interrogate reality. Hillman writes, "Deepening insists: no avoidance and no escape. Stay planted. No leave of absence. Clean up the mess." This was exactly Will's experience in *About a Boy*—a deepening from which there was no escape.

Intensification comes next, and is a continuation of the deepening process, which leads to the third element in the education of the soul: shedding. Shedding can hurt. "Radical shedding happens in those crises that move in on the soul and cannot be easily fixed." Hillman writes of the imaginative risk involved. The task "is to imagine the real, or to imagine as realistically as possible, the consequences of shedding, to visit with the mind the scenarios of catastrophe and letting go of all the security structures, comforting identities, realized achievements, forward planning. See what remains, for only what remains can be truly relied upon for growth."

The fourth element is perhaps the most undervalued in our society: repetition. Good storytelling depends on it. It is the mainstay of ritual. Repetition is often considered negative and, worst of all, boring. Even those who think of it as boring rely on lighting candles and laying down bunches of flowers when something so deep happens that they have no other means of responding to it. Repetition is fundamental for both ritual and the arts. Hillman reminds us that the soul derives "a great deal of pleasure in practice, in precision, in polishing." Think of repetition in our learning to love as a bit like bedtime stories for children. When I read to my children just before they fell asleep, repetition was a very important part of the ritual. Sometimes, because I was tired of a particular story I'd read over and over again, I would change a word or two. There would be cries of protest, and I would have to begin again. The repeated words created not only a safe world but also a deeper one, out of which could grow new and wondrous possibilities.

The fifth element—emptying—is to begin at the beginning. What comes first is nothing. To wait in the primal emptiness is fundamental to spiritual growth. Hillman calls for a different kind of hero, a different kind of leader. The new century requires a courage different from the one suggested by battle, conquest, and victory. We need to find another kind of leadership—still heroic but characterized by service and self-giving.

In my tradition, faith in Christ promises transformation, but this transformation is not exclusively for Christians. This strikes fear into many believers and makes them angry. Jesus does not belong to Christians. He is the property of the world. Anyone can be drawn to the attractive power of Jesus, and there are many paths by which he may be followed. In theologian Walter Wink's wonderful phrase, Jesus Christ is "God's rash gamble that humanity might become more humane." God's rash gamble that deep down we all want to be human on a full-time basis.

The Future Doesn't Need Us

Technology is changing the way in which we understand ourselves. The irony of the miracle of the interconnectedness of the Internet is that more people seem to be cut off from each other. More and

more of us feel unprotected perhaps because of the new interconnectedness. But it's an interconnectedness without either intimacy
or compassion. That's why the subject of hope is particularly
poignant at this time. I don't want to turn September 11, 2001, into
a cliché, but if we place those terrorist acts in the context of other
world events (the Middle East and the darker effects of globalization
will do), we are going through a period of history that *feels* deeply
apocalyptic, even if our time is no more apocalyptic than any other.

It is estimated that only 30 percent of the world's population
have developed beyond the narrowly tribal, while virtually 100 percent of those trapped in the tribal have destructive technologies at
hand as well as cell phones. The old ways and the old Church are
dying—you can feel it. We are caught between loyalty to the old and
fear of the new. The pain is intense when a great ideal that has lost
its power ceases to inspire and give hope. It feels like a terrible loss,
the loss of humanity itself. Bill Joy, cofounder of Sun Microsystems,
wrote an article in *Wired* magazine that was something of a sensa-
tion: "Why the Future Doesn't Need Us." He estimated that within
fifty years, technological advances in genetics, robotics, and nano-
technology might mean the end of the human species. Human consciousness could be downloaded into machines. The feasibility of
this is not the point. Its power lies in its effect on the human imagination. Hope in our time is a battle about the imagination. What
images will form the future?

The Christian hope holds out the promise of a healed imagination—the vision of a world in which there don't have to be winners
and losers. The world defines itself over and over again in terms of
victory or defeat. Christians define the world as communion. Christians also compromise and betray their own deepest convictions.
Also, there are intractable issues such as theodicy (God has a lot to
answer for), judgment, and time that attach themselves to our
hopes and longings. When we add to this the consequences of our
living at a time when the notion of the sacred is being eroded, the
crisis deepens.

When it comes to Christian hope, judgment is part of the deal.
To think otherwise is to betray an emotional and spiritual childish-
ness. Daniel Goldman not long ago pointed out our lack of emotional

intelligence, which leads to hopelessness. "International data shows what seems to be a modern epidemic of depression. . . . Each successive generation worldwide since the opening of the century has lived with a higher risk than their parents of suffering from a major depression—not just sadness but a paralyzing listlessness, dejection, and self-pity, and an overwhelming hopelessness—over the course of life." Time is simply one damned thing after another. And depression starts earlier and earlier, even infecting childhood.

Mystics have always known the flimsiness of our world, and when we pay attention (when we pray), the trapdoor opening to the bottomless pit below becomes apparent. That's why we resist spiritual growth. Western culture has produced people who are continually taken by surprise that life is hard and ends in death. It seems that for many, life feels both desperately urgent and utterly pointless at the same time. There is no avoiding the abyss (*El abismo de la fe*, as St. John of the Cross understood it). In this context of desperation, talk about hope comes as a challenge rather than a comfort. To be open to life is to be open to a series of demands. And it might hurt. Depression, which is a kind of violence turned inward on oneself, can easily become violence against others. And how freeing that violence is when it is done in the name of a cause or a god.

The End of the World

Hope has something to do with how we move through time and how we are judged and shaped by the decisions we make. Time is a part of creation and is a peculiar creature, and our relationship to it can make us mad. Time will not stop, and there's an incurable sadness about it because the past cannot be undone. Time goes on and on but doesn't go anywhere, does it? The Christian affirmation of "the God of history" sounds pretty hollow in light of history's long, bloody mess. And how deadly boring it all is. How easy to kill time with depression or violence. No wonder we fear it. Look what it does to us. It brings us to a dead end, and when people are cornered, they turn nasty. The god Chronos feeds on its own children—moment by moment is eaten up by time, and we along with it. Never a final solution—the future is always coming at us, and we never catch up with it. So many of us live life as if we were on the run—knowing that life will catch up with us in the end and do us in.

We have various coping mechanisms to try to dodge time's decay. Power, money, some form of subservience or slavery in religion and politics—any number of strategies might buy us both time and safety. But in the end we run out of time and there is no safe place. We lose our moorings. It's as if we have lost touch with our own resources. We have mislaid our hearts and put a ceiling on our own growth. We underestimate ourselves and hide from the risk that growth involves. God has a lot to answer for—the slaughter, the holocausts, the senseless waste of human life, the relentlessness of time. I believe that God does answer for these, sort of (but only sort of). For other people, hope may be easier that this. Not for me. The Christian story as it has been told to many of us won't do anymore. We need new stories and a better way of telling them. We also need grace to live with the loose ends and with the mystery and muddle at the heart of life.

Christianity's Attraction

The coming of Jesus as both Baby and Judge offers access to God for all, including and especially those who have no claim of moral or spiritual privilege—the unqualified. The God of Jesus is the God who sends rain on the just and the unjust, who loves everybody—even the desperately wicked. Our hope is that God is building a peculiar community of "unqualified" people. John Dominic Crossan calls this the "unbrokered society"—the promise of a society that does not rely for its workings on control by some privileged class of the means of access to power and acceptability. The welcome of God is like an invitation to a meal with no social rationale, no ritual for ranking guests and marking their various levels of wealth or importance. According to Crossan, "Jesus makes no appropriate distinctions and discriminations. He has no honor. He has no shame." In our terms, he is shameless. And his future keeps impinging on our present—calling us, enabling us to be human on a full-time basis.

And the tragic is real because Jesus' mission is, in one sense, a failure. Yet it turns out to be our failure to discern the true nature of power and authority, the true nature of hope. According to Crossan, "Jesus proclaims the . . . indiscriminate and indestructible regard of God for all, regardless of merit and achievement," and for this he is executed. Yet, what happens? He won't lie down! The action of Jesus reveals a living presence that endures rejection and even death. This is the vision, which could heal the imagination.

What about us? We are to act so the nature of this radically loving, shameless, hospitable, and just God becomes visible. (This is ludicrous. Look at us!) Christians often talk about "the sacramental principle," which is the inherent capacity of the material world to bear divine meanings. But we also know that these meanings emerge from a process of estrangement, surrender, and re-creation —not a bland appeal to natural sacredness. "God's in his heaven and all's right with the world" is a lie.

Judgment hangs over us. The late John Gardner reminded us, "Despite the troubles, our vast society hums with reassuring steadiness. The morning paper is delivered on time. One's favorite program is predictably there. The chain stores are stocked and the highways crowded. It is hard to imagine that under that great throbbing busyness, the clock of doom might be ticking—as it has ticked for every other great civilization in history. There are more dead civilizations than live ones." And most civilizations die from within. They die from the loss of shared purposes, from the lack of imagination.

Tom Paine wrote in his pamphlet *Common Sense* (1776), "We have it in our power to begin the world over again. A situation, similar to the present, hath not happened since the days of Noah until now. The birth-day of a new world is at hand." This is the great American Error—admirable in some ways, certainly heroic, but wrongheaded and, in these times, dangerous. It's time for the West and for American Christianity in particular to take the tragic seriously. To be conscious is to be sad. To be Christian—be fully human—is to affirm a deep joy behind the sadness and the tragic.

In *Approaching the Qur'án: The Early Revelations*, translator and editor Michael Sells writes:

Qur'anic reciters and commentators characterize the tone of the Qur'anic recitation as one of sadness *(huzn)*. This is not a world-rejecting sadness. Indeed the sadness is at its most telling in those passages in which the world's mystery and splendor are evoked. Yet there is a sense that somehow the splendor and mystery are too great for the human to encompass—or that the human heart has somehow forgotten it actually has the capacity to encompass the splendor and the mystery. At this moment of reminder, the text expresses not fear but the sadness, which comes with a personal realization of a loss that is part of the human condition. The day of reckoning contains the possibility that this loss will be overcome with final reconciliation and sense of belonging, or that it will be revealed as permanent—and it brings into the present the reality of that moment of finality.

My friend Al Shands puts it well in describing how a friend of his received the news of a death-dealing cancer. For Al's friend, this is all there is. There is no life after death.

When it's over it's over. What you see is what you get. . . . I was beginning to experience a dark gap widening between us, separating and threatening. Though I was uncomfortable, I also felt he was onto something important. . . . The End is not something [that] is readily accepted in our society. We are loath to accept the tragedy of the End. We want to avoid the truth that life is in part inherently tragic. We see life as some kind of endless fulfilling continuum. But of course that is not the whole story. The truth is that the deepest experiences of the spirit also involve utter darkness and emptiness. It is when we are in the power of death that the mystery of our lives also opens up to us in the deepest ways. . . . We cannot avoid it. We do not want to avoid it because it takes us beyond the shallows of pessimism or despair to the Edge where we gaze trembling into the very mystery of God.

Our hoping, longing heart in the light of the End is a function of our identity. To be a person of hope is to be one who cooperatively enacts the End of the World. And what is the End of the World? It is to have arrived at the place of freedom in faith, hope, and love. This is what it is to be a human being on a full-time basis.

Perhaps the difference is between those who are willing to stand for something and those who aren't. A sign on the calendar at Kim's Auto Body Shop in San Francisco, where I've had my car fixed, reads, "Choose Christ, as I did." I admire that and felt a little ashamed that I wouldn't have such a sign in my office. On one hand, I admire those who make a stand, and on the other, I know from history how we humans betray our ideals.

The Call of Freedom

The Australian novelist Patrick White, in *Riders in the Chariot,* has a character say, "Do you see everything at once? My own house is full of things waiting to be seen. Even quite common objects are shown to us when it is time for them to be." Seeing what presents itself to us in terms of a web of relationship and communion requires imagination. Imagination is the way we take part in the world, not escape from it. Every morning the world offers itself to be seen, and we have to make choices. What sort of world shall we "invent"? A world where we can all be human on a full-time basis?

The poet Dante, in the *Divine Comedy,* celebrates his vision of Paradise as the homecoming for free souls who are "crowned and mitered" over themselves. This is an amazing image for a man at the beginning of the fourteenth century. We are called into so great a freedom that we are, as it were, our own emperor and pope all rolled into one. Dante's vision of a fully human being is that of someone who acknowledges no sovereignty other than God. It gives us a capacity to believe in ourselves because God believes in us. And there are wondrous consequences. True sovereignty over ourselves isn't wanton selfishness (a world populated by little emperors and popes doesn't bear thinking about). True sovereignty is the antidote to the destructive felt need for people to humiliate others. The humiliation of others is perhaps the root of many of the world's ills. It is a failure of imagination. It refuses to see others for who they truly are.

Historian Michael Ignatieff writes that humiliation is the kind of "cruelty which can destroy our very capacity *to believe in ourselves*. People can with great effort rise above inefficiency, unfairness, even exploitation. But systematic humiliation is different: the sense that the whole of the social order is stacked against you can rob you of self-respect, the feeling that you have purposes worth attaining and the right and capacity to do so." Choosing not to humiliate others when we are in positions of power is therefore an important act of the imagination, as is the refusal to be humiliated when we are powerless. Religion reminds us of this and makes clear what we easily forget or repress: our inalienable dignity. Religion wakes us up to what's important. At the end of life people don't ask, "How much is in my bank account?" or "What a pity I can't rush off to work and cut another deal." Buddhist teacher Jack Kornfield tells us that people who are aware at the time of their death tend to ask very simple questions: "Did I love well?" "Did I live fully?" "Did I learn to let go?" These are questions of ultimate allegiance—the questions kept alive by the religious imagination.

How can the religious traditions convey their message about real freedom in today's media-dominated world? Theologian Harvey Cox writes, "We live in the midst of a whirling, fast-paced battle between contending myths, parables, and narratives. And most of them are about freedom, or pretend to be. Cynthia Ozick once said that the future belongs to those who have the best stories." Cox adds that the future also belongs to those who *tell* them best. And who get them *heard*. Advertisers tend to tell the stories that are really heard by the majority of people. Ads promise not only freedom and fulfillment but also an entrance card to a group you would like to belong to. Regardless of your age, you can join the Pepsi Generation, or become one of 50 million who "think different."

Whether you believe or not, there is a question that won't go away. Who or what controls you? Who or what has conditioned you? Who are your keepers? Who keeps you on a leash? How free are you? At the end are the questions. "Did I love well?" "Did I live fully?" "Did I learn to let go?"

In the end, God is to be known not by thinking but by love. Thomas Merton wrote, "We will never be fully real until we let ourselves fall in love—either with another human person or with God." When we love each other, we are more interested in what we *are* for each other than in what we *do* for each other. When we are cherished, we are enlarged in our being. I tend to believe less and less and to *look* more and more. When I look at the picture of my daughter holding her new baby, I think of myself—helpless—being held by my mother, as she was by hers. Beliefs and structures help me to see, but once I see, they fall away. My being needs no justification. Neither does yours.

Where Are the Others?

Someone once said, "We're on earth to help others. What others are here for, I have no idea." Thomas Merton invokes the old maxim that we are here to love and to be loved. He makes it clear that others and we exist in mutuality: "In the mystery of social love there is found the realization of 'the other' not only as one to be loved by us, so that we may perfect ourselves [come to full birth as persons], but also as the one who can become more perfect by loving us. The vocation to charity is a call not only to love but to *be loved*." It is as if Merton is saying "I'm here to love you. You're here to love me, and don't you forget it! Don't let us forget it. When we do, all hell breaks loose."

Meanwhile, the others are crowding in and taking over our space and demanding attention. Stories of heaven and hell revolve around our attitudes toward others. Jean-Paul Sartre's famous *"L'enfer, c'est les autres"* (Hell is other people) is balanced by the question Charles Péguy puts into the mouth of God when we reach the gates of heaven: *"Où sont les autres?"* (Where are the others?). What will God say to us when we go to him without the others? What about these others with whom we share the world? Hell is other people. Heaven is other people. Choose.

New stories, which include "the others," are emerging. And the generous inclusiveness of some of the old stories is being rediscovered. The great religious traditions are beginning to listen to one another. Is there a great planetary story emerging that truly has room for "the others" and that treats the earth as sacred? Is the human race in labor with a new version of its purpose and destiny? Or is it the same old story of fear and conflict?

One of the great images from the New Testament that is peculiarly apt for our time is St. Paul's metaphor of the cosmos in labor (Romans 8:18–25). Paul writes of the sufferings of this present time and of the glory that shall be revealed. What a place to get caught— in the in-between times. Creation waits, he writes, for the revelation of God's children.

Some years ago I was struck by a statement by French theologian Léon Bloy: "There are places in the heart that do not yet exist and it is necessary for suffering to allow these to come into being." This statement is deeply true today. Suffering, in this sense, is neither masochistic nor passive, but rather a way of allowing things to be by permitting, consenting, and submitting to life's processes. As a friend of mine once put it, "If we don't accept our destiny it will return to haunt us as fate." And Lewis Thomas writes: "Mankind is all of a piece, a single species, and our present situation will not do." Now, that's something with which to labor!

The great story of Christianity helps me to remember my first vulnerability. What if I feed the hungry, forgive an insult, and love my enemies in the name of Christ? Carl Jung writes, "But what if I should discover that the least among them all, the poorest of all the beggars, the most impudent of all the offenders, the very enemy himself—that these are within me, and that I myself stand in need of the alms of my own kindness—that I myself am the enemy who must be loved—what then?" When we are given that kind of self-knowledge, love and peace have a chance. There are no outsiders. Here comes everybody.

Epilogue

Spiritual Practice, Spiritual Presence

But there are still the hours, aren't there? One and then another, and you get through that one and then, my god, there's another.

—Michael Cunningham

The elusive quest to turn lifestyle into life.

—Michael Arditti

Stopping the World

How are we get through our days, pass the time? What habits and practices might help us move through a life that at times seems without purpose and, at other times, full of meaning and wonder? We have explored something of the world of images and story to help us negotiate the mystery of being alive and aware. But what about the future? I like the secondary meaning of the word *prophet,* as poet: a person who puts the future into words. A mature spirituality is open and expectant. It isn't naive about the darkness and the despair, but it hasn't lost its curiosity about what might happen next. The future is no longer something to dread. But unless we do something about our addiction to velocity, the future comes hurtling toward us with frightening and seemingly directionless speed.

An important aspect of a spiritual discipline is to find ways of *stopping the world.* Journalist Pico Iyer writes of his being at an economic conference in Davos. He was sitting next to a pioneer in artificial intelligence who spoke of a trip he'd once taken to a monastery. "What moved him most, he said, was just the way the stone of the monastery steps had been worn down, by centuries of monastic feet, all anonymous, but all walking on the same path to the chapel, to sing the same hymns every morning." One way to stop the world and allow yourself to catch up with yourself is to be part of a community committed to repetitive meditative acts

First, Decide Where You're Going to Show Up

You have to show up somewhere. It may be a church, a synagogue, a temple, an AA group, a yoga class, the Kiwanis, the Rotary Club, Log Cabin Republicans, a Quaker Meeting, a Buddhist meditation group—the list is endless. This isn't to say that all these activities are of equal value. They're not. But we have to show up somewhere. Imagine your life as a jigsaw puzzle. We all—most of the time without thinking about it—take the bits and pieces of our lives and try to organize them into some pattern. We try to make a picture and glue it together as best we can. Our spirituality—homemade or bought off the shelf—is the way we choose to arrange the pieces and glue them together. Showing up and interacting with others is the way we find the edges and start filling in the picture. Rotarians, Republicans, and revolutionaries—and countless other groups— provide the glue and even show us the finished picture. Some of the pictures are cruel and destructive, but they provide a kind of relief. It is comforting to find that there is a picture at all, even if it's an awful one. We show up—even if the venue is Nuremberg and an Adolf Hitler paints the picture.

There is a way to avoid the Hitlers, the Stalins, and other despotic storytellers who offer to relieve us of the burden of sorting out the puzzle of our lives for ourselves. Before we show up at a rally or even show up to a date with friends to go to the movies, we need to show up to ourselves, somehow to acknowledge and celebrate our own being. We might not even know why we're there, but we show up just the same because this is what human beings do. Those of us who simply can't do that suffer from deep, painful, isolating depression.

Journalist Andrew Solomon, who himself struggles with depression, recounts the case of Maggie Robbins, who found showing up to herself for repeated meditative acts a way to relieve her depression. In Maggie's case it was the practice of reciting Evening Prayer from the Book of Common Prayer. She says, "Depression makes you believe certain things: that you are worthless and should be dead. How can one respond to that other than with alternative beliefs?" Prayer was a way of slowing her down and helping her keep the chaos of depression at bay.

"It's such a strong structure," she says. "You get up and say the same prayers every night. Someone has delineated what you're going to say to God and other people say it with you. I'm laying down these rituals to contain my experience. The liturgy is like the wooden slats of a box; the texts of the Bible and especially of the Psalter are considered to be an extremely good box for holding experience. Going to church is a set of attentional practices that move you forward spiritually."

Wouldn't aerobics do as well? They might help, but to "get out of yourself and show up somewhere else" you need a story to help you put the future into words. The poem of Christianity is one way of telling the story. The structure of believing can help, too. Maggie goes on: "According to Christian doctrine, you're not allowed to commit suicide because your life is not your own." The poetic insistence that we're not alone but well connected, that God is on our side, can be very potent when we are battling with what seems pointless. Maggie says:

> The Church is an exoskeleton for those whose endoskeleton has been eaten away by mental illness. You pour yourself into it and adapt to its shape. You grow a spine within it. Individualism, this breaking away of ourselves from everything else, has denigrated modern life. The Church says we should act first within our communities, and then as members of the Body of Christ, and then as members of the human race. It's so non-twenty-first-century American, but it's so important. I take from Einstein the idea that human beings are laboring under an "optical delusion" that each of them is separate from the others, and from the rest

of the material world, and from the universe. For me, Christianity is the study of what real love, useful love, consists of—and of what constitutes attention. People think that Christianity is against pleasure, as it sometimes is; but it's very pro-joy. You're aiming for joy that will never go away, no matter what kind of pain you're in.

She sees religion as that which dislodges the everyday and reconnects us to a bigger world. And Solomon comments, "People with a degree of faith before they reach the gutting darkness of the Abyss have a route out of there. Finding your balance in the dark is the key."

Showing up is a big deal. Ask yourself, "Where do I keep showing up? Is this what I want to do with my time?" How should we spend our time?

The Judeo-Christian tradition tells us that time is a creature (part of creation). Time is one of the things over which we have no control. It cannot be stopped or manipulated, and it flows in only one direction. It can, however, be sanctified, given shape and purpose. The minutes, hours, days, months, and years can be woven into a pattern of praise and penitence, giving shape to our joys and sorrows, tragedies and triumphs. Showing up and practicing some simple disciplines also can revolutionize our attitude to time. Some of us are addicted to velocity and stress. Time is running away with us. Taking time for prayer and meditation, for pleasure and enjoyment, for service to others are ways of getting off the treadmill of dread where time is simply one damned thing after another. We need a way to punctuate time at regular intervals. We eventually become what we pay attention to (what we contemplate), and paying attention to our hearts in their longing for God eventually builds us up as children of God and as brothers and sisters of each other. What we read, what we take in from television, provide the architecture of our thoughts and teach us how to experience the world. Therefore we need to be as intentional as possible in how we spend our time.

It has been said that there are only two prayers: *Help!* and *Thank you!* The rest are footnotes. And when I was growing up, we were told in Sunday school that the four elements of prayer are adoration, confession, thanksgiving, and supplication (ACTS). As we think

about where to show up and what to do with our time, these four
elements and two basic prayers in one form or another will keep
showing up, too. Adoration and thanksgiving are primary. They
place us in a right relationship with God and with all things.

Confession and supplication are essential, too, because they are
ways in which we practice self-examination (Socrates said, "The
unexamined life is not worth living.") and pray for others. The old
way of thinking about "confession" was to call it "examination of conscience." I like to think of it as an "examination of consciousness." I
find it helpful to offer my mind (with all its busyness and noise) to
God every day. Our consciousness, with its fixations and obsessions,
needs cleansing and setting back on track. Beginning and ending the
day with a brief time of reflection gives shape not only to the day but
also to our life. Being committed to a daily discipline of prayer that
is common (shared and not merely private) puts us in touch with a
great company of pilgrims through the ages and gives our life a healing rhythm—rather like the ground bass for the music of our lives.
But first decide where you're going to show up.

Second, Decide What to Do with Your Time

There are two poems that I go back to time and time again and that
help get things in perspective. The first is by Naomi Shihab Nye:

THE ART OF DISAPPEARING

When they say Don't I know you?
say no.

. . .

If they say We should get together
say why?

It's not that you don't love them anymore.
You're trying to remember something
too important to forget.
Trees. The monastery bell at twilight.

Tell them you have a new project.
It will never be finished.

When someone recognizes you in a grocery store
nod briefly and become a cabbage.
When someone you haven't seen in ten years
appears at the door,
don't start singing him all your new songs.
You will never catch up.

Walk around feeling like a leaf.
Know you could tumble any second.
Then decide what to do with your time.

The second poem is by the late Philip Larkin:

The Mower

The mower stalled, twice; kneeling, I found
A hedgehog jammed up against the blades,
Killed. It had been in the long grass.

I had seen it before, and even fed it, once.
Now I had mauled its unobtrusive world
Unmendably. Burial was no help:

Next morning I got up and it did not.
The first day after a death, the new absence
Is always the same; we should be careful

Of each other, we should be kind
While there is still time.

The Four Basic Relationships

All the great religious traditions provide means for us to deepen our relationship to God (and if you don't like the word *God*, you can try *mystery of being*), to the world, to others, and to our inner self. These four sets of relationship to God, the world, others, and self are fostered by the three classic practices of prayer, almsgiving, and fasting. Prayer, both private and public, orients us toward mystery and makes it possible for us to slow down and practice the art of self-simplification. Prayer in its various forms is a way of our not only seeing life as a dense mesh of interconnections but also experiencing those connections so that we act differently in the world. The central Christian sacrament of the Eucharist is a banquet that connects us to God and to each other, and, if properly seen for what it is, pushes us out into the world to work for justice and inclusion in our daily lives. Almsgiving, which is the old term for giving to the poor, can be seen as a way of expressing our solidarity with those in need. Fasting has to do with the body and our relationship not only to food but to material things, as well. How far do they rule and possess us? Ask yourself where you need to show up to God, to the world, to other people, and to yourself. One of these four compass points is bound to be neglected. Start there. It is all one circle. The starting point may be something deceptively simple, such as getting up ten minutes earlier to sit still before the day begins. It may mean making a telephone call to say you're sorry or writing an overdue letter to say I love you. It could be facing your eating habits or getting some help from a therapist. You might need to write a check—a big enough one to feel it in your gut—to support a homeless shelter. You might even have to take to the streets in protest. If you're addicted to protesting, the biggest challenge may be those extra ten minutes in the morning. If you tend to be reclusive, joining that march next weekend might be just the thing you need to do.

Finding God in All Things

The metaphors of intoxication and sexual climax have often been used by mystics to describe their relationship with God. The Sufis call the often crazed ecstatics among them spiritual drunkards who hang out in God's tavern. But there are others who are even more revered—those who can see God everywhere while they are sober! The sexual imagery is also very powerful and points to an even more robust way of loving, of which the mystic has caught only a glimpse.

Our relationship to God will involve practices of wakefulness, mindfulness, and compassion. It also takes the intellectual life seriously; you don't have to switch off your mind to be connected in the spirit. It also means familiarizing yourself with the sacred texts of a tradition. For the Christian it will be primarily the Bible but also would include texts and stories from the mystical tradition.

St. Ignatius Loyola tells us that those advanced in the spiritual life constantly contemplate God in every creature. In other words, wake up and start looking at the world. The world presents itself to you every day for wonder and contemplation.

Your first practice might be simply to look at something for five minutes—a flower, a candle, light playing on the wall, your glass of orange juice in the morning. Look.

The second practice, having acknowledged the being of a flower, candle, light, or orange juice, might be to look inside yourself and wait without judgment. This is simply learning to trust the immediate relationship you have with God because you are the place where God chooses to dwell. You don't even have to believe it intellectually at first. Simply imagine that is who you are—the dwelling place of God.

The third practice is to find out who you are and what you are about in the company of others. This is code language for showing up in church, temple, or synagogue.

Here, then, we have three simple practices:

1. *Look long and lovingly at an object.*
2. *Look long and lovingly at what's inside you.*
3. *Show up and be with others on the same pilgrimage.*

Others

"Being *is* communion" is an important spiritual maxim. At its heart, Christian practice is communion—a sharing in bread and wine. This sacrament is actually a sign of the sacramentality of the world—a kind of ecological statement about the sacredness of things. Everything tells us something about God, and there is nothing from which God is excluded, including our social arrangements and our politics. There is no private deal with God, since "Being *is* communion." Therefore our spirituality will inform our friendships and our lovemaking. And because we're not very good at loving, there will have to be opportunities for confessing our failures, for forgiving, and for being forgiven.

Body, Mind, and Soul

Christianity is very much a religion of flesh and blood, although, at first sight, you wouldn't think so. The Christian tradition, like many other religious traditions, has often been tempted to embrace a dualism that separates body and soul. The result has often been to devalue the body at the expense of the soul. A truer vision in Christianity is that we are body, mind, and spirit and that the three are all bound together in a unity. The body has its own wisdom, and many of us have found that wisdom released in, for example, the practice of yoga. Yogic practice at its best integrates body, mind, and soul.

Questions about the body, especially sexuality, often bring up issues of guilt. One of the most important things we can do for ourselves is to sort out the difference between false guilt and true guilt. Psychotherapy can often help us with the false kind. The true kind has much to commend it. Guilt might make us less happy, but to embrace a guilt-free, anything-goes attitude makes us less than human. Judith Viorst writes, "We cannot be full human beings without the loss of some of anything-goes moral freedom. We cannot be full human beings without acquiring a capacity for guilt. To be a human being is to be responsible." Part of growing up is waking up—and, therefore, *knowing* what we are doing. A seven-year-old once complained to his parents: "I'm getting sick of this. Everything I do you blame on me."

Forgiveness is at the heart of the gospel because so is personal responsibility. Without the responsibility we would be less than human. Without the forgiveness human life would be unbearable.

Here are some suggestions:

- Go for a walk.
- Go for a run.
- Turn off the TV.
- Bake a cake.
- Take up yoga.
- Go on a retreat.
- Consider psychotherapy.
- Make your confession.

The Power of Music

I remember with gratitude and affection my training in England as a choirboy in a great tradition of choral music. It changed and shaped my life. I am convinced that the music influenced the way I approach and think about God—in poetic and metaphorical terms. Each of us has, perhaps, a piece of music that speaks to us more deeply than any words. Some time ago I discovered the "Incarnatus" in one of Palestrina's Masses. These fifty seconds of music deepen and strengthen my faith. Music is highly valued precisely because of its power to convert the soul and touch the heart. Palestrina isn't to everyone's taste, but the principle is the same. A teenager describing, on public radio, what her music meant to her convinced me that music is one of the most basic ways we get off the treadmill of ourselves and into another world. I'm not saying it's all equally good or even spiritually healthy, but its power cannot be denied.

Music speaks of three basic human experiences: thoughts about death, the desire for happiness, and the reality of love. We learn, sometimes painfully, that "here we have no abiding city." Appreciation of our own instability in a changing world causes us to reevaluate what really matters. Music can be the point of entry into the kind of vulnerability that opens the heart and teaches it to trust.

Here are some things to do:

- Sing in the shower.
- Go to a concert.
- Take singing lessons.
- Write a poem.
- Go to church.

Waiting on God

One of the hardest yet most basic of disciplines is simply waiting nondefensively in the presence of mystery, knowing that you're going to die someday. "Doing nothing" and doing it deliberately and consciously seems a waste of time, yet all the great religious traditions give high priority to this simple "waiting on God." It brings with it a kind of suffering and the unpopular intuition that suffering is not always to be avoided. Waiting and feeling empty put us in touch with our neediness. Would any sane person want to be in touch with an area of such weakness? But there is a "payoff" for those who wait. Out of the darkness of waiting and attentiveness come new possibilities and new risks for the sake of inner freedom. A person of prayer put it this way: "When I choose to wait in the presence of God and come in touch with my mortality and need, I find that I am freed from being a victim of my own personal history. I am liberated from 'me' and from the maintenance of 'me.'" The vulnerability never goes away. The Dark Night of the Senses and the Dark Night of the Soul are always possibilities, but the soul also knows a freedom and a love that it could not know in any other way. There is terror in it and there is joy. Be alive.

Suggested Reading List

Amis, Martin. *Experience*. London: Vintage Books, 2001.

Arditti, Michael. *Easter*. London: Arcadia Books, 2000.

Armstrong, Karen. "Introduction." In *Every Eye Beholds You* by Thomas J. Craughwell. Orlando, Fla.: Harcourt, Brace, 1999.

―――. *Buddha*. New York: Viking Penguin, 2001.

Bailie, Gil. *Violence Unveiled: Humanity at the Crossroad*. New York: Crossroad/Herder & Herder, 1997.

Baldwin, James. *The Fire Next Time*. New York: Vintage, 1992.

Barzun, Jacques. *From Dawn to Decadence*. New York: Perennial, 2001.

Becker, Ernest. *Escape from Evil*. 1975. Reprint, New York: Free Press, 1985.

Beckett, Samuel. *Three Novels by Samuel Beckett: Molloy, Malone Dies, The Unnamable*. Cambridge, Eng.: Grove Press, 1995.

Berger, Peter. "The Concept of Mediating Action." In *Confession, Conflict, and Community* by Richard John Neuhaus. Grand Rapids, Mich.: Wm. B. Eerdmans, 1986.

―――. "Different Gospels: The Social Sources of Apostasy." In *American Apostasy: The Triumph of "Other" Gospels*, edited by Peter Berger. Grand Rapids, Mich.: Wm. B. Eerdmans, 1989.

Berry, Thomas, et al. *Befriending the Earth*. Mystic, Conn.: Twenty-third Publications, 1991.

Beuchner, Frederick. *Brendan: A Novel*. San Francisco: HarperCollins, 2000.

Brooke, Rupert. *Rupert Brooke: The Complete Poems*. New York: AMS Press, 1942.

Brueggmann, Walter. *The Land: Place as Gift, Promise, and Challenge in Biblical Faith*. Minneapolis: Fortress Press, 2002.

―――. *Spirituality of the Psalms (Facets)*. Minneapolis: Fortress Press, 2003.

Cahill, Thomas. *How the Irish Saved Civilization.* New York: Doubleday, Anchor Books, 1996.

Carroll, James. *Constantine's Sword: The Church and the Jew.* New York: Houghton Mifflin, 2001.

Carroll, Robert P. *Wolf in the Sheepfold: The Bible as a Problem for Christianity.* Norwich, Eng.: SCM/Canterbury Press, 1997.

Chatwin, Bruce. *The Songlines.* New York: Penguin USA, 1988.

Colegate, Isabel. *A Pelican in the Wilderness: Hermits, Solitaries, and Recluses.* New York: Counterpoint, 2003.

Cotter, Jim. *Brainsquall.* Sheffield, Eng.: Cairns Publications, 2000.

Crossan, John Dominic. *A Long Way from Tipperary: What a Former Irish Monk Discovered in His Search for Truth.* San Francisco: Harper-Collins, 2000.

Cunningham, Michael. *The Hours.* New York: Picador USA, 2002.

Cupitt, Don. *After God: The Future of Religion.* New York: Basic Books, 1997.

Davies, Robertson. *Murther and Walking Spirits.* 1991. Reprint, New York: Penguin USA, 1992.

de Botton, Alain. *How Proust Can Change Your Life.* New York: Vintage Books, 1998.

de Waal, Esther. *The Celtic Way of Prayer.* New York: Doubleday (Image Books), 1999.

Drabble, Margaret. *Gates of Ivory.* New York: Viking Press, 1992.

Ecclestone, Alan. *Gather the Fragments.* Sheffield, Eng.: Cairns Publications, 1993.

Erdman, David, ed. *The Complete Poetry and Prose of William Blake.* New York: Random House, 1982.

Fuller, Robert W. *Somebodies and Nobodies: Overcoming the Abuse of Rank.* Gabriola Island, B.C., Canada: New Society Publishers, 2003.

Gardner, John. *National Renewal,* joint publication of Independent Sector and National Civic League, September 1995.

Goldman, Daniel. *Emotional Intelligence.* 1995. Reprint, New York: Bantam Books, 1997.

Greene, Graham. *Monsignor Quixote.* New York: Simon & Schuster, 1982.

Grof, Christina. *The Thirst for Wholeness.* San Francisco: HarperCollins, 1994.

Handy, Charles. *Beyond Certainty: The Changing World of Organizations.* Boston: Harvard Business School Press, 1998.

Hillman, James. *Kinds of Power: A Guide to Its Intelligent Uses.* New York: Doubleday, 1997.

Hirsch, E. D. *Cultural Literacy: What Every American Needs to Know.* New York: Vintage Books, 1988.

Holloway, Richard. *Doubts and Loves: What's Left of Christianity.* Edinburgh: Canongate Books, 2003.

Hornby, Nick. *About a Boy.* New York: Penguin Putnam (Riverhead), 1999.

Iyer, Pico. *The Global Soul: Jet Lag, Shopping Malls, and the Search for Home.* New York: Vintage, 2001.

James, William. *The Varieties of Religious Experience.* 1994. Reprint, New York: Penguin USA, 2002.

Jenkins, Philip. *The Next Christianity.* London: Oxford University Press, 2002.

Johnson, George. *Fire in the Mind: Science, Faith, and the Search for Order.* New York: Vintage Books, 1996.

Johnstone, William. *Mystical Theology: The Science of Love.* New York: Orbis Books, 1998.

Jung, Carl. *Modern Man in Search of a Soul.* Arlington Heights, Ill.: Harvest Books, 1955.

Kammen, Michael. *Mystic Chords of Memory.* 1991. Reprint, New York: Vintage Books, 1993.

Kermode, Frank. *Pleasing Myself: Essays from Beowulf to Philip Roth.* London: Penguin Press, 2001.

Kohler, Lotte, ed., and Peter Constantine, trans. *Within Four Walls: The Correspondence between Hannah Arendt and Heinrich Blücher, 1936–1968.* New York: Harcourt, 2001.

Kuthins, Herb, and Stuart A. Kirk. *Making Us Crazy, DSM: The Psychiatric Bible and the Creation of Mental Disorders.* New York: Free Press, 1997.

Leech, Kenneth. *The Sky Is Red: Discerning the Signs of the Times.* London: Darton Longman & Todd, 2003.

Llewelyn, Robert. *Joy of the Saints.* London: Templegate Publishers, 1992.

Lodge, David. *Thinks.* London: Penguin Press, 2002.

Lossky, Vladimir. *The Mystical Theology of the Eastern Church.* Crestwood, N.Y.: St. Vladimir's Seminary Press, 1997.

Lundin, Roger. *Emily Dickinson and the Art of Belief.* Grand Rapids, Mich.: Wm. B. Eerdmans, 1998.

MacIntyre, Alasdair. *After Virtue: A Study in Moral Theory,* 2nd ed. Notre Dame, Ind.: University of Notre Dame Press, 1997.

Maloney, George. *Inward Stillness.* Denville, N.J.: Dimension Books, 1981.

Mayne, Michael. *This Sunrise of Wonder.* London: HarperCollins, 1995.

———. *Learning to Dance.* London: Darton, Longman, & Todd, 2001.

McEwan, Ian. *Atonement.* Peterborough, Eng.: Anchor, 2003.

McGinn, Bernard. *The Presence of God: A History of Western Christian*

Mysticism. Vol. 2, *The Growth of Mysticism: Gregory the Great through the 12th Century.* New York: Crossroad, 1996.

McLaren, Brian D. *A New Kind of Christian: A Tale of Two Friends on a Spiritual Journey.* San Francisco: Jossey-Bass, 2001.

Merton, Thomas. *The New Man*. 1981, 1983. Reprint, New York: Noonday Press, 1999.

Millbank, John. *The Word Made Strange: Theology, Language, Culture.* Oxford, Eng.: Blackwell Publishers, 1997.

Moltmann, Jurgen. *The Spirit of Life: A Universal Affirmation*. Minneapolis: Fortress Press, 2003.

Mountford, Brian. *Postcards on the Way to Heaven*. London: Society for Promoting Christian Knowledge, 1997.

Needleman, Jacob. *Time and the Soul*. 1998. Reprint, San Francisco: Berrett-Koehler, 2003.

Nye, Naomi Shihab. *The Words under the Words: Selected Poems*. Portland, Ore.: Eighth Mountain Press, 1995.

Oldenburg, Roy. *The Great Good Place. Cafés, Coffee Shops, Bookstores, Bars, Hair Salons, and Other Hangouts at the Heart of a Community.* New York: Avalon (Marlowe), 1999.

Pagels, Elaine. *Beyond Belief: The Secret Life of Thomas*. New York: Random House, 2003.

Pascale, Richard, et al. *Surfing the Edge of Chaos: The Laws of Nature and the Laws of Business*. New York: Three Rivers Press, 2001.

Postman, Neil. *Technopoly*. 1992. Reprint, New York: Vintage Books, 1993.

Radcliffe, Timothy, O.P. *I Call You Friends*. New York: Continuum, 2001.

Rich, Frank. *Ghost Light: A Memoir*. New York: Random House, 2001.

Ridley, Matt. *Genome*. New York: HarperCollins/Perennial, 2000.

Roszak, Theodore. *The Cult of Information*. 1986, 1987. Reprint, Berkeley: University of California Press, 1994.

———. *The Voice of the Earth: An Exploration of Ecopsychology.* Grand Rapids, Mich.: Phanes Press, 2002.

Russell, Mary Doria. *The Sparrow.* New York: Fawcett Columbine/Ballantine, 1997.

Sacks, Rabbi Jonathan. Templeton Lecture on Religion and World Affairs, "The Dignity of Difference: Avoiding the Clash of Civilization." London: Continuum International Publishing Group, 2002.

Sells, Michael, trans. and ed. *Approaching the Qur'án: The Early Revelations*. Ashland, Ore.: White Cloud Press, 1999.

Senge, Peter, et al. *The Fifth Discipline Fieldbook*. New York: Currency, 1994.

Singer, Tom, ed. *The Vision Thing*. New York: Routledge, 2000.

Smith, Huston. *Why Religion Matters*. San Francisco: HarperCollins, 2001.

Sobel, Dava. *Galileo's Daughter*. New York: Penguin USA, 2000.

Solomon, Andrew. *The Noonday Demon: An Atlas of Depression*. New York: Touchstone Books, 2002.

Steiner, George. *No Passion Spent: Essays 1978–1995*. New Haven, Conn.: Yale University Press, 1998.

———. *Errata: An Examined Life*. New Haven, Conn.: Yale University Press, 1999.

Swimme, Brian. *Canticle to the Cosmos*. Louisville, Colo.: Sounds True, 1996.

Turner, James. "Secular Justifications of Truth-Claims: A Historical Sketch." In *American Apostasy: The Triumph of "Other" Gospels*, edited by Peter Berger. Grand Rapids, Mich.: Wm. B. Eerdmans, 1989.

Updike, John. *Roger's Version*. New York: Alfred A. Knopf, 1986.

Viorst, Judith. *Necessary Losses*. 1987. Reprint, New York: Simon & Shuster, Fireside, 1998.

Ward, Graham, ed. *The Postmodern God*. Oxford, Eng.: Blackwell Publishers, 1997.

White, Patrick. *Riders in the Chariot*. New York: New York Review of Books, 2002.

Wilken, Robert. *The Myth of Christian Beginnings*. Norwich, Eng.: SCM/Canterbury Press, 1979.

Williams, Rowan. *A Ray of Darkness: Sermons and Reflections*. Cambridge, Mass.: Cowley, 1995.

———. *On Christian Theology: Challenges in Contemporary Theology*. Oxford, Eng.: Blackwell Publishers, 1999.

———. *Lost Icons: Reflections on Cultural Bereavement*. Harrisburg, Pa.: Morehouse Publishing, 2002.

———. *Ponder These Things: Praying with Icons of the Virgin*. New York: Sheed & Ward, 2002.

Wilson, A. N. *Daughters of Albion*. New York: Penguin, 1993.

———. *God's Funeral*. New York: W. W. Norton & Co., 1999.

Wink, Walter. *The Human Being*. Minneapolis: Fortress Press, 2002.

Index

ethnicity, 21–22, 23, 47, 216
Eucharist. *See* communion
Evangelicals, xiv, 9, 86–87, 101,
　212
evil, 43, 100, 135, 183, 225
　consciousness of, 125–26
　symbols of, 18
evolution, 35, 56, 57
experience, 46–47, 194–95
　doctrine and, xxi, 140–41, 208
　interpreting, 50, 207–8
　as unfinished, 43, 123

faith, 1–13, 85, 139–40, 192, 211
　believing and, 72, 76
　challenges of, 19, 125, 140
　free choice of, 48
　homogenized, 61–64
　human failings and, 82, 141
　imaginative acts and, 156
　questions and, 10–11, 40,
　　58–59
　science vs., 56–58, 67
　transformation and, 224
fanaticism, 35, 65, 80
fantasy, 17, 152, 163–64
fasting, 199, 241
fatalism, 60–61
fear, 21, 71, 152, 156
forgiveness, xviii, 134–35, 243
fox and hedgehog, 65
free choice, 47, 48, 119–20,
　196–97
freedom, 119–21, 159, 197, 243
　call of, 230–32
　in communion, 178, 186–87
　neighborliness and, 127–28,
　　134–35, 181
　primary narratives of, 199
　sacred identity and, 139, 188
free market, 105–8, 220

French Impressionists, 161–62
friendship, xxii, xxiv, 199, 200
fundamentalism, xi, xvi, xix, 2, 3,
　83, 139
　attractions of, 32–33
　consumerist clash with, 108–9
　literalism and, 27–35, 59, 152
　mystery vs., 114, 119
　politics and, 104, 183
　tribalism and, 16–17, 71
future, 33, 164–65, 235

Galileo, 56, 116, 128, 203
gay people, 89, 129
gender, 3–4, 32, 132
Gentiles, 193
global consciousness, 21–25
globalization, 7, 106, 225
God, 1, 5, 19–20, 21, 28
　American religiosity and,
　　97–107
　as artist, 164
　Buddhism and, 12
　Christian meaning of, 24–25,
　　64, 66, 169–70, 172–73, 227
　crucifixion of Jesus and, 168,
　　170
　domestication of, 99
　Eucharist and, 199
　evolving images of, 117
　fatalism and, 60
　hospitality of, 179, 184
　human needs and, 39–52, 79,
　　120, 142
　humans in image of, 141–43,
　　177–78, 181, 196–97
　idea of vs. reality of, 162
　immediate relationship with,
　　200
　known unknowability of, 78,
　　231–32